# A to Z MAPS
# The Personal Story

Phyllis Pearsall c. 1940, by the late Sir Henry Turner.

# A - Z MAPS

*THE PERSONAL STORY
FROM BEDSITTER TO HOUSEHOLD
NAME*

## PHYLLIS PEARSALL

*God is omnipotent.
Aim high, be high ... Ardent desire
and abject humility work wonders ...*

## GEOGRAPHERS' A-Z MAP COMPANY
### MCMXM

Published by Geographers' A to Z Map Company Ltd
Vestry Road, Sevenoaks, Kent TN14 5EP


ISBN 0 85039 243 8

*Printed and bound*
by SMITH SETTLE
Otley, West Yorkshire

*To all the darlings at A to Z with whom I am and have been blessed to work, laugh and cry. Also to the many good friends who have supported us in our pilgrimage and in time of need.*

# CONTENTS

## The First Thirty Years

# ACKNOWLEDGEMENTS

and grateful thanks

To James Stourton who created the book design out of friendship despite lacking time to do so.

To Ian Griffin for seeing the book through from start to finish; and to his equally painstaking proof scrutineers — Hazel Rolan, Fred Bond and Esmé M. Wren.

To every one of my friends (past and present who helped make A to Z Maps a household name), for being the *Dramatis Personae* of the book.

To Ken Palmer for asking me years ago to record my personal story of Geographers' A to Z Map Company.

And above all to Nigel Syrett without whose enthusiasm and practical help (such as setting up my Amstrad Computer/Word Processor) I could well have abandoned this long sustained task.

Title page quotation from *Meister Eckhart: Sermons & Collations* (Translated by C. de B. Evans)

*Boadicea* quotation by kind permission of the author.

# FOREWORD

Deserted by my parents at the age of a penniless fourteen — and with a natural if small talent — I became a compulsive artist and writer. Never would I have been a map publisher had not my father been one (in Great Britain from 1908 to 1920 which he then lost; and in the U.S.A. from 1928).

Inveigled during 1945 into helping him in minor matters relating thereto, I realised how vital it was to his self-respect to be re-established in this country. Which is why all our publications bore the inscription *'Produced under the direction of Alexander Gross'* until his death in 1958.

But as the following story shows, his influence (though perhaps by contraries) stops there.

This is not to denigrate an impossible father (loved in retrospect) in order to magnify myself, but to demonstrate that a business woman true to her nature can be successful in her own right. As living proof (on a small scale, for I'm no Warrior Queen) of Antonia Fraser's brilliant 'Appendage Syndrome' theme of her *BOADICEA*.

> 'Again and again we shall find a Warrior Queen acting out her life voluntarily or involuntarily as an example of the Appendage Syndrome: that is to say, she will either be regarded as officially an appendage to her father, husband or son...' (to the next strong male, in fact): 'or stress the relationship to give herself validity (as in Elizabeth I's frequent stress upon her father Henry VIII).'

# PREFACE

Inadvertently, and without ambition or envisaged aim, I became a map publisher. In 1936. At 30 years of age. Temporarily, I thought; but as the French say *'il n'y a que le provisoire qui dure.'* (Only the temporary lasts). In haste to get back to my painting, etching and writing, I hurled my indefatigable energy — and my total concentration on whatever had to be done — into the plethora of detailed map making. Thread by thread. Mistake by mistake. Into a quarter of a century of ups and downs. Leading to a second 25 years — aided by the integrity, and dedicated ability of colleagues hereinafter portrayed — of gradual but sustained UP.

As to achievement. So emphemeral in this transitory world that I hasten to sprinkle salt on the tail of a few.

A to Z has become a household word. For its maps and indexes clearly show millions of people, including the public services, how best to get from where they are to where they want to go.

Geographers' A to Z Map Company remains independent. Due to the Trust (holding all the shares for the benefit of the employees) formed in 1966; and to Trustees immune to 'offers too good to be refused', by eschewing greed, power, status.

Reputation for trustworthiness. Due to simple truth and care for all others in all dealings.

The majority of staff stay on. Linking their endeavour and pride to the Company's. Eight non-pensioner recipients of the 25 years gold watch include colleagues who have served 42, 40 and 33 years; while twenty eight of the younger generation clock up 20 to 10 years; and some of the youngest up to 5. And may the new arrivals inspired by the enthusiasts amongst us continue to spur A to Z upwards and onwards.

Directors are from our own timber; and continue to work in their own sphere. In the hope, God willing, that any tendency to flounder into prestige pride — instead of just increased responsibility, allied to wider overall view — will be kiboshed by the chastening consequences of wrong decisions. (It is also a Trust 'must' that outsiders are not to be brought in over their heads.)

School leavers are trained — practically not theoretically — by similarly trained experts. To mastery of their craft, and the maintenance and evolution of A to Z's high standards of quality and service. Talents are searched out, nurtured and encouraged to bloom.

Problems are discussed horizontally; not self-importantly down, nor obsequiously up.

Each individual is considered equally worthy of trust — for nothing is lost by trusting. The fine people blossom. Some of the others, if corrupt will take advantage. Thus, to quote a Psalm, 'Mercy and Truth have kissed each other'. And solutions are based on love and truth combined ... For love without truth can be sloppy, and truth alone, cruel.

It is therefore natural that — though Utopia and other systems founder on human nature — we accept as compliment the oft-repeated query from business and professional conformists: 'How can such fools be successful?'

The story that follows of A to Z's first thirty years, is written at my colleagues' request; it is chiefly a tribute to the friends who stood stalwart throughout our testing voyage, whose characters were tried by circumstances and by frailer humans — those still gracing this life; and those who in God's timelessness have joined 'The Golden People on the other side'.

# PART I
## 1936 to 1938/9

# UNCLE FRANK and PAPA

# CHAPTER I

'THE spitting image of Uncle Frank!' I thought as from my window I spotted a burly bonhomous man in mustard tweed issue saloon bar sprightly from the Barley Mow and bee-line for the Regency Place urinal at Horseferry Road. Thence he emerged, buttoning up his fly, and rolled towards my studio bed-sitter on New Street corner.

My bell rang. 'It can't be he! I thought. It was he. One of my mother's elder brothers. I had not seen him since 1920. When for a bribe he had enabled other crooks to oust my father from Geographia — the renowned map publishing firm founded by my father and mother in 1908.

'How's Auntie Billie?' I enquired, vividly recalling my uncle's striking red-head pseudo wife — the last "Auntie" known to me after a varied legion of others. His only legal wife, my Auntie Winnie (and their daughter Alice), he had deserted early this century — a year after marriage.

'Auntie Billie!' he anathematised: 'Phew! That shrew! Do you remember my gashed and bloody phyzog the morning your dad brought me to see you at Roedean? Her doing! Our jug and wash-basin hurled at me before breakfast. "Enough's enough!" I decided there and then; and walked straight out on her! … More fool I! Only a month later her nonagernarian grand-dad kicks the bucket; and Lady Muck, damn her eyes, inherits the brewery fortune … The fortune I'd cowered under her tantrums for, year in year out … Just my luck … But a miss is as good as a smile … Life's all a matter of timing, Phyllis, learn that from your poor battered Nunkie …' A pause; a long salacious wink; and with a lilt in his voice, he breezed on: 'Anyway all's well that starts bewitchingly. It's your Auntie Peg now. You'll like her. Top drawer Indian Army. Poonah and all the rest of it … Where did I meet this paragon of a better half? In my beloved stamping ground … bracing Brighton. While drowning me "lost brewery" sorrow at The Ship. She was sitting up at the bar. Alone. It was love at first sight. Doffing my hat, I gaily ventured "May I dear lady offer you a port? A white port?" And she replied: "How could I refuse so courteous a gentleman?" That for me clinched it. Having quaffed our several "Same Agains", I helped her on with her stylish cloak and ventured further: "Take my arm, oh comforter of a lonely soul; and let us now languidly saunter along the promenade to Hove where I reside"…'

'But with Peg's high moral tone', he glumly added: 'It was marriage or nothing … Never let on to her that your dead-as-mutton Auntie Winnie's still alive … Me and Win being Catholics rules out divorce. The rub is that Win only became a convert to catch this ninny, this toast-of-the-town cycling champion and drag him to the altar ... Talking of which, I still hold the amateur record, Phyllis.'

Why, after all these years, I wondered (in the early Spring of 1935) had he — Frank Crowley — erupted into my life: 'How did you know my address?'

'From your father, of course ... Hasn't he told you?'

Since his loss of Geographia my father lived in the States.

'Hasn't he told me what?' I asked.

'That I'm starting up a map sales business in London. Like the Geographia Fleet Sales I directed in his prosperous days — (As they're still functioning under that name, mine'll be "Field Staff", I told your dad.) — We've kept in touch; but when I suggested he produce a map for me, what does the blighter come up with? A Map of the World! "The Standard Map of the World" he's called it ... "Who wants the World?" I wrote him. So he replies: "I've had it drawn for my American business!" which from him means as I know of old — take it or lump it! ... So, Holy Mary Mother of God that was that, thus and therefore! ... Map of the World, so be it! As Representative worthy of my salt, I don't give a damn what I sell! ... Nor, if they know which side their bread is buttered, will my Sales staff ...'

'I'm an artist and writer ... What's all this got to do with me?'

'Before they invade us though, I must have a look-see at The Map.

'What map?'

'Where is it Phyllis?'

'Where's what?'

'The Map of the World your dad's promised me ...'

'I haven't got it.'

'Good God! What am I going to say to the applicants?'

'What applicants?'

'I was just coming to that ... My Situations Vacant entry — in *The Daily Telegraph* and *Sporting Life* — gives them your address. Today they'll be calling here, dear lovey-dovey niece of mine. Today. From noon on. At half-hourly intervals...'

Ruminatively, he added: 'Spotting my inimitable usage of Shakespeare's tongue, bet you some of my old gang turn up! ... A bloody nuisance though — excuse my French — not to have the actual map to show them. It won't be the first time I've had to make hay out of thin air...'

'What on earth are you talking about?...'

'No time for chit-chat! Got to get this dump looking something like an office ... So give me a hand my girl and HEAVE HO.'

From the model stand we hauled down the screen — ready draped for my next sitter — and carried it across the room 'to conceal your dratted divan bed'; then we pushed my pine refectory table — 'Your Auntie Peg says only mahogany for her!' — to the window: 'Right! Now for your cheap kitchen wheelbacks ... One for my interviewee ... Facing the window you silly billy, so he has the light in his eyes. Mine, opposite, the light behind me. Grasp the idea? And one for you beside me to take down notes and so on and so forth ...'

After a pause to survey his *mise-en-scene* — 'The best of a tatty job' — he told me to set before him — 'on this apology for a desk' — inkpot, pens, pencils, ruler, a wad of paper 'I can appear to study; and last but not least, your telephone at my elbow — if your frayed flex'll stretch far enough ... all set for me to answer you, dear girl, when you phone me from the Barley Mow once or twice during each interview. Nothing more impressive than a busy line ... Yes you'll have to put your skates on, I know, but you wouldn't let your old uncle down, would you ... Furthermore we must shut the doors to your bathroom, kitchen, and cupboards ... as if they opened on to well-appointed Salon after Salon - (how lyrical I wax in this artist's studio!) — a gilded bathroom ... a concert hall for musical soirées à la Lady Cunard ... But HARK! ... Methinks at the very stroke of midday the curtain is about to rise. On la-di-da Thompson known to hop, skip and jump to appointments on the dot at the spot. Do you hear him now taking the stairs three at a time — despite his dicky ticker ... and by the way, ne'er a word, he doesn't know I know he's been in quad...'

Seating himself expectantly at his desk — 'As dignified as the Lord Chancellor, would you say, Phyllis? '— my uncle shushed me: 'All you are, remember is my personal secretary ... When the bell rings, usher the scallywag in.'

On my threshold stood a death's head. Breathless, attired in flashy blazer, white flannels, wash-leather gloves.

'Thompson. The name's Thompson, miss ...' he stammered out in suspect Oxbridge: 'Thompson with a "P" ... Mr Frank Crowley's expecting me' and, sporting a cane, pranced arthritically in. Nor did he take the chair indicated; but skittishly skirted the table to dig a skeletal elbow into my uncle's well-upholstered ribs: 'How's tricks, Frankie boy? When do we unfurl the flag?'

'Three weeks from today, Thompson. If, after this interview, I decide to pipe you aboard ... By then I'll have the gen ... size, price, order book ...'

'And the goods, Frankie? What's the goods?'

'The World. The most up-to-date ever. Here or abroad. New. With all frontier and nomenclature changes. Exquisitely coloured. Beyond compare. That's what. A unique opportunity for first-comers. Not that it's title "The Standard Map of the World"'s a world-shaker — Ha! Ha! Get the pun, Tommy? — But the follow-up is ... With all the hearing you've got left, Thompson, WAIT FOR THE PUNCH LINE! For, beneath that lack-lustre title, glow the electric words: "Produced under the Direction of Alexander Gross F.R.G.S."'

'Not our Alexander Gross? ... THE Alexander Gross?' gasped Mr Thompson awestruck: 'I can't believe it...'

'When have I ever lied to you, you old curmudgeon?'

'Often ... But not now. Please dear God not now ...'

Fearing stroke or heart attack, I burst out: 'It's true, Mr Thompson!' While

Uncle Frank apotheosed: 'Yes! Superman A.G. has staged a COME BACK ...
For his brother-in-law! His boon companion! Me!...'

'Do you mean like the good old days of Sales, Wine, Women and Song!'

'Steady now old gelding! Keep your hooves on the ground'; and Uncle Frank
outlined procedure: 'Our usual form, Thompson ... pre-publication
subscription; half payment on order, balance on delivery. Varnished maps
mounted on linen and rollers.'

'And my cut?'

'Commission as before. 10% of selling price.'

'On order?'

'Half on order. Balance on cash received ... And by the way feller-me-lad
what were you in for?'

'False pretences ...' admitted Mr Thompson: 'Only six months ...' adding
with a leer: "Hell knows no fury like a woman scorned!" As you should know,
Don Juan eh? Talking of which, you wouldn't have a fiver handy? I'm a bit
short of the ready...'

The telephone rang. Uncle Frank — 'Just a moment, Thompson, old man'
— raised the earpiece: 'Who's speaking? Oh! Lady Ashfield? You desire a word
with Phyllis ... I'm her uncle ... Pronto my Ladyship ... Here she is...'

At my recent one-man show, Lady Ashfield had asked me to pay off her taxi
— 'I've stupidly forgotten my purse' — and to lend her tuppence for the bus
fare home: 'When I couldn't pay, and said my husband owned London
Transport, the conductor with a — "I've heard that story before!" — rang his
bell and put me down.' Now, on the phone, she invited me to dine with them
next Saturday; and referring to the Pembrokeshire landscape she had bought:
'To see your beautiful painting hung. We both love it.'

A story to which the two men listened spellbound. 'Did you hear that,
Thompson with a P? Our Open Sesame to the top-notcher at London
Transport! ... Hip Hip Hurrah ... On the doorstep from here, old soak! At St
James's Park tube station.' Whereupon, at my ponderous uncle's 'Let's dance
the light fantastic!' the two buffoons burlesqued a polka round my studio. Only
saved from apoplexy by the phone.

'Answer it, Phyllis ... I'm out of puff ...' panted Uncle Frank, collapsing into
his chair; while the operator asked: 'Would you accept a reverse charge call
from Liverpool?'

'I know nobody there.'

'From a Mr Seymour Benn?'

'Never heard of a Mr Seymour Benn.

'Accept it, Phyllis! Don't let them cut you off' roared old war-horse Uncle:
'Seymour Benn's one of my aces.'

Mr Benn, put through to me, implied close family friendship: 'Dined with
your dad at the Beaux Arts last night before I sailed from New York for jolly
old England. He's in the best of health, you'll be glad to hear. He sends his love.
We've much in common you and I; You an artist ... I, a poet...'

Uncle Frank snatched the phone: 'You always were a waffler, Seymour ... These niceties are costly ... For God's sake come to the point!'

'Oh it's you, Crowley old bean ... Gross told me you were resuscitating Fleet Sales ... I can't wait to rejoin you and your rapscallions of yore. Gross, bless his heart, paid my passage; but not a spot of walk-about. So, the Adelphi won't let me out until my bill's paid ... Then there's the fare to London ... A mere trifle of fifty quid wired me straight away would bring me to you ...'

'Not a brass copper!'

'Worth a try, though, Kubla Khan! ... See you anon ...'

The remaining applicants — unknown to my uncle — he disposed of at breakneck speed: 'Riff-raff, Phyllis...'

'Destitution's not their fault!'

'Spare me your socialist twaddle! Laggards the lot of them! There's plenty of work for those who want to! ... And instead of yapping, show in the next!'

Of the strangers, he took on two. Mr Arnold — a gnarled middle-aged chain smoker with impeccable references; and Mr Nolan in rags.

'Paddy my boy that fig leaf won't even get you to first base!' jocosed Uncle Frank: 'I've seen better than you crawl from a stilton...'

'I'd have you know my wife's the daughter of a Church of England Rector, Mr Crowley ...' smiled the Irishman — his blue eyes unsmiling

'A mixed blessing, eh? ... But you'll do. Nothing like Irish gift of the gab to blarney orders out of stone! Come along with me and I'll buy you a reach-me-down. No good giving you a fiver, you'd drink it ... Ta ta Phyllis tararaboom-deeaye ... No, drat it! I've lost my wallet ... Must have left it in my plus-fours after golf on Saturday ... and in the rush this morning to catch the train from Hove forgot to switch it ... So, oh pretty banker mine, pluck a tenner from the Petty Cash and hand it to your Nunkie.'

'What's "Petty Cash"?' I asked. My uncle laughed: 'You see Paddy she's quite a caution ... You'll have to watch your step ... But cough up niecey, there's my gal ...' and snapping open my handbag, helped himself.

Then, with hug, kiss and tuneless singing of Sedley's '"Phyllis is my only joy"', arranged for us all to meet next week — 'same day same time,' — and before I could demur, followed his protegé out.

A brisk rat-a-tat brought me to the door again. A telegraph boy, chin-strapped pillbox at a jaunty angle, and whistling 'Tiptoe through the Tulips', rifled through the document pouch on his belt and handed me a cable from papa:

*DON'T TRUST FRANK LETTER MAILED*

It arrived next day. With three requests *'you'll be only too happy to carry out for your loving father ... viz:*

'1. *Open a bank account — You and Frank to be joint signatories.*

'2. *Buy a sixpence Cash Book at Woolworths. Write "Money In" at the top of the left hand page, and "Money Out" at the top of the right.*

'3. *Prepare a crucial Inset for my world map.*

*(a) Obtain statistics showing decreased immigration from Europe to the U.S.A. for the last ten years.'*

*(b) Take these to my map draughtsman, C. H. Fountain. Instruct him to columnise the information obtained — he'll know what to do — and draw its heading, The Diminishing Glamor of the West in handwritten BOLD.'*

The last, the most complicated, I tackled first. A friend at the American Embassy — secretary to the Naval Attaché — tracked down a librarian at another U.S. building in Grosvenor Square. Showing me the required figures, he apologised: 'As no documents can leave these premises, I'm afraid you'll have to copy them out here.'

That done I phoned Mr Fountain, took a bus to Maida Vale, climbed the stairs to his top floor flat, and rang the bell. Sixtyish like papa, he opened the door and stood there motionless. Tall, slim, his sour elongated face inflexibly grooved, neat in brown suit and mirror polished shoes, his good head of hair too polished black for real, he did not ask me in; and after quick perusal of my scribbled copy, sent me packing: 'Come back when you've re-written it legible!...'

That done at a nearby Post Office, I soon rang his bell again. Again his lips curled: 'I need it printed in 10 point don't I? And three pulls on good white paper?'

'Who'll do that?'

'The City 24 hour Service Trade Compositor...'

'Where?'

'Off of Fleet Street as everybody knows...'

No problem either over Woolworth sixpenny Cash Books.

As for opening a dual account, I chose the bank nearest me. A Midland branch in Victoria Street. But the form needed Uncle Frank's signature as well as mine. So that when he billowed in for our Friday rendez-vous — 'Hallo ducks! The early bird catches the worm, what!' — I asked him for it.

'Why your's at all!' he exploded: 'Doesn't that dad of yours trust me? Fancy him tying me to his daughter's apron strings! I've a good mind to resign!...'

'Papa insists ...'

'So the old skinflint's backing me with a few thousand dollars, I don't think! ... Not on your sweet Fanny Adams!'

'He's giving you the World...'

'I've already got seven orders in the bag ... Not bad for your evergreen uncle what? At three guineas each ... always guineas for high class goods, remember that Phyllis; and I soon nosed out that three guineas is the highest the market'll take. At 10 per cent commission, you owe me — give or take a little — £2.10.0.'

'Sorry, Uncle Frank. We can't draw on the £5 minimum I put down to open our account.'

'When can I promise my lads the maps?...'

'I haven't the faintest idea.'

'Phone the draughtsman then.'

Through the earpiece we could both hear Mr Fountain's considered calculations: '... another week on my black original ... a fortnight to three weeks to draw the colours in black — wot with blue coastlines and lines for sea screens — a few days for the transfers to be made ... three weeks at the printers ... say two months at the earliest.'

Face suffused — 'These dawdling draughtsmen drive me hopping mad!' — my uncle wagged his forefinger in my face: 'You're not going to take this lying down I hope! ... Your dad didn't make his fortune letting grass grow. No! You gee up that peppery Fountain like Alex always had to!'

Calm again, he donned his coat: 'But alas! Alack! No funds, and no map on the horizon yet ... Which puts paid to our niftiest gambit: "Pre-publication Sales!" ... But we Cavaliers of the Road take hurdles in our stride ... So Frankie boy, back to the treadmill of flogging Cash Boxes. And to you until the great day dawns, Oh sweet Phyllis of the Phyllis Blue Gown, it's "Toodledoo Goodbyee!"'

'Wait for the others please, Uncle Frank!' I pleaded, as he made for the door: 'They'll be here any moment ... What shall I say to them? ...'

'Tell them to hold their horses till the drop of the starter's flag ...' he called back and vamoosed.

But he was right. Though jolted from dreams of affluence to niggardly dole, they did not outwardly repine.

'With enough poteen in, a man can take even that' laughed Mr Nolan, dapper in new suit.

'Never say die!' croaked Mr Thompson.

And Mr Arnold, bravely chipper too: 'When you're ready, Mrs Pearsall, whistle us up, an' like ole Man River we'll just come rolling' along.'

His origination ready, Mr Fountain, phoned me to fetch it. 'Half a mo', he said, neatly rolling several tracing paper sections (including the white panel 'with your father's ridiculous title') into one, and inserting it into a cardboard tube: 'Take this with my written instructions to Mr Weiss for transfers.'

'Transfers?'

'For the printers ... Weiss knows ... Done well for hisself he has. Married a baker's confectioner with rooms over the shop ... Where he and his Lily still live ... In Shepherdess Walk. I've forgotten the number...'

Shepherdess Walk, pastoral only in name since Islington's mid-1840 expansion, stretched busy and noisy to the Grand Union Canal.

In his workshop lined by a graveyard of almost obsolescent lithographic stones, Mr Weiss — his lilting accent and pedant speech dubbing him Hungarian — welcomed me warmly the daughter of papa: 'an exile like me at the turn of the century from the Austro-Hungarian Empire ... How proud we of the Hungarian colony were of him. Still are. For founding the Geographia

Company and directing it to spectacular success. And then to lose all he'd built up! What a colossal tragedy! It should never have happened! Not to a fine gentleman like him. Give him my warm regards please when you write ... And may I hope my dear that your visit to me harbingers the restoration of his good name ... his re-ascendance to foremost British Map publisher ... By you his daughter ...'

'Never! I'm a compulsive painter and writer. And earn my living at what I love to do! ... But papa himself may well be contemplating a come-back...'

Fervently he prayed: 'God grant it may be so...'

Then 'to work!' he said; and unrolling my original: 'Now what have we here? ... 54″ x 40″ ... Four colours ... I'll get down to it straight away ... should take me two to three weeks ... Will ring you as soon as it's ready for the printer. But few printers have presses that large. Who are yours?'

'I don't know.'

'I suggest Greycaines at Watford ... What run are you thinking of?

'What does "run" mean?'

'The number of maps you print at a time.'

'Mr Fountain hasn't told me.'

'Don't let that bully Fountain intimidate you. With make-up and wash-up for four colours the economic minimum's five thousand. But before placing the order, you must let tham have written specifications, and receive a written estimate.'

'"Make-up? Wash-up? Specifications? Estimate?" ... What do they mean? ... Sorry to be so stupid, Mr Weiss.'

'To admit one doesn't know is half the battle. As my old professor used to say: "Without humility we can neither learn nor teach ..." Ah me! Yes I was a student at Budapest University ... That's where I met your father ... he wanted to be an actor; I, a lawyer. But "man proposes, God disposes." Enough though of reminiscences. We must live in the present. And for Mr Gross's dear daughter I myself will draft the specifications.' Briskly he jotted them down: 'There you are, kishlany ...' (Hungarian endearment for little girl) and advised: 'With printing in the doldrums Greycaines should quote you at cost.'

'Quote?'

'Give you a price ...'

Out at Watford, before preparing the estimate, their Director asked: 'Who's supplying paper?'

He had sufficient MG in stock, he told me.

'"MG"?'

Showing me a sample of a white paper, smooth and shiny one side, rough the other, he licked a corner: 'No good buying a pig in a poke, eh?' and reeled off equally arcane particulars: sheet size, weight per ream, percentage of "overs" required ... and I enquired what was wrong with the paper 'for you to be landed with it?'

'The bankruptcy of the advertising client we bought it for ... that's why it's well hung...'

'Like meat and game,' I laughed; and he laughed too: 'Never thought of it like that! Your specifications are so precise, I took it for granted printing was an open book to you ... I'll take you round the works...'

Accustomed as I was to a small etching press, the vast machines enthralled me; particularly the two colour: 'How do you prevent smudging?'

'They're dried through these ducts.'

Impressive too — as craft versus art — was the discipline of limiting multiple colours to four; and subjecting primary colours by screens to the required mix: such as red and yellow modified to an acceptable orange ... yellow and blue for green. Together with ''Register'' — another technicality new to me.

'What's it mean?'

'Fit. See the yellow sliver along the top of this flower reproduction? It ought to be green. So the blue's out. At the bottom, though, you've still got a yellow sliver; yet down both sides the fit's perfect ... so we can't adjust any better. Tracing paper, transfers, zinc plates, and paper all shift differently. Depends on the weather. Hot, cold and worst of all humidity...'

'How soon can I have the maps?'

'With all these machines idle — no wonder my hair's turned grey! — within a month from receiving copy ... I'll give you a tinkle when I want you to pass the colours. Please be ready to get on the train at once ... It costs the earth to keep a machine waiting.'

I placed the order.

To Mr Fountain's fury: 'Are you barmy? ... Greycaines belong to Hutchinson's, and they own Geographia! So you can bet your life you've given your dad away to his old firm! What blooming idiot recommended them to you?'

'Dear Mr Weiss...'

'Dear! I like that! Quite right too with the prices he charges! Not cheap, ha ha! He always was one to poke his nose in where it wasn't wanted ... Don't suppose he told you that Greycaines must first run off good black copies of each of the colours — including black — on a handpress? And for why? The plates have got to be pristine as base for Mr Gross's American edition ... But don't just stand there on the doorstep! I've got a bone to pick with you! Mrs Fountain will get us a cup of tea.' Hair hennaed, and voice high pitched, she touchingly played girlish lead to his *jeune premier*.

'You be Mum!' she giggled, placing the tea-tray before me; and at a nod of dismissal from 'hubby dear', withdrew.

Choleric as ever, he began: 'Why didn't you let me know that bamboozler Frank Crowley's wormed his way back in ... Did you know that at the Geographia crunch he sided with your father's foes! ... That thief, multiple bigamist, boozer — lazes in Turkish Baths to sweat out the alcohol. Why am I expected to make maps for a crook who only looks after Number One ...

10

Answer me that!...'

'I thought the only map was The Standard World? Drawn mainly for papa.'

'Now it's an England and Wales, your dad's put me on! ... You can't tell me that an E. & W.'s for America! Anyway, I got stuck into it this morning. You're to index it, he says ... That's why I asked you round ...'

'But when? I've got my own work ...'

'You can't yet. Not for a few months. Not till I've got it drawn with index squares and references...'

To his criticism of Uncle Frank relayed by letter, papa replied:

> *'Fountain's a fine one to talk. A punter. Left my employ to make a fortune on the horses like his brother-in-law. Returned to me broke, begged me to let him go on drawing maps at Geographia. Didn't realise he'd played into my hands. For he's hopeless with staff ... puts everyone's back up: "Very well then" I said: "But not as Head Draughtsman!" ... He left me several times afer that, but always returned.'*

Greycaines kept to their date.

I've got the first World hot off the press!' I phone Uncle Frank.

'Eureka!' he rejoiced: 'I'll hie me to thee on my trusty Brighton Belle!'

# CHAPTER 2

ON close perusal of The Standard Map of the World, my uncle's jubilation turned to horror: 'What's this abomination? This inset! ... Has your father taken leave of his senses! ... How could he — an educated man at that — think up "Diminishing Glamor of the West?" And Oh my God, add insult to injury by leaving out the "u" in Glamour! It'll make me the laughing stock of the City! ... I could howl!'

Reminded that the map had been produced for papa's American business — 'or you wouldn't have a map at all!' — he laughed bitterly: 'A Yankee Doodle Dandy, that's what the blighter's sunk to ... When I think of the blood and sweat we Crowleys put into turning that uncouth Csurog peasant into an English gent! Into a gentleman worthy of my favourite sister Bella — your mama. How is she by the way? Am I going to give Alex a piece of my mind! And forthwith!'

Expostulating many a 'Preposterous', 'Scandalous', 'Blasphemous', he penned his tirade, and finally — pen spluttering — signed with a flourish: 'If only I'd got him here, I'd tell him to his face what's what!' Then, in caged lion stride back and forth across my studio, muttering: 'Mustn't let anything rattle me ...' he asked me to address and stamp the envelope: 'Your Auntie Peg, bless her heart calms me with her dulcet voice: "You're not as young as you were, dear one", she says: "though always young at heart!" ... Folding his letter into the envelope, he skipped rejuvenated to the door: 'I'll just pop out and mail this blistering epistle ... Nothing like a breath of fresh air to bring down the blood pressure!'

From 'the breath of fresh air — euphemism for a few double whiskies at the Barley Mow — he returned rosy, his proboscis purple — 'My troubled spirit soothed' — and resolute: 'No good crying over spilt map ... So let's talk turkey.' Which he did. From the start, incomprehensible to me.

'First Phyllis get 250 Worlds mounted C.R.V. ...'

'What's C.R.V.?'

'Mounted on cloth, varnished, attached to rollers top and bottom. With pink tape loop at top for hanging on the wall ... Secondly, 50 mounted Cut to Fold.'

'Cut to Fold?'

'Don't you savvy anything? ... For desk or car use. A luxury item to prevent maps tearing at the folds ... bound in bottle-green leatherette case with gold embossed title ... But don't bog me down in map mounter lore!'

'Where do I find one?'

'That's your pigeon! My priority is to prepare a Sales Sample ... So hand me some shears ... Oh no! Well if nail scissors are all you've got, they'll have to do ... And while your're on your pretty feet trot out for a pot of paste...'

Side by side we knelt on the parquet; he handing me the ragged pieces he cut out — 'Like Napoleon planning a campaign!' — and I pasting them together.

Over each choice he cogitated aloud: '... British Empire red for Board Rooms, exporters, Town and City Councils. Ocean names for shipping magnates. The title in full for House of Lords, London University, and public libraries etcetera; with beneath it your dad's resurrected insignia "Produced under the direction of Alexander Gross"'

At which, dismayed, he stopped mid-cut: 'Phyllis, why's that ass Fountain omitted the vital "FRGS" after his name? ... Our *ne plus ultra* selling point! ...'

In 1923 papa had been removed from Fellowship of The Royal Geographical Society — ostensibly for non-payment of his annual subscription; in reality to avoid Council embarrassment at his bankruptcy. An added disgrace to his downfall, I would not divulge. Particularly not to 'Born Betrayer Frank' as mama called her brother.

Instead, I reverted to the completed 12 inch by 3 collage: 'Why so elongated?'

'The key to my success!' he exulted: 'To fit into my poacher's pocket!' and, unbuttoning his jacket, demonstrated: 'I tuck my sample like so into this slit in the lining!' and re-buttoning: 'Nothing to show from outside, see. No give-away bulge! ... Unlike those run-of-the-mill sales buggers — excuse my French — who, weighed down by samples of their goods, are spotted at first base, and booted out ... To be unencumbered is the nub of my whole strategy ... And thus m'dear nonchalantly to stroll past the Hindenburg Line of commissionaires, clerks, secretaries. Straight through to Chairman, Lord Mayor, Peer of the realm ... For I always go to the Top, Phyllis. As equal to equal ... But time is money, as my mater used to say when washing up. So quick march to a mounter with my Selling Section ... Ask for CRV and CTF Estimates and delivery dates ... And ask them to throw in a dozen of these Sections gratis and for nothing!'

From mounters listed in the Post Office book, I chose Harding & Sons of Camberwell Green; where in his workshop, Mr Harding père in white coat, could not, he told me 'quote off the cuff ... It'll depend on the materials you decide on'; and, producing a swatch of linens and a linen-tester magnifying glass, asked: 'How many threads to the inch, Missie?'

My ignorance obvious, he patiently explained: 'The tighter the weave, the better the quality ... and of course costs more...'

'Which do other publishers use?'

'The best ... and I'm not just saying that to increase my profit ... Cut-to-Folds need the best marbled paper ends as well; and for the case, elegant leatherette indistinguishable from real leather; with the title embossed in gold paint ...'

Completed ones he displayed — gruesome to my aesthetic sensibility — clearly satisfied his business magnate customers. Though not, apparently the recent suceessor to the throne: 'For our new monarch, only the finest calf and gold leaf chasing! ... We had to put it out to a specialist.'

He was referring to a Map of the Mediterranean destined for King Edward VIII at Fort Belvedere: 'His Majesty's planning a summer cruise, his equerry says ...'

'Do you mind if I watch? ... I asked.

'Comes easy when you know how', he said, spreading out a large sheet of finest linen: 'First, allowing for an 8th of an inch border for each section to be folded, I calculated size and number of sections needed. With this square map for example — the job I'm just starting on — it'll be four folds down and four across ... Now come with me ...' And leading me to a series of high wooden partitions, demonstrated: 'Nailed to this board by nails spaced two inches apart along each edge are several sheets of linen (for the several maps in hand). Sponged with water, so as to shrink. And here, the map sections, pasted with water-based paste, and allowed to stretch. Which I then place in positon on the still wet linen so they can shrink together. Only when completely dry, do I take down each Cut to Fold map, trim it, fold it, and marble board the two outside ends.'

At my tentative request: 'How soon please can I fetch the Sales samples?' a young handsome well-tailored man, who had joined us unnoticed, chimed in: 'The moment the varnish isn't tacky, and dad's got them in their cases, I'll deliver them to your office, what!'

'To my home', I indiscreetly said: 'I haven't got an office!' 'Good-oh!' he smirked — 'Must be off, though! Or dallying with you, my beauty, will make me late for my appointment' — and swiftly departed.

'My son seems to have taken a shine to you', said Mr Harding: 'You give your children the chance you never had, and blow me if they don't come back from Cambridge despising their mum and dad...'

Details agreed, I phoned Greycaines to deliver 500 Worlds to Hardings.

'And where's the van to deliver the rest of the load missus? ... asked their warehouseman.

'Please give me a couple of days to find somewhere to put them...'

'Means unloading the bloody van! Women! Can't make their cock-eyed minds up!'

'I'll phone you as soon as possible...'

I phoned Uncle Frank. His suggestion — 'There's room on your model stand' — I turned down: 'Sitters for their portraits on Saturday and Sunday...'

'Take the bull by the horns then, spitfire, and rent an office ... As near your dad's old 55 Fleet Street as possible ... Not on any account in the seedy Strand ... Ring me when you've found it, and I'll zoom there in my jalopee a la Aix to Ghent!'

No vacancies to be found in Fleet Street, I walked up Chancery Lane to High Holborn; where for a £1 a week a newly decorated light and airy fourth floor office — with lift, caretaker, central heating, telephone and Ladies and Gentlemen lavatories — seemed ideal.

Uncle Frank also approved: 'And a jolly good address! Napier House, 24/27 High Holborn! And another pleasant feature — I took a recce — is its proximity to Henekeys. Only a couple of doors along! ... Many an important deal's clinched over a round or two...'

My trepidation at signing a two years lease, he pooh-poohed: 'You can't make an omelette without breaking eggs!...'

So I signed, phoned the delivery address to Greycaines and to Mr Harding.

Uncle Frank undertook the furnishing: 'You wouldn't have the foggiest, Phyllis!'

Next afternoon, as I approached along High Holborn — from painting Chelsea Old Church — Greycaines' van drew up at the kerb. With ten parcels of 54 inches by 40. Which the vanman, our caretaker, a fellow tenant and I dragged acorss the pavement, through our narrow entrance, into and out of the yet narrower lift and into the office.

Where my uncle, swivelling in a swivel chair directed us to pile them in the furthest corner from him.

That done, and the others gone, he crowed: 'Cast your hazel eyes — I know they're hazel like your mother's — on the tasteful furnishings around you ... Class, eh? ... My desk, genuine teak; its right-hand drawer a filing cabinet, see. My carpet — your Auntie Peg swears by Wilton — show's who's boss here! What's more, its red based pattern provides the perfect setting for this green leather armchair ... in which my important visitors will recline ... Peg always trusts me to match her embroidery silks ... Not dear artist that you've been forgotten!'

Linoleum floored, my Lazarus area contained a minute ink-stained leather-topped table on casters which careered away at the slightest touch; and rickety chair with straggly wicker seat. Five replicas along the wall, were destined for 'My Sales Staff' explained my uncle: 'a few nails, a lick of varnish, a chair-caner, and hey presto write-offs become antiques! Guess what I paid for the whole caboodle in Holloway Road? £29! And on tick! ... "You should feel honoured to have my custom!" I told them.'

In sauntered young Mr Harding with the dozen Sales Sections — 'Hope they're in order, Sir' — and with a large bouquet of red roses for me: 'How about dining with me at the Savoy tonight? Their diner dansant. I've booked a table overlooking the river ...' Ardour which remained undimmed — as he and I in evening dress watched the lamps light up across the river spiralling their reflections in the water — by my unromantic request after coffee for three months credit.

'I can't refuse you anything, dear innocent ... adrift in this cut-throat world of arrogant business men.'

'Now to action, Phyllis!' commanded Uncle Frank the following morning: 'Open an account at Gibbs & Mast...'

'Where?'

'The stationers at the Holborn end of Grays Inn Road, for heavens sakes!

And sprint back with six order books and extra carbons '(the mucky things peter out so darned quick), six London maps — if only we had our own! — drawing pins and a box of coloured pencils.'

'The allotting of territories is crucial! ...' he declared on my return; and kneeling on the floor pulled me down beside him:

'Unfold a map for me and one for you ... Here goes! ... Now for me, the Generalissimo, the best of course! The City! Excellence to excellence ... Good ground too for training new boy Nolan ...' To Mr Thompson he alloted Holborn — 'to save the old lag's puffer and decrepit pins.' To Mr Arnold, Acton and Shepherds Bush: 'Not too far from his Ealing digs ... For the others, who may well fall by the wayside, a few streets at a time — So ... so ... and so ... Whereupon — 'You can use my desk' — he set me to colour the designated areas — 'Your hand's steadier than mine!' — followed by: 'Print the reps' names in the centre of his area', and a slap on my hand: 'No, Phyllis! They're plaguey touchy my buccaneers. Not just ''Nolan'', ''Thompson!'' but if you can do it neatly add ''Mr'' before each ... That's better ... Now pin up our chef-d'oeuvre on the wall behind my desk. Right...'

My next task, to colour each a map for each rep with his particular territory, he left to me: 'And before you go, don't forget to display our *piece de resistance,* our World, gloriously to stun our Sales Force as they enter!'...

With final command: 'Let them know we all foregather here Monday moring sharp at 8 ackemma', he bid me a week-end farewell: 'Your Auntie Peg's cooking our Saturday sirloin — you should taste her Yorkshire pud! Can't let her pride and joy spoil in the oven...'

More than an hour later, I stepped out into High Holborn. To behold my Falstaff uncle reel from Henekeys midst crony chorus: 'Pack up your troubles in your old kitbag and smile, smile, smile.'

'We're in business my hearties!'

So on the Monday morning did Uncle Frank address his motley crew: 'First take an eyeful of my Forces Deployment Map'; and pointing his Royal Flying Corps swagger cane to each man's territory, warned: 'No forays across another's frontier you swashbucklers or there'll be the devil to pay! ... I'm issuing each of you with a personal area map to keep you on the straight and narrow; and to work out your routes ... So much for Admin! Now walk over to this other wall. Here as you will observe hangs the superb STANDARD MAP OF THE WORLD. Our mission and livelihood is to introduce it to our élite clients. ''CLIENT'', note. Never ''customer''. Nor of course, do you ever say ''Sir'' ... It's you who are doing him a favour ... nay, an honour. Not for the *hoi polloi* has the world-acclaimed cartographer Alexander Gross produced this magnum opus! But only for the cognoscente ... So much for the Spiel! Now down to practicalities. Here are your Selling Sections — I take it you've got your wives to sew in poachers' pockets — See how easily they slide in. Here are your

Order Books and Receipt vouchers ... Both slim enough to conceal in any pocket ...

'Now then, the drill. You've won over your client. "What does the map cost?" he wonders or even asks. "For you uniquely," you infer, the reduced price of three guineas ..." That goes for both the C.R.V. and Cut to Fold. Forgive him any chance to hesitate and you've lost your fish...'

'What if customer's compare notes Sorr?' mused Mr Nolan.

'Didn't I tell you to delete "customer" and "sir" from your vocabulary! Anyway, to men of standing three guineas is too paltry to question ... As I was saying, your client's taken the bait, and you're playing him skilfully. "Half-payment on order" you mention off-hand. "Balance on delivery." Better still if you can swing it to bump up the kitty, suggest full payment on the dot — "From Petty Cash, to save the paper work" — with delivery promised within ten days ...'

His briefing obsequiously followed by all but Mr Arnold, my uncle rap-a-rap-rapped his cane on his trousers (*faute de* wartime winged breeches), and bellowed: 'Arnold! Pay attention to my pearls of wisdom!'

Mr Arnold, though, true to his history master past, remained absorbed in the Map itself. 'Good!' we heard him mutter: 'Manchuria in North East China — nation created by the Japanese in 1930 or 1931 ... And good! The 1932, I think, new Kingdom of Saudi Arabia ... And yes! Ankara shown as the capital of Turkey — as it became after Kemal Pasha's troops advanced to Constantinople and deposed the Sultan. Yes! And correct here too the change of the Sublime Porte's name to Istanbul. Good!...'

'"Sublime Porte" indeed!', ridiculed my uncle: "What's the use of all that ballyhoo?'

'I'm a pro who can sell only what he believes in, Sir.'

'Didn't you hear me forbid the use of the word "Sir"! ... But now old-timers! All ready and correct? Zero Hour! Over The Top you go!' and as they trooped out, he held Mr Nolan back. 'Well Paddy, that leaves only you. I'll show you the ropes. Gird your loins! Straighten your tie! Smarten up! First call: The Lord Mayor of London. On then, Dick Whittington, on to the Mansion House!'

'A grand total of two hundred and forty-six guineas!' exulted Uncle Frank at the end of the first week: 'Not a bad haul for kick-off eh, Phyllis? And, praise the Lord, enough shekels to pay my gang's commission ... As for mine ...' and he lowered his voice, 'Here's my tally. Plus of course my delivery charge for the lot — a mere bob for each map ... And that still leaves a sumptious sum to line the coffers ...'

'To pay the printers, stationers, furniture ...' I reminded him.

'Spoil-sport!' he glowered.

Blue smoke from gaspers hung heavy in the office, amidst hubbub of scoops: 'Six from Coreys plus six more in the offing!' Of brush-offs: 'You know what you can do with your bloody World!' Of special requirements: 'For their boardroom to pull up and down like blinds!' Of requests for other maps: 'an up-to-date London ... there's nothing later than 1919'; an England & Wales.' Ignorant of my own ignorance, I entered Cash In and Cash Out into my Woolworth Cash Book as I received or paid it ... Foxed though by variations; particularly advances and expenses Uncle Frank bestowed at random; by my own asterisks, alphas, betas, which, though meant to clarify, added to the confusion, rendering the vital totting up of columns chimeric. Nor, with offhand 'Double Entry, old gal ... That's the ticket!' did my uncle help; and saved from answering my 'What's that?' by the arrival of a dreamy good-looker, stood up to greet "reverse charge caller" Seymour Benn.

Guileless and grudgeless the poet had hitch-hiked from Liverpool — 'Via Aberystwyth, would you believe ... Lovely place. Spent a week there contemplating the Ocean ... inspired me to pen a few sea shanties. Now for London to inspire me! A la Francis Thompson and his "Jacob's ladder pitched between Heaven and Charing Cross", or T. S. Elliot's:

"Sweet Thames run softly till I end my song.

Sweet Thames run softly for I speak not loud or long ..."'

But at his self-interruption — 'Oh dear! I've forgotten how it goes on' — and my prompting:

'"But at my back in a cold blast I hear

The rattle of the bones ..."'  he clasped my hand; and ignoring my uncle's — 'You two eggheads may have all night, I haven't!' — swanned to a Shakespeare sonnet: 'Ruin hath taught me thus to ruminate'. With which, turning deathly white, he dropped into the green armchair.

'When did you last eat?' I asked.

'Lack of food does make one a little light-headed...'

On our return from the cafe downstairs, Uncle Frank, addressing me as Florence Nightingale, told me to 'give our Poet Laureate gen. and impedimenta.'

'What area have you chosen for me, Old Top?'

'Mayfair of course, my Keats.'

As he signed the chit for an advance, he smiled: 'This signature will be valuable one day.'

Rowdy Friday meetings thereafter became routine; with Mr Thompson's choler ever on the trigger: 'Benn! You've pinched my client damn you!' and at our poet's excuse — 'an introduction from one of mine' — demanded the commission. Nor did his grumbles cease at Mr Benn's disarming: 'But of course, old chap; my intention from the start...'

By using a separate Woolworth Cash Book for each different batch of complications, I thought them solved.

Letters took five days each way across the Atlantic. Long enough for Uncle Frank's outrage at the World Inset to abate. Papa's reply —

*'Tell Frank to repeat "The Distinguished Glamor of the West" to himself two hundred and fifty times, and he'll learn to like it',* he happily dismissed as 'Poppycock!'

# CHAPTER 3

A<sup>N</sup> extended interlude devoted to painting — except for the Field Staff invasion every Friday — ended with a phone call from Mr Fountain: 'Come round at once. England & Wales is ready to index.' At the door of his flat he handed me a long brown paper roll: 'Get three sun copies made of each section.'

'What are sun copies?'

'Wot's the use of wasting time on wot's above your head. Give these written instructions to Norton and Gregory ... Their works are in Castle Street round the corner from your digs ... Wait for the finished job — they don't take half a jiff — and bring them back with my original.'

There, a girl assistant explained the process. The tracing original, placed onto sensitized paper, is wrapped round an upright hollow glass tube, and held in place by a strip of canvas clipped round them. Then, a high powered light, timed slowly to descend inside the glass tube creates an image on the sensitized paper. The light, switched off, the canvas unlatched, and the original and paper image removed, the latter is placed face down onto a continuous canvas-backed jelly bed (a big table pasted with jelly), and rubbed by hand. The paper peeled off, printing ink is rolled onto the jelly bed image; and copies pulled on cartridge paper — again by hand. Ruefully, she concluded: 'And who's given the lousy job of scraping off the dirty jelly and throwing it into the dustbin? Old muggins here, of course!'

Mr Fountain, after checking the sun-copies, allotted me one set: 'For you to index ...'

'How?'

Despite his reply: 'I'm a map draughtsman ... not a pen-pusher', he showed me: 'You see the squares I've drawn across the map — 3 & 9/10 inch each, though that don't figure — What does is the A, B, C, D to N along the top and bottom margins; and numbers 1 to 17 down both sides. Now let's look for ... Newbury — Where Mrs Fountain and me will be investing a bob or two on the gee-gees Saturday — There it is. Where square H and square 6 converge. See? So you'll write "Newbury H6". Got it?'

At home, in my amateur fashion, I tried the impossible. Simultaneously to alphabeticise the places (with their references) while listing them on writing paper. Until no longer able to squeeze new ones between each other, nor by littering the margins with arrows to where they belonged — I appealed for help. From my efficient Communist neighbour. (Momentarily in the news for leading a group of unemployed to lunch at the Ritz — having raised cash from sympathisers.) He and I often popped in on each other to borrow sugar, tea, bread or chairs for guests — in his case usually politicos.

You'll have to scrap the lot', he said, and at my woebegone look: 'Don't lose heart. Put it down to experience! Unswerving aim progresses step by step. Even in prison sewing mail bags I concentrated stitch for stitch and never got bored ...'

'You should spout from a soap box ...' I laughed; and he laughed too: 'Tovarich dear, I was trying out my Speakers' Corner speech on you!...'

He earned his living, he told me — possibly to avert suspicion of Soviet funding — selling the latest refuse vans to local authorities: 'The commission on one every three years pays my keep ... freeing me to propagate my gospel ...'

Reminded about my index, he said: 'Ignore alphabetical order until you've indexed every place — crossing it out on the map as you go, and each completed square ...'

'Do I have to cut each one out of this confused list?'

'By Lenin and Karl Marx no! ... Haven't you heard of card indexes?'

'What are they?'

Wrily, he sympathised: 'I too learnt the hard way ... compiling a directory of British Party members'; and fetching me a packet of cards 'to start on', suggested I add the Administrative Authority to each place name, — 'except for Parish Councils' — with population as at the last census.

'Where do I find them?'

'It's all in here', he said, lending me his Municipal Year Book. That done, he told me: 'Only now do you shuffle the cards into A piles, B piles and on to Z; finally each pack into its proper order: Aa, Ab to Zu right through to Za, Ze, Zo, Zu ...'

'So how do you think I'm going to fit that lot into the space available?' fumed Mr Fountain at sight of my cards: 'At minimum acceptable 10 point type face? Who on earth could read 6 point up on a wall, I ask you?'

'I definitely want it included. So what am I to do?'

'Abbreviate, of course! ... To initials. Like so. "C" for City, "MB" for Municipal Borough, "RD" for Rural District ...'

Leaving the capital letters standing, I quickly deleted the rest. 'More haste less speed!' he scoffed: 'How do you expect me to make head nor tail of your heiroglyphics! Let alone the poor devil of a comp! ... He'd send them back to you any road; and it'd cost you ... If I was you I'd copy out new cards. Clean and neat like so ...'

Twenty four hours of application, and the task completed, I returned to him. Instead of approval, his lips curled in *Schadenfreude:* 'Now wot have we here? The cards unnumbered. Everyone knows each one's got to be. And for why? They're fiddling things to handle, and the comp's bound to drop them. So wot does he do? Puts them back any old how ... Z's amongst M's ... Rather you than me to sort that jumble out on the proofs ...' and shunted me back to the three thousand five hundred and ninety cards — as the total proved to be.

But, his next demand unreasonable — 'Now type them out in list form as type-setters charge more for cards' — I jibbed: 'You should have thought of that before.'

Finally, type-set and printed on good white paper by City 24 Hour Service, Mr Fountain panelled my text, positioned it on the Irish Sea; Mr Weiss made the transfers — 'one step nearer to you vindicating your dear father!' and the E. & W. was ready for printing.

'But not at Greycaines!' instructed Mr Fountain: 'You'll have to find another printer able to handle 54 x 40.'

Quest I mentioned to my American sitter Keturah — with her adored Portalloch terrier Angus on her lap.

'Right down my alley, dear! As representative for Fishburn's Printing Inks, Campbell knows every doggone printer in the U.K. ... I'll have him call you ...'

Campbell, her husband, introduced me to Weiners' Managing Director at Shepherds Bush; who, shown the E. & W. original, murmured: 'Never tried our hand at anything like this before! ... We're poster printers by trade ... But, with advertising in the doldrums, I'd like to have a go at the quality market.'

Not so, his Works Manager: 'You to pass the colours, Miss? Not on your life! We can't have silly customers — begging your pardon — traipsing around here to tell us how to run our business...'

In from the shop floor trotted a machine minder handling a 54 x 40 sheet of paper: 'Want you to pass the blue, Sir...'

It was Gainsborough's 'Blue Boy' enlarged to advertise a well-known brand of confectionery. The manager, after cursory comparison between the hot mauvish blue of the vulgar pull and the cool blue of the commercial artist's copy on his desk, signed 'O.K.'; and nodding his subordinate out, reverted to me:

'As I was saying blue's blue, red's red — though that dratted red ink always runs — and yellow's yellow!'

'The register?' I ventured.

'Don't talk to me about register! ... The originals you customers land us with, zinc plates, the paper, every bloody material shifts different. Some shrink, some stretch, others do both ... So how am I to make 'em fit? ... Nor God Almighty neither!' Though Campbell's chum, as I placed my order for 7500 copies — 'You to supply paper' — struck a more hopeful note: 'Our revolving paper hanging system dehumidifies ... It's *dernier cri,* and cost a bomb!'

Outraged by the dirty, torn state of the original returned to him, Mr Fountain fulminated: 'A fine kettle of fish! Nobody cares about the work gone into it! They treat a map like it was a trashy design or throw away snapshot. If only your dad was here! He'd soon put a stop to all this aggravation! ... I can't for the life of me understand for why you didn't stick to Greycaines ... That original's got to last through years of reprints! And how's it going to stand up to me making changes on it? Scratching out on tracing paper with this sharp knife destroys the surface anyway ... have to burnish down the fibres to write on after ... A tetchy job at the best of times I could do without thank you ... A job an apprentice wouldn't have the skill to do ... to blend in the new with wot's already there, and it'd stick out like a sore thumb! — Not that I've got an apprentice ... got to do all the donkey-work myself — For a map draughtsman there's nothing like creating a new map ... able to see every evening wot you've produced that day ... and in the end something to show for it ...' Already he was straightening out Weiners culpable crumples and creases, rubbing out thumb marks, smudges — 'Didn't you tell them never to talk over an original drawing. Spittle dissolves the ink!' — re-drawing obliterated characters and line-work: 'Got to do what I can to restore it...'

As fiercely did he condemn Weiner's printing of this Standard Map of England & Wales: 'Garish! That's wot! They haven't a clue! Black thickened up, red slopped, register out by inches!...'

Whereas Uncle Frank delightfully acclaimed it: 'Spiffin'! ... Gorgeous strong colours!' — (disclosure to me of universal tribal warfare twixt Craft and Sales) — 'Phew! Phyllis! And in the nick of time! ...' he continued: 'We'd just about scraped the bottom of the barrel with Alex's bloomin' World! ... Watch us rake in the shekels! ...'

Indeed sales surged immediately. Cash receipts too; and large outstanding bills paid off, I rejoiced in freedom from debt. (For never before had I owed a penny — even as a starving student sleeping under Paris bridges.)

The Field Staff also rejoiced. At increased earnings. Bumped up by the unhoped for commissions I paid on repeat orders mailed or phoned to the office: 'Another England & Wales for our Boardroom, please' ... 'Six Cut-to-Folds for our van drivers; clarity of the main arteries saves us time and money' ... and, from a Sales Manager: 'The population figures on my wall map are just the job for area planning; but I need ten Cut-to-Folds for my Reps...

'Sweetener to the daily grind!' laughed Mr Nolan; and Mr Seymour Benn: 'Manna of blessed leisure to wait upon my Muse...'

'Ridiculous largesse, Phyllis!' jeered my uncle: 'Everybody knows that Office orders must be credited to the Company and not to staff.'

Alone together, he continued: 'At one blow you're rifling the kitty and spoiling my good-for-nothings! ... Haven't you tumbled yet to high-falutin' Benn? He stops selling the moment he's earned six guineas to meet his pifflin' basic needs — even if it's on a Monday!'

'Without their initial order, how could there be a repeat? It would be robbery!'

'Oh holier than thou! ... Thou thorn in my entrepreneurial flesh! You wait until your father hears about this — as he will in the monthly report I'm penning ... Meanwhile, fie to sentimental mush in business ... and for the sake of the blessed Virgin Mary, Saint Joseph and all saints, hie thee to thine art ...'

# CHAPTER 4

'BEFORE I can start on my next job!' phoned Mr Fountain: 'there's errands for you to run...'

'Next job? ... Oh, for America, I suppose?'

'America my eye! It's our great metropolis I'm embarking on!'

'But you said you'd rather die than draw another map for Mr Crowley.'

'For goodness sake leave me alone!'

That papa would never again entrust him with American work, he did not disclose; nor the humiliating reason. As did a letter from papa:

> 'Fountain's cost me thousands of dollars in damages and costs. He's landed me in a law case for infringement of copyright. The silly ass, imagine, in spite of a lifetime's experience, copied house number errors from a competitor's Manhatten ... I don't ever dare use him for the States again. So I'm handing him over to you ... Learn from me and watch he doesn't land you in a lawsuit. From now on of course you'll be paying his £7.10s.0d. weekly wage. I told him to start on London. Frank's been pestering me for it!
>
> Love,
>
> Father

'An up-to-date London map and street atlas!' I thought aloud to Mr Fountain: 'Why not? It's a public need!' And unaware that my decision would slice my life into compulsive map publisher as well as artist and writer, I agreed: 'Let's cover the London County Council area.'

'That's a lot of 6″ Ordnance Sheets you'll have to buy ...'

'Where?'

'Stanfords ... Don't you know anything yet!'

Shuffling forward in the long queue at their O.S. counter, I overheard a man some way behind me say: 'If that isn't Mr Alexander Gross's daughter I'll eat my hat! ... Haven't seen her since she was a nipper ... her parents let me look after her in the shop when they were busy ... But Holy Moses! Come to think of it! Does her presence here mean our old Guv's going to start competing with us? If so, unless stick-in-the-mud Bain pulls his socks up, it'll be goodbye Geographia and goodbye to my job as shop manager!'

My purchase made, I looked for the speaker; and, despite balding head and increased occupational stoop, recognised papa's shop manager of old: 'Mr Ayres!' I greeted him: 'How kind you always were to me ... how patient with the horrid rich brat I must have been! ... You gave me globes to twirl, map jigsaw puzzles to work on, and you even pretended to let me help serve customers!'

Spontaneously he responded: 'You were a dear little girl ... It might have been yesterday we were all out on the balcony of your dad's office watching the Lord Mayor's Show. With you in a pretty kind of flowery dress I remember, white socks, black patent leather shoes. Your mother always turned you out lovely ... How we miss your dad! The life's gone out of the place since he left ... Please tell him so when you write to him ... and that I'd jump at the chance to open a shop for him over here ... Meanwhile, a small favour he could do me. Next time he sails to the Old Country, I'd like a can of the miracle American car polish (I've forgotten what it's called but he'll know) that's unobtainable here...'

The queue moved forward: 'Don't forget, Miss Gross! Any time you're in Fleet Street pop in for a cuppa and a jolly old chin-wag ...'

Nostalgic encounter that wrung merely a snort from Mr Fountain — 'Typical of Ayres! Always on the make!' — And, beginning to unroll and check the 72 weighty six inch sheets I had managed to heave in and out of buses to his flat, he chivied: 'Don't just stand there goggling! Run along to Hunter Penrose in Farringdon Road. For more stick ink and tracing paper as per this chit ... While I check these ready for you to take to Norton & Gregory.' For them, more complicated specifications: the O.S. maps to be reduced; the reduction bromides then to be sun-copied — a dozen of each pulled on good white paper. 'Wait there for them, and return as soon as poss...'

These he then sorted into sets; rolled up two, parcelled and labelled them: 'Take them as addressed! ... A vast undertaking, London! If I don't farm out some of it, I'll go bonkers!...'

After the 1914-18 war, papa had bought the New Eltham printers ''Gilbert Whitehead''. To initiate a map department there and run it, he transferred two of his Fleet Street draughtsmen. Where, under new Hutchinson ownership (following papa's and Geographia's bankruptcy due to premature calling in of an overdraft), they remained employed. Remained too in the nearby homes, papa had helped them buy.

The first I called on, recently retired Mr Scowen agreed at his front door to free-lance for me: 'on condition I don't have no truck with Fountain ...' adding: I'd like for Mr Gross to know I've come up in the world. My son's a Major in the London Scottish...'

But Mr Stewart — papa's first ever draughtsman — warmly greeted me, invited me in and declared: 'Though I'm still Geographia's manager at G.W., my first loyalty is to Mr Gross and always will be ... When those villains — including Messrs Frank and Chris Crowley — voted him off the Geographia Board, I cast the only vote on his behalf with my one share. Furthermore, when Bain that jumped-up nincompoop sent a circular to every employee forbidding contact with Mr Alexander Gross on pain of dismissal, I told him in no uncertain terms where he got off: ''What I do in my own time is none of your business!'' Written, signed and delivered! For all to see! ... So that when, soon after, your father returned from America for his bankruptcy proceedings, I openly met him ... As I did six years later when he arrived in London to institute legal proceedings against those sordid plotters of his downfall. What an achievement! To have earned and saved enough within the statutory seven years! ... From an English night-school he founded for teaching Polish immigrants in Chicago's rail and stock yards. 'Then, two days after his arrival here, Nemesis! Out of the blue every cent of his hard earned savings down the drain ... all he'd denied himself for. He who'd been used to every luxury — Claygate mansion, butler, gardeners galore — down and out again! Through the American Stock Exchange crash. His bank gone bust. He showed me the fatal letter from his manager, a University student, glad in such a holocaust to have got a job as street-sweeper.

'That put paid to your dad's long nursed hope of clearing his name: of re-instatement as Chairman and Managing Director of Geographia; of moral and financial retribution from the dastardly conspirators who'd robbed him — (no longer anything to do with our firm, I'm happy to say ... They just went off with the boodle.) How I admire his courage! How vividly I remember his words to me as this second great calamity hit him: ''Fate has decreed that I face map publishing again ... My one expertise. I've shied from it for too many years. I either make a fresh start now on the verge of fifty ... or I never will! ...'' And swallowing his pride, asked: ''Would you Stewart draw me the maps I need to start up in New York?'' I was too full to answer straight away ... a pause that made him doubt even my loyalty: '''I'll quite understand Stewart if you say NO.''

'''On the contrary Mr Gross'', I said: ''Just send me the material; and don't think of paying me until it suits you.'' Never to my dying day will I forget the look he gave me ... As you know he can't thank or praise; he thinks it'll go to one's head or cost him too much! That day I told Bain straight: ''I'm working for Mr Alexander Gross evenings and week-ends.'' So our director knows where I stand ... Let's see what you've got for me.'

'But this is in direct competition with the firm you're working for ... Surely that can't be right with Geographia?'

'When your father suggested I help out Fountain on your E. & W., I let Bain know. It's common practice for map draughtsmen — when there's no overtime — to increase our earnings wherever we can. Competitors or whoever. We know all about trade secrets and when to keep our mouths shut ... So that's that!' Unwrapping the package, he mulled over its contents, — 'tell Mr Gross when you write that he can count on me' — and reverted to reminiscence: 'Please excuse a personal remark, but suddenly, with your resemblance to Mrs Gross I'm flooded by fond memories. You were a wee lassie when she first brought you upstairs to our drawing office at 55 Fleet Street ... I lifted you onto my high stool, put a pen in your hand, guided it to the ink saucer on my bench, to the tracing paper and to draw a map outline on it. Do you recall? You were only three years old ... And when we applauded, you clapped your little hands with glee. "Mrs Gross", I said, "How I hope your daughter follows in your footsteps!" A prayer which to-day seems answered ... Your mother was always the lady. How we all loved and respected her ... elegant ... brilliant ... genuine — when she spoke to you, only you existed for her. And what a remarkable business women she was! Here and now I must pay her a tribute she was too modest to claim. Her vital part in the founding and development of Geographia. I was in at the start so I know ... Though your father — a live wire if ever there was one — never gave her credit ... How is the dear lady, may I ask?' Too sad to confide that her latent manic depression had deteriorated into certified madness at Bethlem, I prevaricated: 'As brilliant as ever! ... She's married again. An American artist. He's painting King Edward VIII for the Queen Mother. In Coronation Robes.'

Nor did I mention her recent horror at my doing 'a spot of indexing' for papa: 'Working for that megalomaniac! He'll use you as a drudge and then destroy you! You'll end up a wreck like me! Competitive in everything he says and does. Envious of my popularity, wit, repartee, unpredictability! Men resent successful women, Phyllis. But that devil! ... That Hungarian father of yours! ... He's the worst of the lot! Smash! Smash! Smash!'

The sanity of the mad is rarely heeded. Mama's ravings — although I knew them justified — could not, I felt, apply to me. For I was neither married to papa, nor emotionally, mentally or financially dependent on him. Thus, his intrusion into my career only spasmodic up to now, I ignored her wisdom; and succumbing to his next persuasive request — '... there's nobody else I can count on' — agreed to index London for three separate publications he itemised:

'1. PREMIER LONDON
'Fountain to give you copy of area covered. Centred on Charing Cross you to draw one inch squares to the outer margins and reference them: A B C etc. top and bottom; 1 2 3 etc. down both sides.

'2. STANDARD STREET GUIDE of LONDON
'Fountain to let you have copy for a smaller central London area. On the Premier index cards falling within that area, add "Nearest Main Street"; and, next to it, "Nearest Station and Bus Route", with appropriate railway and/or Underground Line (abbreviated), and bus numbers after each street name. Work that out for yourself from the map — though the map itself won't be connected to this Guide; and you'll have to tell the compositor to leave out the references. Use your common sense.

'3. O.K. STREET ATLAS of LONDON
Area to be increased outside the L.C.C. area where necessary to make a complete rectangle. Plus Croydon and Harrow as insets. Fountain to give you paginated copy combining this outer area with the Premier's, for you to index from sun-copies.'

Simple, I presumed. But confused from the start by ambiguous abbreviations — did C denote Close, Court or Crescent? M, Mansions or Mews? — I bolted to Mr Fountain who shuddered at a more serious inadequacy — 'A right botch you've made of your reference squares! I thought you was an artist!' — and ruled them correctly on another set of sun-copies.

'Abbreviations?' I asked.

'Obvious my dear Watson ... Look them up in a couple of other indexes ... As to your scrawl, words fail me. How many times on the E. & W. proof did you have to correct your "D" for 'O", "C" for "G", "I" for "T", "P" for "R", and so on and so forth and vice versa? ... At least try can't you to print each letter. And neatly. And with serifs.'

'What are serifs?'

'Like so ... If I was you I'd start all over again!'

'Oh no!' I groaned: 'You draw the squares in for me, please ... and the O.K. pages too and number them ... To set me off right, at least.'

Top pressure concentration day in, day out lulled me into false security; into growing fascination with London's history implicit in its many names: Blue Anchor and Bleeding Heart Yards, Hanging Sword Alley; and from Amen Corner to Paternoster Row, the Lord's Prayer word for word (in brick — perhaps originally in wood); Charterhouse Square — witness of Carthusian friars burnt at the stake during Henry VIII's persecution...

The indexing at last finished, I began to alphabeticise. Only to be stopped short by the plethora of identical names: Abbey Roads and Streets, Aberdeens, Acacias, Addisons, Adelaides...

'How differentiate them for the user?' I asked my long-suffering neighbour.

'By Postal Districts ... No good putting your cards into alphabetical order until you get such problems cleared up...'

'How do I find the Postal Districts?'

'In this years's Post Office List of Streets ... Hold on a mo' and I'll fetch you mine to work on ... though with happy-go-lucky English inefficiency, its area differs from the L.C.C.'s.' Inconsistencies proliferated. Well beyond the odds of chance.

Surmising a fundamental flaw in Mr. Fountain's base, I sped to him: 'What's the date on the Ordnance Survey sheets you've used?'

'Wot you getting at?' he rasped; and having flipped through the 72: 'The majority ain't been revised since 1919 ... The remainder 1917 or 1918 ...'

'That accounts for it!'

'Accounts for wot?'

I laid the open Post Office book on his bench: 'The discrepancies ...', and pointed out a few.

'Teaching your grandmother to suck eggs!' he mocked: 'Have you looked at competition? Geographia, George Philip, Bartholomew, Bacons? They're no better ... So wot? ... Every map-maker knows you can't be sued for copyright if two other map publishers print the same mistake...'

'Surely our aim is to show people the way ...'

'Wot's good enough for Mr Gross should be good enough for his daughter ... Anyway, it can't be done. And I'll tell you for why. What's the good of a list to me? How can I know where to draw in a street if I don't see it mapped?'

'Who maps the changes as they take place?'

'The Borough and County Surveyors. Who else?...'

'Where?'

'Town Halls and the like ... They got to know where there's sewer man-holes, fire hydrants, street lamps, water and gas mains ... What we're fleeced for rates for...'

'I'll go.'

'You'd be biting off more than you can chew! ... Twenty years of changes to copy onto another lot of sun-copies...'

'We've got to get it right', I persisted; and flouting papa's latest prod:

*'How can you take weeks on a job I could accomplish in a trice!'* — I set forth.

Most of the 31 Borough Surveyors (28 L.C.C.; one each the City, Croydon and Harrow) welcomed me — 'Up-to-date maps are long overdue. We look forward to yours' — sat me at a desk in their sanctums; and provided me with meticulously hand-updated O.S. sheets: 'Take as long as it takes, my dear.' Helpfully too they advised me of developments under construction or proposed: 'The local Estate Agents will give you the plans.' Which they did — 'easier to sell a house if it's on the map' — or, if unavailable, drove me to the site. Where, scale, shape and grid awry, I drew my inept own.

The majority I covered within a day or two. The rest took longer. Slapdash or non-existent records, or petty bureaucrat's refusal of entry sent me checking on the ground — chaotic after checking maps. Often in the maze of many a turning off many a side street I found myself back where I started, or, completely lost, had to ask the way.

'Tell me the name of the Company you represent', laughed one joker: 'and I'll know what maps not to buy!'

The herculean task completed, I bearded Mr Fountain with my annotated sun-copies: 'to alter on your original, please...'

'If any clot had told me I'd take orders from a woman I'd have knocked his block off!', he capitulated.

Whereupon — too often deposited at the wrong end of a long road by car, bus or tram — I proposed another innovation: 'House numbers!'

'Strike me pink!'

'I'll garner them for you...'

'Just like your ma! Ready for anything! Very well then, Madam, I suppose that while you go gallivanting again, I'll have to twiddle my thumbs! But off you go on your new Marathon! And when you gets back I'll try to fit in the finnicky figures you compile ... And that's a promise! ... And I'll tell you for why ... Your enthusiasm's catching...'

Envisioning a quick gallop up and down the radials out to Edgware, Finchley,

Tottenham, Barking, Croydon, Ealing, Harrow and the many in between, I set off from Marble Arch up the west side of Edgware Road, jotting down the house numbers at each intersection. Despite inconsistencies galore, such as names instead of numbers, unnumbered blocks of flats, churches, continuation into side streets, I did not falter till 453 suddenly plummeted to 35 — due to the start of Maida Vale; which, ending at number 245 plummeted to Kilburn High Road's Number 1. Shoot up Hill started at 27; Cricklewood Broadway at 1 again; and when Edgware Road (understandably forgetful by now of where it had left off) resumed, it did so at 329 instead of 455 — thus duplicating 126 numbers — differentiated only by Postal District change from W2 to NW2.

Similar anomalies beset the even numbers along the east side on my rush back towards Marble Arch. Finchley Road, however, (though bedevilled with many self-numbered Parades), at least ran consecutively from 8 to 1201 on the left, and 2 to 872 on the right. In fact, every radial sported its very own system or lack of it. As did the horizontals I next tackled; and finally the any-which-ways of Central London.

'That lot'll obliterate the street names!' demurred Mr Fountain leafing through my notebooks.

'Fit in the first, middle and last ...', I pleaded: 'so that people can see at least if the numbers run in sequence or odd one side and evens the other...'

Without a quibble, he acquiesced; shamefacedly admitted: 'A little hitch I'm afraid ... You remember the reference squares I drew on the Ordnance sheets for you to index? ... Well, when it come to drawing my original, I had to re-position many names; so you'll need to get it sun-copied. For why? To check your index references along the edges of each square...'

'Why didn't you warn me?' I quailed: 'Or I wouldn't have started till you were ready ... rather than face that whole dog-eared lot again!'

With tissue protecting each sheet of the original, he deftly rolled them together, inserted them into a cardboard tube, instructed me to get the sun copies; said: 'and then you can begin to check.'

A Sisyphean task. And although my cards were not alphabeticised but in square order, it proved quicker and more accurate to re-index the whole bang shoot.

Through with that enormity, another zoomed. Via my well-informed and cooperative neighbour: 'Did you know that the L.C.C. are changing 2000 street names?'

Confirmed by County Hall's Surveyor: 'It's to eliminate duplication. Adam Street Adelphi, we'll retain for its architectural relevance. But, for example, Adam Street off Baker Street we're re-naming Robert Adam...'

My request for a full list elicited a hollow laugh: 'We only started last year; and though we at the L.C.C. propose, the local Councillors dispose. Each has his own idea; maybe to immortalise wife or child — Catherine, Cedric, Celandine — or enshrine some preferred saint, apostle, flower, tree, bird, mountain range, locomotive, sport, poet — often misspelt, no affair of mine, thank goodness ... It's going to be a long process. But here's a list of the few already ratified; and, as others become so, I'll make sure you're sent a memo; or, better still, I suggest you subscribe to our fortnightly journal ... Though remember, dear lady, that however highly we cartographers aspire to perfection, never can we be up-to-date. Like Alice's Red Queen, "it takes all the running we can do to keep in the same place." 'It's no good fretting. Go ahead regardless!' I did so. On what — after supplying Mr Fountain with the definite changes, and incorporating them in my index — I believed the last lap: the delayed alphabeticising of that daunting mass of index cards.

It took days to shuffle each into its separate pile of A, B, C, to Z; then to subdivide these into second letter piles from 'a' to 'z'; and even third and fourth letter piles from 'a' to 'z'. All spread out on the floor like a gigantic game of patience. Thus did I become addicted to A to Z. Obviously the only possible title for the London Street Atlas, I decided. And wrote so to papa. Who, remaining enamoured of his own O.K., objected furiously by return:

> *'Why?! Why?! Why can't you ever do what I tell you?!!! Bad enough when you don't think! But worse when you do! What a dunce to suggest so abysmal an alternative! What customer's going to have the nerve to ask a shopkeeper for the first and last letter of the alphabet! Ludicrous! He'd be laughed out of court. Whereas "O.K." is on everybody's lips. Synonymous with "fine" ... inferring excellence. Without fail you're to use the enclosed cover design I've had especially drawn for you. At my prompting, the artist has placed the lettering — THE OK STREET ATLAS & GUIDE to LONDON — over an open Tower Bridge. To symbolise that The O.K. ... opens up London to the purchaser ... So bury your malapropism; and let this be the last I ever hear of A to Z!'*

Mr Stewart agreed with me — 'Living in the States, how could the Governor recognise "OK" as an Americanism that's hardly taken on here! — and deftly substituted A to Z on the design.

Anxious to clear the studio for my sitters, (their fees now helping pay Mr Fountain as well as my keep) I stacked the awesome mass of index cards into shoe boxes — (provided by my neighbour: 'The extortionate price of index cabinets is another example of capitalist exploitation!') — and on a borrowed push-cart, trundled them from Horseferry Road to High Holborn.

The cards already numbered to the end of the S's, I was well into the T's, when — the air foul from Field Staff smoking — I leant across my rickety table to push the window open.

Disaster! For, precipitated by its unruly castors, the table hurtled forward ... and — 'Oh No!' — catapulted the flimsy cardboard box of T's out through the window — emptying its precious contents as it fell.

The traffic lights at red, I raced down the four flights of stairs. Out into High Holborn. Out into the road. To retrieve within seconds the cards most at risk. By sweeping them off car roofs, bonnets, boots and running boards before —

the lights turning green — the traffic surged forward. Only then, with the help of passers-by inspired by my frenzy, did I gather up the quiescent cards. From road, gutter, pavement. All except for a few escapees on the top of a bus I watched sail away into oblivion. For, un-numbered, they could not be traced.

'Can't be helped ... Kiss them goodbye', I counselled myself. While our vigilant caretaker — ever lifeboat quick to the rescue — counted blessings: 'Thank God it wasn't raining! Imagine the sodden mass we'd be carrying up in the lift ... and the ink smudged or washed clean away...'

The recovered truants re-alphabeticised, I resumed tabulation. Reaching the grand totals of 23,000 for the A to Z index entries, and 19,000 for the Premier.

# CHAPTER 5

MY elated letter to papa: *'The index is done!'* brought the reply: *Done? What do you mean done?! You haven't begun yet!* And, paternally assuming my further bondage, he instructed me in ten cramped pages how to publish: *'the manuscripts you've managed at long last to finish.'* Lore so compressed and jargon studded — 'perfector', 'quad demy', 'imposition', 'gripper', 'stereos' — that I was flummoxed. Even after several re-readings.

*'It's all double Dutch to me',* I replied. And he: *'I give you the benefit of a lifetime's experience and you don't even bother to read it ...'*

Inexperience remedied by one of Mr Arnold's clients. A clean-shaven softly spoken caller at the office who apologising — 'We bought your England & Wales wall map, and wondered if you had any printing to put out ...' handed me his visiting card:

*Harry Williams. Representative.*
*Lowe and Brydone*
*Music and Book Printers & Publishers*

'In these hard times', he said: 'either we technical men become representatives or go on the dole ... I wouldn't like you to think I'm poaching for your England & Wales reprint. In fact its 54 by 40 size is outside our range. But if you're contemplating quad demy or smaller, we'd provide altogether better quality, though I say it myself ... A new German photo-lithographic process our Mr Brydone bought the British rights for is sharper than any other I know.'

'What's quad demy?'

'45 by 35 inches.'

'Our Premier London size!' I exclaimed: 'I'm in dire need of a good kind printer...'

'How many colours?'

'Six.'

A moment's pursed lip cogitation, and he replied: 'Our presses are two colour, but no matter. To keep them busy's the priority so we wouldn't charge you more for running through three times.' Wherewith, he produced from his portfolio four-colour samples of illustrated nursery rhymes, in sheet form — for hanging on nursery wallls — and as book: 'I think they speak for themselves...'

I phoned Mr Fountain: 'We have a printer for the Premier.'

'Who?'

'Lowe & Brydone'.

'Never heard of them. What do they know about maps?'

'Nothing', admitted Mr Williams.

'Black! That's wot they all fall down on!' sneered Mr Fountain.

'My draughtsman would like to see your black ...' I euphemised to Mr Williams.

'If your Chief Draughtsman could let us have a sample, we'll supply a bromide...'

To Mr Fountain I suggested they try an A to Z page.

'Fetch and deliver it yourself then! A sun copy of course. You don't think I'm going to trust my original to the tender mercies of another lot of butchers who call themselves printers! If Lowe & Brydone or whatever they call themselves want to waste time and money on it who am I to stop them!'

But the resultant bromide next day — peered at through his linen tester — he grudgingly approved: 'Not too bad ... No broken lines ... They'll do.'

Mr Williams apprised, hurried to my office. Giving him papa's letter of instructions, I asked him to interpret 'what my father wants me to ask you to do'.

Only after long and concentrated study did he sum up: 'Most urgent seems to be the Premier ... A few good black copies first as drawing office base for the A to Z street atlas. Then a black, blue, red and yellow 15,000 run ... 5,000 of them on good quality paper for mounting; the remaining 10,000 on cheaper paper for the trade. No problem. We can adjust the machine ... Your father certainly knows the ropes. By running the 5 and 10 thou' together, he's cutting out double make-ready and wash-up.'

'What's make-ready?' I asked — having received no explanation from Mr Weiss.

'Getting the ink in the ducts, matching colour to your copy, getting register as good as possible ... It can take four hours for each colour...'

'And wash-up?'

'Like what it says — cleaning the machine for the next job. It's got to be spotless ... black after yellow's all right, but yellow after black's diabolical ... you wouldn't do it. My dad — in his day of one colour machines — learnt that soon enough!'

Next he asked: 'What about paper? You'll be needing reams, if not tons...'

'Reams?'

'500 sheets to a ream.'

Never had I bought more paper than half a dozen sheets of Whatman's hand-made water colour and box of typing paper; and hopefully told him: 'Greycaines and Weiners used paper they'd got in stock...'

'You probably had to pay a handling charge ... As you'd have to do with us. Cheaper for you to buy direct from a supplier. I'll introduce you to Mr Brown of John Dickinson ... He delivers in good time for us to stack, hang, and — as

far as ever-changing humidity and temperature allow — to acclimatise ...
Minimising our perpetual headache of shrink, stretch, cockle, he's God's gift
to us ... Any trouble with it on the machine and there before you can say Jack
Robinson is Mr Brown ... If I can use your phone I might get him here
right away...

Mr Brown, neat in his brown suit, proposed 'Dickinson's new twin wire
Evensyde for your 5,000 quality edition; and for the trade, 7,500 Croxley white,
with 2,500 thin scrim for cloth-lined.'

'Thin scrim?'

'Loose woven cotton. About 40 threads to the inch', he explained; adding to
Mr Williams: 'I'll need 10% for overs.'

'What are overs?' I asked.

'Wastage. Particularly on make-ready ... I'll bring your estimate and
samples round tomorrow', he promised: 'So long, Mr Williams. Thank you for
thinking of me ...' and left.

'That settles the photolitho side of your father's instructions', resumed Mr
Williams: 'Now for letterpress and binding ...' and sloughing off his ill-cast
selling role: 'We're too pricey in that department at Lowe & Brydone. Gordon
& Kerensky are letterpress and binding only. Mr Short's the man you want. I'll
give him a tinkle ... ask him to join us...'

While we waited, Mr Williams chatted on: 'Short, like me, left school at 14,
and bound himself for seven years as apprentice — ''to be at your Master's
bidding 24 hours a day'' — Quite a hoo-ha! Indentures on parchment, signed
and sealed with the Company Seal ... In those days one had to pay half a crown
a week to be an apprentice ... or rather, in my case my mother did. By taking
in washing. Now in this present slump Mr Short's also had to combine getting
print orders with seeing them through. Otherwise our firms couldn't afford to
pay us...'

Mr. Short — short in stature too, but cairn terrier abristle — on reading
papa's letter quickly gleaned his main problem: how to fit 19,000 names and
references into a minimum number of pages. Out came his printers' rule —
Let's measure the longest lines, Missee. In ems, not inches begging your
pardon. Which settles choice of type-face ... 3 columns Roman 6 point, on a 5
point base ... That's 12 lines to the inch.'

'Inch? I thought you said ems? I interrupted.

'Inches for verticals; Ems for horizontals ... number of letters along each
entry including spaces, punctuation etcetera ... Am afraid we'll have to charge
more for cards than typescript as they're fiddly for our Comp., sorry,
Compositor, and no offence meant. But we won't charge more for having to sort
out the Premier Index from the two other references crammed on each card ...
Let alone handwriting not typed. Am I to quote for paper?'

'Shouldn't we have asked Mr Brown while he was here?' I asked Mr
Williams.

'Your father specifies newsprint; which Croxley Mills don't manufacture.'

'What about Walter Makin in Queen Victoria Street?' suggested Mr Short: 'We've always found him reliable ... I'll ask him to send Mrs Pearsall a quote ... I hate to say it, Mr Williams, but between you and me and the gatepost, she'll get a squarer deal that way than if it goes through our office ... Wish my bosses were like your Mr Brydone. Everybody in the trade trusts Mr Brydone.

Grateful for the patient guidance of these two friends, I accepted their Premier estimates. But with the proviso: 'subject to my father's approval'.

Which was not forthcoming. Instead, censure:

*'So you've let yourself be hoodwinked! Beat them down! ... Get comparative prices from other paper suppliers and printers. And make the printers quote for each process, not in lump totals ... And you place each process with the cheapest!'*

With a father in America I seemed a sitting duck to the scores of other printers I approached. Pin-stripe Chairmen and Managing Directors in panelled offices, flattered, patronised — 'Young lady, you can trust us to look after you' — while their estimates for the same job puzzlingly ranged between £280 and £2,000 ... 'or shall we quote you in dollars?'

No ground under my feet with these effete elite, and once again defying papa, I confirmed my orders: 'full steam ahead.''

At Lowe & Brydone — by tube to North Acton — I passed the colours. At my office I corrected galley proofs brought by Mr Short.

In the margin of the Tr's the ''reader'' queried: *'Is Trafalgar Square left out deliberately?'*

In horrified relief, I thanked him: 'It whizzed away on the top of a bus ... Let's hope you'll spot the others.'

Page proofs followed.

'Do you want stereos?' asked Mr Short.

'Stereos?'

'Papier maché moulds of each page made when type and furniture are clamped into the chase.'

'Furniture?...'

'Pieces of wood or metal fitted round the type and into blank spaces to hold the page firm.'

'Chase? ... And why would I want stereos?'

'If future editions need alterations you'd best leave the metal standing — though we do charge a small rent — and print from stereos. Then changes for a new edition made on metal unworn by use, won't stick out black like a sore thumb! ... For further editions, a new stereo can be made every time until the cows come home...'

Soon he delivered the 5,000 Field Staff indexes. On papa's instructions, pinned into staple-ringed covers with a tasselled cord — either to hang on the wall beside C.R.V.'s or slip into Cut to Folds. And shortly after, Mr Williams delivered his 5,000 Field Staff Premiers to Hardings for mounting: 'We're home and dry!'

# CHAPTER 6

'SUPERDUPERIFEROUS! ... Splendoriferous!' gasped Uncle Frank at first sight of the Premier London; tears of joy aglisten on his Bacchus cheeks: 'El Dorado at long last! ... or as my poetic Peg would say: "the pot of gold at the end of the rainbow!"'

Scenting release from lifelong salesman struggle, this old campaigner in his jaunty sixties, effervesced into Midas dreams fulfilled: 'Oh Phyllis, how I'll adorn my beloved! With jewels, furs! Couturiers' coutures! ... And in Silver Cloud waft her away from our poky Vallance Road nest to country mansion set in parkland with herds of deer ... And what-ho businesswise: luxury offices, minions galore ... While thou pain in thine Uncle's neck, can avaunt thee hence from sordid commerce to ladylike smock, easel, palette!...'

Jubilantly too did he greet Mr Arnold: 'As I was saying Arnold old chap, this superb London is the cat's whiskers ... Yes, take a good look, dear fellow. The Punch Lines stare you in the face: "Bang up-to-date including latest L.C.C. street name changes" ... "House numbers along main roads (for the first time ever in commercial mapping)" ... and — our unique symbol of quality — "Produced under the direction of Alexander Gross." A winner, eh? And how do I, your Supremo, intend to back this beauty?! By increasing the staff tenfold and slashing territories! That's how!'

'No Sir! And break the spirit of every rep you've got! ... The boys trust me. They've done more than their fair share of drudgery — on the wretched World and the limited market E. & W. — No Mr Crowley Sir! I refuse to be a party to inhumanity!'

'You jumped up pip-squeak. You must be a Protestant!'

'I'm a Quaker.'

'Worse!'

At my intervention — 'I agree with Mr Arnold about inhumanity' — Uncle Frank smouldered; but forced a laugh: 'No need to get hot under the collar, old man ... You know how reasonable I am. And magnanimous. Always ready to listen ... As to heresy, that's your own affair! Hard luck on you, though, when St Peter pops the question: "Are you a good Catholic?" and bars you from Paradise! Ha! Ha! We know the only true faith, don't we, Phyllis? ... But to return to your insubordination, Arnold. I run this outfit, and don't you my man forget it...'

Calmly Mr Arnold rejoined: 'My strategy is to preserve territory and jobs by combing street by street — ruling each off on the map when completed. As to picking out important people or companies to call on, how to keep track of where one of us has or hasn't been? And anyway my not inconsiderable experience shows the prominent less likely to buy than the little man beavering away in a shed — who needs the map to save him time and money.'

'Have you finished!' rasped my uncle; and, at my 'Mr Arnold's right, you know', turned on me: 'Stop putting in your ten cents worth where it isn't wanted, can't you, woman! Arnold and I understand each other, don't we old stick-in-the-mud?...'

Whereupon a *contretempts* allied them against me. Opening my mail, I dropped a draft cover design for the future trade edition of the Premier London. On the floor. Where they spotted its retail price of half a crown.

'Betrayal!' bellowed my uncle. While Mr Arnold appealed to my conscience: 'You can't mean to put these on the market and compete with our three guinea London, Madam! Surely with such a winner at last, you'll give us a fair crack of the whip!...'

'It won't come out for ages ...' I reassured them. Having decided to keep it back until the A to Z Atlas and the Standard Street Guide were ready. Against papa's advice — 'Never wait to sell! Get the money in!' — But on the advice of my sitter, B. H. Binder, eminent Chartered Accountant and Chairman of a retail chain: 'Phyllis, until you've got at least three publications to launch simultaneously, don't tackle the closed ranks of the book trade ... And I know what I'm talking about!...

Meanwhile the Field Staff Premier sales exceeded rosiest hopes; resulting in wild Friday night carousels at Henekeys. Until arch manipulator, Uncle Frank — with Cheshire cat 'Fill up your glasses lads! This round's on me!' — bragged of 'a sensational *coup* I've personally perpetrated ... Can't keep my Peg pining for her knight errant any longer...'

On the Monday he gathered us together 'to spill the beans ... A week today the Cold Sell champion of the world is going to flog the London with us...'

Simultaneously Mr Arnold and I queried: 'What territory are you giving him?'

'Me giving him?! That's a laugh! He's a law unto himself! ... It's your Uncle Chris, Phyllis! My elder brother! My alter ego! Winkled out of his Devon retreat ... Cheerybye!'

In a ten days whirlwind Chris rampaged through London, ruthlessly plundering every territory; and loot pocketed, roared back to Devon.

Once again, Uncle Frank not daring to face the victims — 'This situation calls for feminine tact.' — left me to deal with them. But instead of righteous indignation, bedazzlement: 'Begod what a virtuoso!' praised Mr Nolan for them all: 'In a Brooklands Bugatti! And he the spittin' image of his bulldog sittin' up beside him! As he careered in and out of streets horn hooting, scattering pedestrians, snarling up the traffic! ... A much greater man indeed, than his bone-lazy meanie brother Frank we're saddled with...

Criticism — encouraged by Mr Arnold's 'give the little lady an eye-opener'

— he proceeded to specify: 'Never a one of the orders you paid him commission on was his. Stolen from us on pain of dismissal if we croaked ... Even on my first training trip he drew up at the Mansion House, and sends me in to sell; while he indulges in a little shut eye. When out I come triumphant, he snitches half the juicy orders for himself: "unless you want to be out on your uppers again!"''

'Which applies more or less to all of us', confirmed Mr Arnold.

'You too, Mr Thompson?' I asked.

'As long as you don't peach to His Lordship, Ma'am righty-ho ...'

'And you, Mr Benn?'

Though above personalities, his Blake quotation — 'Cruelty has a Human Heart!' — corroborated the ghastly accusation.

What can I do to put things right?' I floundered: 'If I confront my uncle I lose you your jobs...'

'Nothing hasty, Miss ... You'll be given the opportunity...'

Opportunity which, though shrouded at first, unfolded from a telephone call. An unknown man, his accent true Oxbridge, asked for the Chairman.

'Perhaps I could help?'

'I don't speak to subordinates'; and he gave me his number.'

Thrilled, my uncle phoned the important caller back: 'Chairman speaking ... What can I do for you dear fellow?'

'A proposition of mutual interest ... I'd like to put it to you personally. Would 7 o'clock this evening be convenient?'

The gang expelled — for Mr Arnold often kept them late to delay returning to his unhappy home — my uncle set the stage: 'Open the windows, Phyllis, 'this place looks and stinks like a Wild West corral ... Now stand beside my desk to take down an important letter in shorthand...'

'I don't know shorthand...'

'Holy Mary Mother of God, do you always have to quibble!'

A knock at the door, and in walked a presentable youngish man, right hand outstretched: 'Mr Crowley, I presume ... My name's Morgan. I'm deeply impressed by the exceptionally high quality of your Business Executive maps. Those I saw in the Lord Mayor's parlour far surpass the Philip's I've been selling for years ... As free lance agent. May I offer you my services, Mr Crowley? You can ask George Philip for a reference of course...'

'With your credentials, quite unnecessary, old chap ... What area have you in mind?'

'Of no consequence. I have excellent contacts everywhere ... So long as I'm not stepping on anybody's toes, and the territory you allot me is exclusively mine...

'What about Bromley and Croydon? Hitherto untapped.'

'Capital! ... As to terms, Mr Crowley? I gather your E. & W. is selling at five guineas ... For me then 25% commission ... let us say £1.10 each map ... payable on order, it goes without saying.'

'When can you start?'

'Monday next.'

Handed his Selling Section and Order Book, he professionally slipped them into his poacher's pocket; but refused the Receipt Book: 'That's not my way. I refer my clients to our Accounts Department...'

'Shake on it!' heartily responded Uncle Frank: 'Till Friday week then ... Au revoir ...'

'If it's the last thing I ever do, I'll justify your faith in me!' smarmed the paragon departing.

'How unfair of you Uncle Frank to give better terms to a newcomer I protested.

But, self-satisfaction oozing, my uncle waffled on: 'A gift from above ... That'll put George Philip's nose out of joint ... Eton or Harrow I shouldn't wonder ... What style! ... And I bet you a million — let's make it a fiver — that his orders'll be astronomical.'

They were. One hundred and twenty five maps. Mostly London at 3 guineas, but quite a sprinkling of the other two — the clients' names, addresses and Special Requirements methodically recorded in a clear hand.

'If only you, Nolan, could be as neat!' apostrophised my awestruck uncle: 'A bumper crop. Congratulations, Morgan!'

'To work for so appreciative a Chairman is indeed an inspiration, Mr Crowley! ... My goal next week is to double, treble, nay quadruple my orders! ...' And, producing his gold-cornered crocodile wallet, asked me to pay his commission: '£185, I calculate...'

'Only half on order; the balance on payment ...' I resisted. To my uncle's suppressed annoyance: 'My agreement with Mr Morgan, Phyllis, is for Payment on Order. And a gentleman's word is his bond. So pay up fair secretary mine! Pay up and play the game! ... And while you're about it, how about the fiver you owe me! ... As to you, Morgan, associate after my own heart, let's hie us to Henekeys and celebrate!'

'Deliveries?' I asked.

'God grant me patience, oh spoil-sport niece ... Haven't I always attended to that side of the business! ... Monday will be soon enough.'

It was not.

Monday night, Auntie Peg phoning me from Hove, bewailed: 'Your Uncle Frank's suffered a severe warning from the old ticker ... He returned home absolutely whacked last night. All due to that dreadful Mr Morgan ... Have you ever known your dear uncle down in the dumps? ... Well he is now. He wants a word with you.'

His voice, shaky at first — 'Didn't I tell you, Phyllis, that Morgan was too smooth by half ...' — took on resonance as he warmed to his story: 'Every one of those 125 orders phoney! Every address, street, house name or number brilliantly invented. Let that be a lesson to you niecey. One hundred and eighty

five smackers down the drain! Next time you'll harken unto thine old uncle ...
Meanwhile post me my commission...'

I promised to do so. Recognising that here was my opportunity to abort for
ever his power to exploit; and proposed: 'Why don't I base your commission
in future on Field Staff turnover instead of on your personal orders?'

'Alex would strangle you! ... And so would I if it meant a drop in my takings!'

'It can't! Not with a dozen men now under your able command! Besides,
Auntie Peg longs for you to take things easy. And so do I, dear Uncle Frank.
To save you stress and harrassment, exposure to bad weather, pounding up and
down stairs, interminable waits for lifts...'

'So you love your old Unkie Dunkie! ... Very well then!' he agreed; adding
ruefully: 'I phoned George Philip about Morgan ... He could hardly answer me
for laughing: "Called himself Morgan for you, did he now? It was Smith for
us; Davis, Allen, what have you, for his other dupes! That Old Etonian's a
byword in the trade! So he conned you too!" At least I cottoned on to Eton,
Phyllis! Trust me to recognise top drawer when I see it!'

Mr Arnold in charge, the Premier sold consistently well. But Mr Nolan, now
our ace, voiced the general feeling of flatness: 'Sure there's no sense in it
— swiping my orders as that mountain of a man did ... and never a grudge in
me — but how I miss the roisterous bastard, so help me God!' He alone added
light relief. By quip of the week stories: 'So the Berkeley Street Rolls Royce
Director, fancying he can turn me down, says: "Three guineas for a map!
That's daylight robbery!" ... "For the Rolls Royce of maps!" ses I ...'

'Did he buy?' asked Mr Thompson.

'Arrah he did! Six Cut to Folds, so. And more to come, one to each Rolls
Royce purchaser — with compliments of the Management!' Even the poet
could not help earning more than his low set maximum: 'Alas! All is seared with
trade! ... I'll join the *London Library.*'

# CHAPTER 7

'I'VE finished drawing the extensions for the A to Z Street Atlas', phoned Mr Fountain: 'So fetch them to have sun copies made. And while Norton & Gregory are at it, nip over to Lowe & Brydone for the black only Premiers. Then bring the lot to me. For why? So I can get stuck into the loose ends ... cut the pages out of the blacks ... draw border frame ... ''continued on page so and so''...'

A few weeks later, he summoned me to take the finished work to Lowe & Brydone — 'It's been a slog making up the names round the edges, I can tell you' — and phoned Mr Williams: 'I'm sending Mrs Pearsall along with written instructions. But so there won't be no cock-up, here's wot: Quad demy. Both sides of the sheet. 96 pages. 48 to view. I've allowed for gripper and gutters ... Give me a tinkle if there's any query ... Oh! You want a word with her. Hold on a mo'.'

'Mr Brydone would like to meet you', said Mr Williams: 'So please call at Admin, instead of going straight through to our works as you do to pass the colours...'

In striking contrast to the modern, spacious gleaming single-storeyed factory was the administrative block.

A draughty sentinel-box housed the commissionaire; shivering with cold though muffled in greatcoat (hung with Boer and Great War medals), thick woollen scarf and gloves. Having announced my arrival on an inside phone, he showed me through the outside door of a ramshackle brick house into a fusty cubby-hole. A room ashake and ablare with clip clop clap of distant printing presses; roar of thousands of marbles hurtling around the sprung engine-powered metal tray, graining the zinc printing plates — as seen and deafened by on previous visits.

Thence, Mr Williams — 'excuse the din ... it's music in a printer's ear — led me through an ill-hung swing door into Dickensian working conditions: 'Our Governor ploughs every penny into plant ... at least what's left after paying off the Green brother's who financed our move here from Windmill Street.'

At closely wedged miniscule desks sat numerous clerks; their ages ranging from 14 year old school-leavers to ancients nodding off — 'kept on for their loyalty', approved my escort. Cramped too were the seniors seated six a side hierarchically at a narrow well-worn refectory table piled high with ledgers. Mr Brydone's office, where the head of the firm — in his mid sixties — stood tall, pencil slim, blue suited, his starched wing-collar digging into scrawny neck, and as he drew up chairs for Mr Williams and me. On the entrance of a Junior with tea-tray, he stood up again to introduce her: 'Judy Smith.'

'Sorry it's slopped, Mr Brydone, Sir.'

'Never mind Judy. I'd have spilt it worse', he cheered her.

'Always the gentleman', said Mr Williams for my ears alone.

Delicately, Mr Brydone — unlike Greycaine and Weiner maulers — leafed through Mr Fountain's pages, perused papa's technical letter, and at length voiced his thought: 'Mr Gross specifies a Perfector. It's by far the cheapest method for printing black both sides ... Unfortunately, ours is booked ahead for years on the Hindi Bible ... But that's our problem. Harry, could we put these A to Z black on a one colour?'

'They're all full, Sir.'

'I agree with you then. That we run it through twice on our two colour at Perfector cost ... What about paper, Harry?'

'Walter Makin to supply.'

'Imposition?'

'Probably "H". Mr Short of Gordon Kerensky — they're doing the index and binding — will let me know...'

'Imposition?' I queried.

'Impossible to explain in words,' pondered Mr Williams: 'Folding machines vary.' While Mr Brydone, folding a 35 x 45 sheet of paper in two, then four, and over and over down to A to Z size, explained: 'the simplest way is to demonstrate!' Whereupon 'Look!' he numbered the top right hand corner of each segment from 1 to 96: 'The numbers are consecutive, you see ... And now', he stressed, opening up the sheet, and showing both sides to me: 'Unconsecutive! You try it' As in a kindergarten, the three of us did. Then holding up the completed sheets in turn, he expertly applied scissors: 'Abracadabra! Cut into pages! Ready to be sewn into covers ... Though the guillotine does a much neater job than my jagged edges!'

No longer the conjuror beaming at a delighted audience, he addressed me sternly: 'Why haven't you asked us for a written estimate for the A to Z, as you did with the Premier?'

'Should I have?'

'We'll never let you down', he promised: 'But there are rogues about. I know that to my cost ... As the Scriptures say, we must be wise as a serpent and harmless as a dove ... An honest person can be too trusting when starting up in business: and then, disillusioned, end up a misanthrope ... To prevent either extreme, Mr Williams will make you out our estimate; and, to avert slip-ups between our two firms, your specification for Gordon & Kerensky.' Tactfully too he saved me from another pitfall: 'Have you insured your staff, original maps, stock?'

'Never thought of it...'

'I'll phone my dear friend Duncan Porteous to call at your office ... He's looked after us for years ...' said Mr Brydone.

There, waiting for me on my return, a jovial Mr Pickwick greeted me: 'Jamie Brydone has told me you need protecting ... I'm his friend, Duncan Porteous. He's asked me to look after your insurance.'

'As an artist I hadn't realised how kind and honest so many businessmen can be...'

'Now, my dear, I don't want to land you in any unnecessary expense ... You're just starting, he tells me ... So forgetting these sticks of furniture, let's concentrate on vital cover only ... Firstly, your irreplaceable map originals. Secondly, stock in hand or in progress — here, in transit and at your suppliers. In both cases you need cover against loss of profit till replaced. Thirdly, staff must be insured against injury — on the premises and in the course of their duties...'

'I'd never have thought of all that!' I thanked him.

'Why should you?' he smiled: 'But there's one more person to insure. The most important! You. You, yourself.'

'Me? An ignoramous? I don't draw the maps or sell them...'

'You weave the threads together. Without you there'd be no business ... Willy-nilly your life's got to be insured. Jamie'd never forgive me if not!' On parting, he wished me an encouraging farewell: 'Your humility, integrity and enthusiasm are bound to succeed ... but believe me, my dear, it'll be a long haul...'

In vivid contrast were the directors of Gordon & Kerensky. Savile Row clad, and ensconced in palatial office, Mr Kerensky, the emaciated senior rose at our entry, while florid rotund Mr Gordon clucked round me till I was comfortably seated. Mr Short he left standing.

'Mr Short's been very helpful', I began. Jocularly Mr Gordon cut in: 'Now I've the honour of meeting you, dear lady, I understand why the rascals's been spending so much of his highly paid time at your office!'

'We look forward to discussing business with your father', intervened Mr Kerensky: 'Are you expecting him over here soon? ... I hope we quoted you in dollars...'

'You've got it wrong ... I may even have to ask you for credit.'

Mistaking the truth for poor-little-rich-girl jest, Mr Kerensky smirked; and 'Hee! Hee!' guffawed Mr Gordon.

'Is your imposition "H", I asked.

'Imposition for what?' asked Mr Kerensky.

'For Lowe & Brydone's 96 map pages, 48 to view...'

'Detail is Short's preserve ... Short! Accompany Mrs Pearsall to your den!''

So crammed and shoddy were the printing works, I could not help remarking: 'Topsy-turvey to Mr Brydone's 'craftsmen first, admin second...'

'That's how things are ...' accepted Mr Short; and loyally excused his directors: 'Experts in foreign languages. But no orders from those sources at the moment, they're happy to have yours ... Though they're not quite up to tabulation ... Me neither, for that matter ... Look!' From his bench he picked up some A to Z index galley proofs, explained: With three columns in your typespace there are too many widows...'

'Widows?'

'Lines which spill over onto the line below.'

'Why does that matter?'

'More pages, higher cost ... Unless you can abbreviate. For instance, take Addison Brdg.Pl., W.14.10.0.59...'

'Not if it means altering those 23,000 cards again?' I almost wailed — just surfaced from alphabetically inserting the additional 4,000 outer area A to Z cards into the Premier ones, and renumbering the lot.

'No, no, my dear. Compositors follow publishers' house style. Cut down the punctuation on one and they'll do the rest ... So here goes. No need for the comma after "Pl." nor the full stop after Postal District letters and reference and page numbers...'

Checking with printer's rule, he smiled: 'Looks daft, but does the trick ... In fact', he calculated, 'it'll leave you fourteen empty pages to fill...'

'Why? Can't you just have fourteen less?'

'For binding we work in sixteens...'

The next day I spent in Westminster library compressing London's vast fascinating history into a brief guide to places of interest. Anticipated changes included:

> BLACKWALL TUNNEL: *'The narrowness of the roadway allows only two streams of traffic, but the building of a parallel tunnel at a cost of 3 million pounds has been planned to relieve the congestion';* and WATERLOO BRIDGE: *'Rennie's bridge became unsafe in 1924. It is hoped that the new bridge designed by Sir Gilbert Scott will be completed in 1940.'*

'How many pages?' asked Mr Short, given the copy.

'Thirteen and a half.'

'How are you so sure?'

'Because as you taught me I counted twelve lines to the inch downwards with a line space between the entries; and from left to right 82 ems as you call them...'

'You're learning ...'

'The remaining half page is GENERAL INFORMATION.' In this I included:

> *Main Line Railway Termini — (Great Western: Paddington. London, Midland & Scottish: Euston and St Pancras. London & North Eastern: Fenchurch Street, Liverpool Street, Kings Cross and Marylebone. Southern: Charing Cross, Holborn Viaduct, London Bridge, Victoria, and Waterloo) — Taxis (minimum fare for one or two people, 9d.); and Parking Places.*

'Where do you want this new section placed?' he asked.

'Between the maps and index, starting at page 97.'

'I thought that's where you wanted me to put last minute L.C.C. changes.'

'Till then we won't know how many there are...'

'Wiser not to number those folios ...' mused Mr Short: 'What I now need from you are three Lowe & Brydone's A to Z imposition sheets for me to pass and sign — one for them, one for you and one for us.'

Meantime I had finished correcting the A to Z proofs — Zoffany Street the last entry — and begun on the Standard Street Guide. Its cards extracted from the rest and re-numbered, I asked Mr Short to quote for 10,000 copies.

'Sewn or pin binding? Your father doesn't specify...'

'What do you advise?'

'Pin is adequate for that number of pages, and costs less ... What about cover boards? And don't forget the cover for your trade Premier map, I'm holding the index for ... I'll ask Mr Makin to pop round to your office with some samples...

Mr Makin, sent to me as promised by Mr Short for the A to Z newsprint — already delivered to L. & B. — and for cover boards also inspired confidence: 'For the bulky A to Z you need a four sheet board; a 3 sheet for the Premier cover, and the same for the Standard — though a 2 sheet'd do but a bit skimpy ...' and, giving me a sample to feel: 'Don't you think?'

'Yes, three sheet', I agreed; and, ignoring papa's fashionable predeliction for gloomy dark greens, reds and browns, chose pale yellow for the A to Z, turquoise for the Standard and for the Premier, cornflower blue.

'When and where do you want us to deliver?' demanded the lanky, spotty assistant accompanying Mr Makin; and whom he introduced as Mr Ted Bould.

'The first two to Gordon & Kerensky ... The blue, I don't know yet ... I'll have to find out where maps can be folded, and inserted into covers with indexes...'

'Make it snappy, then!' grinned Mr Bould.

'Whenever and wherever it suits you, Mrs Pearsall', intervened his employer, reproving him on their way out: 'Overstep the mark again like that, Ted, and we'll have to part company...'

But our caretaker — shepherd of his tenants — had, while sweeping the hall, overheard my quandary; and provided the answer: 'Caroline Moore in the basement is what you want ... You remember the gentleman who helped us drag those wopping packages of maps into and out of the lift, when you first come ... He told me he could provide a service you might be needing ... I'll ask him to come straight up.' Which he did; in white overalls.

'Mr Moore?' I enquired.

'I'm not Mr Moore...'

'Is your boss a woman then?'

'I'm the boss. Why?'

'Who's Caroline Moore?'

'Never thought of it ... Possibly the founder's wife or fancy woman ... We're a long established firm ... What do you want us to do?'

Bumbingly I told him. He, more precisely, recapitulated: 'Letter-press blocks of your Premier cover designs — you to supply; print 2,000 for your paper edition, and 1,000 for your cloth; trim index pages (Williams & Lea to supply), and pin to spine; fold quad demy map — (Lowe & Brydone to supply) — and tip into third page cover...'

He could start 'the moment I get the goods ... In these hard times I've got plenty of girls to call on for piece-work...'

'What's piece-work?'

'Paid by the quantity they turn out...'

'Slavery!' I objected.

'They like it that way...'

The three trade publications now well *en train,* an afterthought of papa's precipitated an A to Z crisis:

> *'Tell Fountain'* he wrote, *'to draw a Pictorial London two colour double crown, to be printed on cheapest newsprint and folded and tipped into O.K. back cover.'*

Mr Fountain, stimulated by pressure — 'like the good old 1914/18 days of war maps' — churned it out 'in no time'; and all my suppliers — as Mr Harry Williams described the flurry — 'put their skids on'.

Thus were born — after long and complicated gestation — my first three trade publications.

# CHAPTER 8

COPIES of the A to Z, the Premier, and the Standard, tucked into a school satchel, I set forth to bestow the acme up-to-date maps on long deprived London.

Via its shops. Starting with prestigious Bumpus. Where the commissionaire's arm prevented me joining the elegant throng within: 'ere's a penny Missy to get yourself a cup of tea.' Across the road, at Selfridge's, no rep could be seen without an appointment: 'Who you from anyway?' At Hatchard's, impossible to push through a milling crowd: 'Queen Mary's just gone in ... always looks so regal ... wonder what she's buying ... That's her Daimler ...' So on to more democratic Foyle's, where after half an hour — 'Second-hand or new?' — Mr Foyle courteously received me. But having with growing concern scrutinised my wares, dismissed me: 'The map trade has been undisturbed for years ... We're not going to let someone new upset it...'

The woman Buyer at Barkers after a cursory look at a cover posed a riddle: 'What does W.C. in your address stand for?'

'West City?...'

'West Central. An inaccurate map publisher! Good day!'

At another the buyer's secretary took my publication into her boss. Bursting out of his office he brandished them at me with a roar: 'Alexander Gross! That bankrupt! ... That infamous scoundrel! Back in this country again!

My attempt to stem his wrath — 'My father was the victim of a City conspiracy' — increased it to Goebbel raving: 'A dirty Jew! Polluting our and Shakespeare's 'emerald isle'! Everyone of you with a drop of that iniquitous blood should be exterminated! ...

A Mosleyite, I realised. In person. Not just in Blackshirt formation marching through Whitechapel while we mob of anit-Fascists — chanting 'They shall not pass!' — fled before the spurred-on horses of the mounted police.

'What's more, I'll start the great purge now!' he screamed pushing me down the narrow winding stairs; and threw my samples after me: 'Take that! Take that! And that! And don't dare ever set foot in any of my shops again!'

Known names might have been too high an aim, I thought. Yet faith in my wares intact, I combed the suburbs. Only to be perpetually turned down. Or even shooed out, as pitilessly as a gipsy:

'Didn't you see the NO HAWKERS NO CIRCULARS sign outside? ... Or can't you read? Warmer-hearted though was a Mrs Naylor, widowed newsagent on the corner of Clapham Common South and Cavendish Road:

'Here's a bob, ducks, I'll buy one of your street atlases. Not that I'd be able to sell it. But, as customers keep asking me the way, I could use it myself...'

'My first A to Z sale!' I rejoiced.

'Hope I'll bring you luck! Tell you what. I'll put it in the window. If it sells, I'll order another five ... That would be half a dozen. At 33 1/3 discount of six bob, I'd owe you 4/-'

'My father told me the retail discount would be 5% ...'

'Oh you poor suckling babe ... The sharks'll gobble you up...'

Raising her counter flap she joined me on the customer side, invited me in 'to a bite of dinner while I put you wise'; and led me into her private quarters: 'You see this Players Capstan advert? The jolly bearded face could be my husband. That's why I've hung it up over the mantlepiece. He was Royal Navy ... a submariner in the war — "Lost at sea on convoy duty presumed dead" said that terrible telegram ... Brought to me here the 1st of November, 1917 ... a Black Thursday I'll never forget ... I still dream he'll come walking through the door: "Cheer up, old girl", he'll say hugging me: "I'm proud of you. Keeping the white ensign flying here without me! ...''

Over chump chop, potatoes and cabbage followed by junket and cream, I recounted my sorry saga. Our hilarity subsiding — 'I haven't laughed so much for years!' — she gave me salutary advice: 'Never interrupt a chap busy on a job! Never expect an order at the first call; but like Robert Bruce try, try and try again ...' winding up: 'Why not have a go at wholesalers?'

'Wholesalers?'

'The middleman between us shopkeepers and you manufacturers ... You have to give them an additional discount, of course, or how else could they function? ... 'I'll jot down a few names and addresses for you ... I'd leave W. H. Smith to the last — it's difficult to get a foot in there, I hear.'

Replete, off I set in renewed hope. To further rebuff: 'Can't you see I'm busy?' ... 'What do I want more maps for?' ... 'Reps come by appointment which is never!' ... I'm satisfied with Mr Stevenson of Geographia, thank you! ...' and more curtly: 'Bugger off!' ... Mr Toler though, of Toler Bros. promised 'to buy your A to Z when the Great British Public ask for it! As if they ever would! Ha! Ha! And by the gross.' ... Simpkin Marshall's buyer objected to light coloured covers: 'Handled once and they'll be soiled!' ... Mr Larby in Old Bailey dashed out of his warehouse, leafed through the A to Z, and running a dirty thumbnail down the outside edge, assessed: 'No go! Look at your index! Bled! Half the last letter in the third column guillotined off ... also on the maps! The continue on page so and so cut in half!...'

'Like the tumbril victims in the French Revolution', I laughed; and he, with a 'I haven't got all day!' called for his assistant, Nancy, to drop what she was doing and take over. An attractive, efficient twenty six years old, she took pity on me: 'Get the next edition right, and we'll distribute for you. Either we business women stand together, or we don't stand a chance!'

Which left W. H. Smith & Son. Their head office Strand House, Portugal

Street, swarmed with employees working at top pressure, who, nevertheless, courteously directed me, re-directed me via a warren of lifts, staircases, packing rooms, the Magazine Binding Room — its workers on high stools — to the Subscription Office 'probably what you're looking for.'

Drawing-pinned to its locked door, hung a faded typed notice:

REPRESENTATIVES SEEN 9 A.M. TO 12 NOON

Too late. Next morning I was too early. After half an hour's wait, the door at 8.30 was unlocked, unbolted and thrown open. By a freckled lad whistling Ivor Novello's 'Keep the Home Fires Burning'. Who, as I entered the bare, windowless cubby-hole, shot away through an opposite door, locking it behind him.

Gradually, men with bulging briefcases, filtered in; and with the wary formality of competitors greeted each other; exchanged publisher gossip — 'Andre Deutsch is leaving Simpkin Marshall to start his own publishing Company' ... 'The Lane Brothers have left their dad's Bodley Head. On some wild goose chase of ditching case-bound books for paper covers. It'll never take on!' — and finally, jammed sardine tight into this Black Hole of Calcutta, proffered cigarettes to each other, which, lit and puffed, soon hazed us in blue grey, choking smoke.

Nine o'clock struck. A hatch in the inner door snapped ajar: 'Mr Cruise is ready to see the first of you!' announced a cheeky boy, letting the first man through, having barred my entry — 'Beats me what a female's doing here! —' And continued to do so at each call for 'NEXT'

Noon struck. Omniscient freckles, cocking a snook at me and a few other disappointed petitioners, chivied us out; and whistling Rule Britannia vanished behind the door he shut, locked and bolted behind him.

Treatment meted me several mornings running.

Until, just before noon about a week later, Mr Cruise's deputy, on hearing that a woman stranger was haunting the place, fetched me into his busy office to ascertain my purpose: 'What can we do for you? Whose secretary are you?'

In answer, I showed him my publications: 'Perhaps please you'd submit them to Mr Cruise...'

'A lady representative!' he exclaimed: 'Most unusual!' But a contented rep emerging at that moment from the buyer's sanctum, ushered me in: 'A young lady to see you, Sir.'

Over six foot tall, the inscrutable arbiter of A to Z destiny waited for me to speak. Handing him my sample, I burbled: 'I know it's bled ... I know I know nothing about publishing ... But I have strived ... or is it striven? ... to be accurate. I personally compiled the information ... much of it on the ground. It's up-to-date — including L.C.C. stop-press street name changes ... I've been the first to revise it since 1919! Even the Ordnance Survey! ... And look! House numbers along main roads; I've walked them from start to finish; you won't find them on any other London map!'

His reaction nil, his expression still poker-face, I faltered: 'Stupid of me to praise my own work...'

'If you don't, who will?' spoke Zarathustra — and scanning my three publications, inserted a carbon between two pages of his W. H. Smith & Son Subscription Order Book, wrote out an order, handed me the incredible top copy:

> 1250 *A to Z Atlas* @ 1/-
> 500 *Standard Guides* @ 6d.
> 250 *Premier paper* @ 2/6d.
> 50 *Premier cloth* @ 5/-

'Fancy!' I whooped: 'Thank you! Thank you ... That'll help me pay for them!'

'Before you thank me you'd better hear our terms: 33 and a third and 15...'

The discounts decreed by papa were the 5% retail my Clapham widow had ridiculed, and 10% wholesale. To pressurise me into keener bargaining, I realised, as with supplier costs; and asked: 'Do the other map publishers give the same discount?'

He nodded: 'And worse to come. The order is on Sale or Return. Payment only at the end of the year when we assess what has and hasn't sold.'

I blenched.

'Don't be shattered, my dear. This Subscription Order allows our managers to buy direct from publishers. They pay 30 days from invoice ... Here are our lists of W.H.S. wholesalers, shops and bookstalls for you to call on.'

'You think they'll sell then?'

'If anybody thinks he knows what'll sell, he doesn't know the trade.'

Jubilant, I dashed out into Portugal Street, across Lincoln's Inn Fields, along High Holborn to the office, packed the large order, piled it into the lift, borrowed a hand barrow from Henekeys, loaded it and wheeled it back at a trot to Strand House. Where, as I negotiated the curb, an urbane tap on my shoulder halted me. I looked up. Mr Cruise, well muffled against the bitter East wind — I'm just off for a bite of lunch' — bent down like a hairpin to my height: '"GOODS IN", my dear, have to be delivered at "ENTRANCE C" ... Keep up a delivery service like this, and you're bound to succeed ... A worker ready to do anything! Your dad can be proud of you, Miss Gross...'

So those hooded eyes had noticed "Under the direction of Alexander Gross" on the covers. 'I'm glad to see him back in map publishing', he warmly continued: 'I always had the greatest respect for him. An outstanding person. What a tragedy he lost the fine business he and your mother built! ... Ever since he left, it's been going downhill ... Give him my regards when you write. He may remember me, though I was only Deputy Buyer in his day...'

Forthwith, I sped to every W. H. Smith listed; reaped a harvest of orders; and invoiced, packed and delivered them — including same-day repeat orders phoned in from Main Line Railway Termini bookstalls: 'We've sold out!'

On my second delivery to Victoria Main, the manager asked for at least three calls a week: 'Unless of course you let Mr Jones here look after me...'

'As most publishers do ...' prompted cheery, plump Mr Jones: 'And that goes for my other Main-Line friends...'

'Your commission?' I asked.

'One percent.' Readily I agreed; and he: 'Let's shake on it then ... Why not produce a vest pocket guide to Places of Interest for Londoners and Visitors? You can take the info lock, stock and barrel from your A to Z! And inside the month you'll have another winner!' He was right. A Subscription Order from Mr Cruise and it joined our best-sellers. For all of which repeat orders flooded in from every other W. H. S. outlet. Nor did the half crown and five bob Premiers encroach on Field Staff sales. In fact, they stimulated enquiries, such as: 'A friend showed me an excellent London map he'd bought ... I'd like a mounted one for my boardroom ...' For which Uncle Frank, on a rare State visit to the office, gorgeously claimed credit: 'Learn from your old uncle, Phyllis. The art of management is DELEGATION ... While keeping my hand on the tiller, I leave the trivia to Arnold...'

F. W. Woolworth & Co. Ltd. were the next great multiple to tackle. Their nearby Holborn Branch manager told me how: 'Our Buyers hang out at Bond Street House Head Office. Take the lift to the third floor and ask for Mr Prescott. You'll like him though he is a Yank.'

The American-style lift opened straight into a light, spacious half-moon waiting-room with floor to ceiling windows. The uniformed and bemedalled commissionaire at a central desk juggled with a perpetually ringing battery of Inside and Outside phones; waved representatives to armchairs or at a summons sent them to their buyers; and in a lull beckoned me to his side: 'Who do you want, lady?'

'Mr Prescott ... I suppose I'll have to wait my turn...'

'Nobody else here for books ... Go right in.' But seeing me hesitate — 'New here?' — he led me along a corridor of named doors — 'There's his' — and marched back to his Sergeant Major quarters.

Timidly I knocked.

'Hi there! Walk right in!' called a voice.

Lean, electric keen, in his early forties, hair receding, Mr Prescott hurried forward to take my samples — 'Show!'

Jacketless, shirt-sleeves rolled up, he deftly leafed through the A to Z; paused at a page, turned to a second, pursed his lips, destroyed me: 'Honey, you don't have my street in the index; and what the heck, nor the map neither...'

Abject I turned to leave: 'That's torn it then ... Goodbye.'

'Not so fast sister!' and pulling me by the hand, he drew me back from the door: 'Darned fine books these. What you think, Miss Wilson? ... We try them?'

From a shadowy background of filing cabinets emerged an enormous woman dressed in black — alert of eye and light of limb — who now riffled through the A to Z for her abode. A sequal of delight ended our growing suspense: 'You've got it in! Look Mr Prescott! There's my tiny mews!'

Thrill of recognition over, she gave me back the Premiers — 'price outside our shilling limit' — told me the generous terms, '33 1/3 and a penny discount; payment ten days from invoice'; and explained: 'I'll be giving you our usual trial order: six dozen of each title for each of our three main stores. Right Mr Prescott?'

'Right! ... Followed by repeats for all our London stores, little lady, if the public go for them ... Right Miss Wilson?'

At my 'thank you', he shook his fist at me: 'You Brits with your ''thank yous''! They drive me hopping mad!'

'Better than the way other suppliers pester us for bigger orders!' said Miss Wilson.

Delivery proved complicated. Mr Short's packages of ten — tailor-made for the W. H. Smith order — I unwrapped and re-packed in twelves; then on Henekeys' barrow trundled them from High Holborn to Bond Street House. Only to be told by the commissionaire: 'No goods accepted here!'

'Where then?'

'To each separate store is our rules.'

Negotiating my load through the crowded Oxford Street entrance, I panicked an assistant: 'Round to the back! Before the manager catches you! Or you'll cost me my job!'

And, back door wiser, on to the others.

Within three days, in fat Woolworth envelopes came the repeats — together with orders from their other London stores. Which, still inexpertly packed, I wheeled at top speed to the many areas I knew so well since compilation exploration.

Pride in my accomplishment, however, Miss Wilson punctured by an irate summons over the phone: 'Come round at once!'

In her formidable presence, out of breath from running, I panted 'Anything wrong?'

'Everything!!! I'm going to give you the biggest wigging of your life! Here goes, then! ... Can't you read? Where were you at school?'

'Roedean ...'

'That explains it. A privileged la-di-da who doesn't have the courtesy to read our Order Form instructions.'

'I was too excited! ... Too busy packing and delivering...'

'Causing pandemonium throughout!'

'Quit nicking at her, Muriel ... She's quite a doll. Don't you see she's trembling? ...' intervened Mr Prescott. She retorted: 'I'm doing it for her own good.'

'Oh you limeys!' he groaned: 'What you cook up for each other's own good has me beat ... Those doggone Eton infants bent over a stone and caned Like crazy!...'

'If you don't teach her here and now, she'll end up in Carey Street!' continued Miss Wilson; and handing me an Order Form, commanded me to study it: 'Read it to yourself! And again! ... You've digested it, I hope? ... Now read it aloud! Right. So I'll sum up what you've got to do: First you get our printer — who knows the ropes — to print (a) Labels for each of our London stores ... (b) Invoices for you to send us ... Here's his address. He's reliable, prompt, cut-price. Secondly, you send us a written receipt for each order the very moment you get it. Have I made myself clear? ... If you don't abide by our rules we cease to buy from you! ... As decreed by our founder. For never are we allowed to stray from the detailed, handwritten procedure he laid down for his 5 and 10 cent stores. Misguided attempts to improve on him have simply landed us in the soup. What a mind! If his foresight wasn't genius, I don't know what is!'

Public demand grew. Leading not only to ever increasing W. H. Smith and Woolworth repeats — and half dozens from Mrs Naylor — but orders from the retailers and wholesalers who had initially repulsed me; followed too by repeats.

Amongst individuals buying direct from our office, was a down-at-heel hawker, reeking of sweat and beer: 'One of your bob street atlases Miss. Here's my tanner. Ta.'

'At my 'Eightpence is rather a big discount ...', he turned his empty trouser and jacket pockets inside out: 'A tanner's my last word!' he proudly said; grumbled: 'You're no better than Ma Burgess! Takes 'er cut, I can tell yer. That's why I comes to the likes of you. See?' and left.

Three A to Z's were missing I noticed, a couple of Standards, and five of my new 6d Ideal Guides. Admiring his sleight-of-hand, I raced down the stairs after him, asked: 'Who's Ma Burgess?'

'Our wholesaler.'

I went in search of her. To a narrow sleazy alley south of the Strand. Where grease-stained suits on hire to waiters flapped from clothes-lines hung across it. Crammed into a bluebottle infested shop window lay a jumble of Old Moore's Almanacks, postcards, streamers, paper sunshades, miniature coronation coaches and Towers of London, rusty razor blades and other fly-blown bric-a-brac. Here Mrs Burgess lived and plied her hawker wholesale trade.

A swinging bell above the door stridently announced my entry. Into penumbra. Into a shop lined almost entirely by glass cabinets, their shelves chock-a-block with the knick-knacks displayed outside.

'Got to keep everything locked up for my boys!' cackled a woman's voice: 'The dears pinch whatever their grubby hands can lay hold of ... A lesson you've already learnt from my Arthur, I shouldn't wonder. He warned me you were bound to call after he'd helped himself to a guide or two...'

Flipping over a counter flap, she appeared. As diminutive as I. Wrapped in woollen shawls, her black skirt floor-length, she confronted me: 'Let's see your samples ... What's your terms?'

'33 1/3 ...'

She shook her head: 'Stuff and nonsense! Shut the door behind you.'

Woolworth trained, I added: '... and a penny ...'

'50% like your dad always did.'

'How soon do you pay?'

'When other map publishers refuse me credit! That's when! Now take my order: The Premier's too pricey ... 9 A to Z's, 24 Ideals, 9 Standards ... My lads'll have to scrape the price off of them; they got to ask for wot they reckon they can get! 3'6d or 5 bob for A to Z on Sundays when shops are shut ... So no-price covers for the next lot or nothing doing!'

Throughout our talk, hawkers sleep-walked in; deliberated long and aloud as to the best investment: 'razor-blade or streamer? or 'Wot's the weather going to do at Ascot? If sunny, dark glasses or paper sunshade? ... For rain, a royal coach? ...' Arthur and I greeted each other as friends.

# CHAPTER 9

PAPA'S abrasive letters proved merely an hors d'oeuvre to his presence.
To my embrace on his descent from the Mauretania boat-train, mid-August 1936, he turned away: 'What a sight you look!' and peering eagerly around for his son, asked: 'Where's Tony? Surely after all these years he's come to meet his father...'

'How lovely to see you again, papa! ... and what a relief to hand over the business to you!'

'I don't know what you're talking about! ... I've been running it!'

Having booked him in at a Bloomsbury hotel and deposited his luggage, we took the taxi on to the office.

There, forewarned by me, sat Uncle Frank in state — as if permanently on the bridge, instead of hardly ever: 'Great to see you, Alex old scout. I've got things buzzing here I can tell you...'

'How's your sex life, Frank? Take it from me, Testosterone' — and papa spelt it out 't-e-s-t-o-s-t-e-r-o-n-e — works miracles at our age. If you can't buy it in England, I'll mail you some from the States when I get back ... But to business! Whoever's heard of a publisher in High Holborn! Why didn't you rent one in Fleet Street, Phyllis?'

'As I told her to ...' sucked up my uncle. While papa surveyed the avalanche-prone flotsam and jetsam I had accumulated since my World Inset start, in growing horror: 'Can't you learn from your uncle's tidy desk!'

From the 'trash can' as he called it, he picked out a discarded envelope. It contained a ten shilling Postal Order: 'So you throw away actual money! My money! ... Don't you know to slash open the three sides of every envelope to make sure nothing's left inside!'

Delving at random into a higgledy piggledy pile of papers, he grasped and perused a batch of unpaid bills: 'How much are you owing?'

'Too much for comfort, I'm afraid ... over a thousand...'

'You'll go bankrupt! Don't expect me to bail you out!' he fumed; and at another corker: 'So my millionaire daughter chooses the highest estimate for photolitho!'

'Purnell's sample was a black mulch; Lowe & Brydone's sharp and clear,' I explained.

'What's the good of quality if it puts you out of business! ... And what's this and this and this: 33 1/3% & 15% discount to W. H. Smith & Son! I told you 10% maximum to wholesalers! ... And their Main Line station bookstalls handed over to a Mr Jones! Every silly ass knows that multiple customers are the publisher's perquisite!'

'I'm only paying him 1% commission, papa!'

'A fortune for him on that turnover! ... And what's this! 50% to old gipsy Mrs Burgess!'

'She told me that's what you used to give her...'

'And you believed her!'

He also objected to an arrangement with a new book publisher's rep to sell our maps in the Midlands until he earned enough with them full-time.

'What publisher?'

'Penguin...'

'Never heard of them! ... And with that sob story he's wheedled you; into giving him 5%! ... Monstrous outlays! Repay them from your salary immediately!'

'Salary? I've never had a salary...'

'From your expenses then.'

'Expenses?' I've paid them all myself...'

'What are you living on then?'

'Painting and writing...'

'Still that old story! ... Your brother's the artist of the family! Shall I tell you what he thinks of you? That you've no talent at all ... That you're only a copy-cat, jealous of his success!'

His next find justly provoked him. An A to Z cover — 'So you've defied me! Called my "OK" "A to Z" ... cannibalised my design!' ... And the next: The galley proof queried by William Lea's reader — 'Good God! How could anybody with a glimmer of grey matter leave out Trafalgar Square?'

At my explanation — 'The Tr's fell out of the window and some got away on the top of a bus' — he groaned: 'Stop! I can't bear it ...' Then, flicking through an A to Z to make sure the howler had been corrected, he found worse; and head clutched, switched from mock drama to alarm: 'I'm ruined! You've ruined me! Every page bled!'

'Yes papa, I know ... and I'm sorry.'

'Is that all you've got to say! I take it you've demanded compensation from the binder?'

'Dear me, no ... Mr Short's been so kind and helpful...'

'Namby pamby in everything you do! Didn't you have him pass the imposition sheet?'

'I think so...'

'What's the good of thinking? ... Either you did or you didn't.'

'Not a single customer's complained as yet ...' I giggled.

'I don't like your flippant attitude to business...'

Totally independent of him — having fended for myself since fourteen — and my work not only bought, exhibited, published and acclaimed by critics and the cognosciente, I kissed and hugged this "all sound and fury" droll Hungarian.

His sing-song accent stronger than I recalled, I asked him why.

'Are you criticising me?!'

'I find it endearing, papa...'

'In the States one tends to mix with one's compatriots ... I feel at home with Hungarians ... Less lonely, I suppose ... One comes abroad, marries a foreigner, and doesn't even understand one's own children...'

'Goodbye to business!' I rejoiced; and apologised: 'Sorry I'm no good at it papa! But it's been fun; and I've particularly liked helping you re-establish your name...'

'You! ... Help me! ... Faugh!' he derided.

Laughingly I embraced him: 'Anyway I won't be upsetting you any more... I'm through!'

At the threat of losing his intended if unwitting king-pin, his demeanour changed. From hectoring to wooing: 'You wouldn't leave your old father in the lurch my darling Phyllis would you? ... You've not done too badly for a novice ... For instance how much are you owed?'

Aloud, and on my fingers I totted up the larger accounts: 'Victoria Main, 22 pounds, 13 shillings, and fourpence halfpenny; Tolers, £7, no shillings and tuppence...'

'After the fortune I spent on your Rodean education' he interrupted, 'and you can't even do mental arithmetic! ... In any case you ought to know to the last penny what you're owed and what's owing ... As I do every day...'

But the total pleased him: 'Then you're solvent!'

'What does solvent mean, papa?'

'How can a daughter of mine be such a duffer!'

'Don't be too hard on the gal, Alex'' intervened my uncle: 'she's done her best to be useful — fetches and carries for me while I run the show...'

'Don't teach me how to treat my daughter, Frank! ... And what do you mean by inveigling her into paying you commission on turnover instead of on your orders...'

'That was a dirty trick of yours Alex to produce a trade Premier competing with my Field Staff', Uncle Frank retaliated; and glancing at his watch, suggested: 'Time for a snifter, what?'

After a Scotch or two at Henekey's and peace restored, he off-handedly remarked: 'Can I touch you for a little doh-re-mi old scout ... The big end's packed in on my jalopee...'

Papa invited us both to Blooms for lunch — 'How I've been longing for their boiled salt beef!'

'Somebody's got to hold the fort,' piously declined my uncle: 'but I wouldn't say ''No'' to another double ... 'Thanks, brother-in-law! ... Cheers!'

After a chatty lunch together, papa on parting — I've an important matter to attend to' — told me to make an appointment for 10 o'clock tomorrow with the A to Z binders: 'But don't let on it's about the bleeding ... and meanwhile search that Augean Stable of yours for evidence to confront them with ... Be at my hotel at 9.30 precisely...'

The appointment made — 'We much look forward to meeting Mr Gross,' said Mr Kerensky — I eventually found Mr Short's signed imposition sheet and his letter of confirmation.

To papa's malicious delight when I called for him next morning: 'Leave all the talking to me ... and do exactly as I tell you...'

Ignoring me, Mr Kerensky and Mr Gordon shook papa's hand: 'Now Mr Gross what can we do for you?'

In dulcet tones papa led off: 'I've come about the unfortunate bleeding of my London street atlas ... In view of my daughter's inexperience you might feel inclined to allow her a token discount...'

Dulcet too gushed Mr Kerensky's riposte: 'We'd dearly like to. Oh that we could! But to obtain your esteemed order — and to keep our presses busy — we quoted below cost.'

'How extremely good of you ...' smiled papa.

Suavely, Mr Gordon offered him and Mr Kerensky a Corona Corona, took one for himself, lighted up; and while the three puffed contentedly in meretricious truce, papa apparently conceded: 'That then has to be that! ...' But after a further pause, stepped up his deceit. 'So let us suppose for the sake of argument that there had been definite proof ... What discount, gentlemen, in so purely hypothetical a case would you have allowed?...'

Mr Gordon, less wary than his senior partner, took the bait: 'Seeing as how it's a dead cert ha! ha! that no imposition sheet was submitted to us ... and I'm speaking for Mr Kerensky and myself ... we'd have considered 20% discount fair.'

'Very well then, my friends, the farce is over!' purred papa: 'Phyllis, show them their signed sheet and letter'; and at my — 'I can't papa' — snatched the papers from me, and did so himself: 'Incontrovertible, I presume!'

Scarlet in the face, Mr Gordon summoned Mr Short, and let fly at him: 'Why, Short, didn't you tell me that you'd passed the A to Z imposition sheet for Mrs Pearsall?'

'The carbon's in the file I gave you, Sir...'

'Well it isn't there now! Explain that, my man!'

'Mr Short's as straight as a die!' I exploded, snatching the folder from under the bully's nose — mauve by now — and turning over letters and carbons to the date concerned, where, round the punched holes clung tell-tale wisps of paper: 'You've torn it out! How could you!...'

Outside in Worship Street, papa — triumphantly brandishing the wrested Credit Note — slated my outburst: 'Just like your mother! Unstable! Scenes in public! ... It's time you learnt that righteous indignation has no place in business ... nor has sentiment.

'Now I'll teach you how to run a business!' proclaimed papa; as he rented two extra offices to form a suite with ours; engaged ex-vicar Mr Norton as representative — from a mass of unemployed applicants; buxom Miss Hemelryk as secretary, Miss Fox as filing clerk; bought desks, chairs, a Remington typewriter and a filing cabinet: 'You, Phyllis and the two young ladies will work in the back office...'

'But it opens onto a well ... there's no view' I objected.

'You're here to work, may I remind you. Not to look out the window...'

'Out the window, papa? How American you've become!'

'Don't interrupt ... To continue. The third office will be the warehouse. Frank's just taken on a Field Staff delivery boy. He'll help you move the stock and the rest of your paraphenalia into it right now.'

Done in a twinkling by him alone, I applauded: 'Marvellous, Mr Lester!'

'I'm not a mister ... Call me "Lester" ...' Seventeen years old, lopsided from head to ill-shod feet, his cheap suit dangling on his slight frame, its sleeves and trouser cuffs inches too long, he marked time at a gallop awaiting his masters's bidding: 'What next, Guv.?'

'There's a good chap ... No malingerer you!' encouraged my uncle — with an aside to papa: 'I've always had the nack of picking winners, eh, Alex? — Lester, here's your orders! Wrap up thirty seven of the London roller maps ... Well done! Now. From these delivery notes and this A to Z, work out your route.'

'Cor! I know London like the back of my hand!'

'Good. But don't tear off yet ... Here's two delivery notes to put with each: one for the customer to keep, and the other for him to sign and return to you. And an invoice each ... The drill is to collect the lolly on the spot if poss. — Makes no odds if it's cash or cheque ... Just chat them up — "it'll save the trouble of postage etcetera ..." Got it?'

'Back in a jiff!' promised the paragon: and staggering under his unruly load, flashed off — as if "to put a girdle round about the earth in forty minutes."

'Who's paying these extra expenses, papa?' I asked.

'You are. Efficiency's bound to increase turnover ... Plus additional publications ... a smaller London map to start with Fountain can extract from the "Premier."'

'No papa. You can't take him off the 35 Miles Round London. The Field Staff are screaming for another mounted map to sell at every call!'

'It's title, Phyllis, "The Authentic" ... black and red ... the old adage "penny black, tuppence coloured" still applies. Your litho printers can draw the red...'

Mr Fountain informed, protested: 'They'll make an unholy mess of it ... Printers are printers Mr Gross, not map draughtsmen ... I'd rather give it to Stewart ...'

'You're talking rot. Stewart's on my urgent "Philadelphia"'...

'Be it on your own head, Mr Gross. And what about the rise you promised me?'

'So you're determined to put us out of business!'

Papa's 'important matter' after our lunch at Bloom's had been a meeting with his solicitor. Where a few days later he took me. On foot along bustling Fleet Street into the stillness of Serjeant's Inn.

With a tap of Number 15's gleaming brass knocker, we walked into a fusty reception office stacked high with cobwebbed black Deed Boxes — evoking Jarndyce versus Jarndyce inheritance litigation; and 'Abandon all hope ye that enter here.'

No spectre, though, was the pallid sombrely clad clerk who took papa's hat — 'Mr Webb is awaiting you, Mr Gross' — and ushered us into an office dwarfed by massive Chippendale bookcases, desk and chairs. Having greeted papa, a portly gentleman affably addressed me: 'You're a lucky little lady to have such a radical father. Who instead of settling the whole Company on his male heir — your brother Tony — has given you 50% ... For he's just taken the important step of incorporating GEOGRAPHERS' MAP COMPANY LIMITED Under the 1929 Companies Act.'

'What does that mean?' asked I.

'The business has thereby become an entity.'

'The name "Geographers" is too close to "Geographia"', I demurred.

'Rubbish!' said papa: They're totally different. A Berlin camera shop named "Photographia" inspired my "Geographia". Whereas "Geographers"' obviously means "of interest to geographers" — as long as you never omit the apostrophe after the "s".'

'Because it's similar I've been accused of sharp practice...'

'So I, your father, have had to live to hear my own daughter impugn my integrity!'

'It's why Mr Namier threw me down the stairs.'

'He was always a difficult customer ... Besides Phyllis, when I bring my old firm to its knees — they've not produced a single notable publication since they ousted me — I'll buy them up.'

'What alternative would you suggest, Mrs Pearsall?' asked Mr Webb.

'"ALEXANDER GROSS", of course ... Like John Bartholomew, George Philip...'

'Never!' agonized papa: 'A name dragged in the mire by those sheep in wolves' clothing! Mann, Livingstone, Legge, the Crowleys! Vilified! Desecrated! Pilloried in Carey Street! Never!'

'Oh poor papa, how you've suffered!'

'It makes me ill to remember how respected my name once was ... Foremost British map publisher, Freeman of the City of London, Fellow of the Royal Geographical Society...'

To celebrate the birth of the new British company, he invited Tony, Tony's French wife and himself to dinner at my studio; and the table cleared, ceremoniously handed Tony the MEMORANDUM and ARTICLES of ASSOCIATION OF GEOGRAPHERS' MAP COMPANY LIMITED:

'This, Tony, my son and heir, is a vitally important moment in your life! ...
So please pay attention...'

'Don't be pompous papa. What's this mumbo jumbo got to do with me? As
you know I'm a painter and etcher...'

'I'm an artist too, Tony. Van Gogh. Sunflowers ... Beethoven...'

'And the play you've written, papa', I intervened to salve his hurt.

Tossing the document over to me, Tony said: 'Your dung heap, Phyllis,
I think.'

'That's where you're wrong, my son ... Five hundred £1 shares for you as
well as for her.'

'Hurrah, Daisy chérie! Tomorrow we'll buy the Renault you've set your
heart on...'

'Not in cash, Tony ... Nominal value ... A £1 share for each of you paid
up ... But get rid of your biased view against business! It'll pay you to think how
those shares are going to rise in the not too distant future ... If I hadn't lost
Geographia you'd automatically have joined me, eventually taken over. Phyllis
is too airy-fairy to run it properly. I need a man there. Not full-time, of course
— your art has to come first! — but now and then to offset your sister's
sloppiness ... The irresponsible way she lets suppliers and customers pull the
wool over her eyes is hardly credible...'

'Fuck business papa!' roared Tony: 'And Phyllis another bottle of wine!'

The chance of a car too good to abandon, Daisy wheedled: 'for my little
daughter ... to take her to the good country or sea air? So generous a
grandfather!' ending with a threat: 'If I not get my Renault, as I tell Tony, I
commit suicide...'

'It's easy Tony to be generous with other people's money', concluded papa.
Whereupon — 'Voyons! Help me on with my coat, Tony!'

After their departure papa warily asked me for help: 'As a travel writer Phyllis
you know that when one applies for a new passport some responsible person
must sign the form and the back of two photographs ... Well, it's the same for
my American visa ... Here's my form, duly filled in; and the photographs —
which, as usual, make one look like a criminal — Perhaps you have a friend
who'd do that trivial service for your father?'

'Of course, papa, But why not Mr Webb? With his high opinion of you?'

'Beware of solicitors, Phyllis. Their friendly manner's only skin-deep ...
Cultivated pseudo-sympathy for bereaved relatives at will-waving sessions —
(Not my *mot juste,* but Samuel Butler's in his Way of all Flesh, remember?) —
Beneath that veneer, they're plying their trade like anybody else ... Tradesmen
in sheeps clothing ... A charge of 7/6d for every letter in and out, for every
telephone call ... and astronomical fees for legal advice or action. But that's all
in passing ... You asked me why I didn't ask Webb to vouch for me. The
haunting truth is that I've never been cleared by the United States Immigration
Department. I've never had the courage to approach them ...' Like most
Hungarians born and bred under Emperor Franz Joseph, papa dreaded

bureaucrats: 'How I envy you! You British born can have no inkling of dictators; of the petty dictators they spawn: soldiers and police, their brutality unbridled; and civil servants down to Post Office officials revelling in power ...' He paused. Then, seeking rescue from immediate torturing dilemma out burst a gnawing secret undisclosed for years: 'For us Hungarian born, the U.S. Immigration Quota is full. So the only way to enter the States is on a Visitor's Visa. But as this prohibits one from working there, I'm running my New York business illegally ... A perpetual menace! Imagine what it feels like to live under that Damocles Sword! ... And the perpetual shadow of possible blackmail ... Now you realise why not a single acquaintance or friend of mine must ever know ... To quote Aristotle: "Have you any enemies?" ... "No" ... "Have you any friends?" ... "Yes" ... "Then you have enemies!" Only you Phyllis can I trust ... Never, but never divulge this skeleton in my cupboard to a living soul. Not even to your brother, infatuated as he is with his covetous French wife ... Many a prominent statesman has been toppled for confiding State Secrets to such a bedfellow.'

Artists' clients often become friends. As with B.H. and Amy Binder. From booking clerk at Nottingham railway station, he had Dick Whittingtoned to London; where, by incessant toll, parsimony and exceptional flair, risen to pre-eminence in accountancy; and with socialite partner Ralph Hamlyn (for high class connections) founded his own Chartered Accountancy firm "Binder Hamlyn & Co." 'They have a house and garden in Hyde Park Gate, papa — gorgeous to paint — a Rolls and chauffeur, so he should be the right person for you ... I'll phone him right away.'

B.H. agreed to see us next morning at 8: 'I can't vouch for your dad unless I've met him! ... You know my office address: River Plate House, South Place.

Outside the imposing building, papa quailed: 'I hope I'm not going to be patronised ... as my daughter's father ... instead of in my own right...'

B.H. after embracing me and warmly greeting papa, put him at ease: 'Phyllis has always spoken so highly of you, Mr Gross ... of your successful New York publishing firm ... Surely I can do more for you than sign this official form ... like for instance asking the Consul to grant you a special visa allowing you re-entry to the States at any time — seeing you have businesses to attend to both sides of the Atlantic ... Can you give me any idea of your financial position there ... of recent tax payments?'

'Here, Mr Binder, are my auditor's figures: turnover, tax paid and cash position for the last five years ... these should enable you to describe me as well-to-do?'

' "Well-to-do" from Binder, Hamlyn & Co. would dub you a multi-millionaire! At the last count, I was Chairman of 66 Companies ... One more than my runner-up ... But I'll be happy to dub you a financial asset to to the U.S.A., as well as a personal and professional friend. Goodbye, Mr Gross. A great pleasure to have met you ... Phyllis, Amy would like you to phone her about some dinner party she's arranging ... And Mr Gross, I'll ask my secretary about some dinner party she's arranging ... And Mr Gross, I'll ask my secretary to get the U.S. Consul on the phone. You can rest assured all will be well...'

It was. And, his papers in order for the first time since fleeing to the U.S.A. from Geographia holocaust, papa sailed for New York ineffably relieved: 'No longer to cower at Passport Control...'

1936. A year of crisis for our Constitutional Monarchy. And though the American press had for months featured articles and photographs — particularly of host and guests on an Adriatic cruise aboard the Nahlin (for which Mr Harding I recalled had been mounting maps) — not until October did the fraught situation burst upon the British public. With the Belvedere Castle's comings and goings of Prime Minister Stanley Baldwin, The Archbishop of Canterbury, Winston Churchill — all minds focused on King Edward VIII's dual desire to marry his twice divorced enamorata, Wallis Simpson, and to make her his Queen. Until the dramatic finale of the 11th of December: Edward's abdication; and accession to the Throne of his brother, King George VI.

MAP IT cabled papa; and I to him:
MAP WHAT
MAP CORONATION ROUTE

# CHAPTER 10

AN intimidating spin-off from Geographers' Incorporation struck eighteen months later. An "ON HER MAJESTY'S SERVICE" buff envelope addressed to me as Company Secretary — which I had not realised I was — enclosing a large unintelligible Inland Revenue form. Official documents conceived to meet every foreseeable contingency bewilder the lay recipient. But official censure from two other sources we had understood — infringement through ignorance of a statutory regulation to depose a copy of every U.K. publication at the British Museum and other national libraries; and to pay Royalty to the Ordnance Survey with specified acknowledgement. And by prompt compliance, apology and promise never again to err, absolution was granted.

But Inland Revenue stumped us: 'I can't make head nor tail of it', said placid Miss Hemelryk, dropping their insoluble puzzle into her waste paper basket; as she did with its many successors. Until a RED Final Demand scared us both.

If tax due was not paid within seven days, it threatened, legal proceedings would be taken against us. And the tax due was formidable. Assessed by them in default of submission of accounts. And so — following my mother's precept 'Meet your problems head on!' — I took the tram to the Collector's office; whence, after being deliberately ignored for a few hours as a member of the public — that despised species, victim and paymaster — I was directed — 'Everybody knows we're not responsible for assessments' — back across the river to the Holborn Inspector. Into limbo. Amongst whitefaced fellow-apprehensives, misdirected like me — in little false-hope bouts of activity between protracted waits — from one tut-tutting official — 'This looks pretty noxious' — to another and ever yet another. From floor to floor and back again, up and down flights of stairs or in recalcitrant lifts, along endless corridors blocked by trollies overloaded with bulging files tied with red tape and trundled along by disabled ex-servicemen enslaved forever to this Dante purgatory.

In zombie trance on one of these fruitless treks I bumped into a bowler-hatted gentleman issuing from a PRIVATE office.

Courteously he raised his hat, apologising: 'It's my fault.'

'No it's mine! ... In this Kafka Castle I'd forgotten to look where I was going.'

'Kafka! How refreshing in this God-forsaken catacomb to meet another fan of his. And at that a charming lady ...' and, ushering me into his sumptiuos carpeted office — for he was the grand panjandrum — asked what he could do to help.

His solution to my predicament — 'Only a Chartered Accountant can get you out of this pickle!' — brought B.H. to mind: 'One of my friends ... He and his wife collect my pictures...'

'Oils or water colours?'

'Both. And etchings.'

'Let me know when you have an exhibition. Here's my card. I've always wanted to be an artist ... What's your friend's name?'

'B. H. Binder.'

'Of Binder Hamlyn? They're top notch. Why not ring him now?'

'But that'll be keeping you from your lunch?' I said; and he: 'You'll join me for it at the Holborn, if that's all right with you ... Here's the phone.'

B.H. immediately responded: 'Put the Inspector on to me, Phyllis...'

'He's a poppet like you B.H.', I said, doing so.

'From now on' I overheard B.H. tell the Inspector: 'I'll attend to the dear girl's accounts ... You know how unpractical artists are ... I'll send you my written undertaking straight away.'

'Your word's good enough for us, Mr Binder ... She's asked to me put her onto you again...'

'B.H., dear, I'm having the same sort of trouble with the Board of Trade...'

'These damned uncivil small fry Civil Servants!' guffawed B.H.: 'Don't worry. Leave it all to me. I'll get son Harry to sort you out.'

Thus early did my career as artist intertwine with business.

Harry Binder, B.H's son by a first marriage, had caused family ructions. Not only by marrying his stepmother Amy's sister Eileen, but worse still — the sisters being Irish Catholics — by giving her grounds for divorce, and re-marrying. But peace ultimately restored, B.H. — with Amy's approval — took him into his firm: 'Not that he's much good, Phyllis ... I gave him the education I never had the chance of ... Public School ... Cambridge ... What did he learn there? ... Wine Women and Song or in modern parlance: Hard Booze, silk pyjamas, sycophancy! ... And still in his mid-thirties sowing the same Bacchic oats!...'

Exquisitely tailored, silk shirted, his face prematurely bloated, Harry strolled into the office about noon: 'Can't say I'm at my chirpiest, sweetie-pie ... Revelled till the early hours ... Did myself rather jucily, I mean what...'

At sight of the plethora of bills, receipts, carbons, I.O.U.'s littering the place, he winced: 'Deucedly discouraging.'

'Isn't it? agreed Miss Hemelryk.

'I've put quite a lot on spikes ...' I interrupted, and she continued: 'There's simply not been time to file since Miss Fox left us for Gamages...'

'For their Lingerie Department', I explained: 'she'd always pined to sell ladies crepe de chine knickers, nighties...'

Sparking up — 'Girlie knick-knacks!' — he dug me in the ribs with cuddly elbow.

'At least, Harry,' I disengaged myself: 'I've kept track of every penny in and out'; and grabbing the top Woolworth Cash Book from its leaning tower toppled the lot.

'Oh no!' screamed Miss Hemelryk: This is too much Mrs Pearsall! How often have I warned you!'

'Do you mind if I take a seat …', languished Harry. But as I opened the current Cash Book for him, he leapt up, eyes organ-stop protruding: 'Jumping Jehosophat! No Double Entry! No bally bottom line balance. No balance, mark you, any dratted where! The mind boggles! … A desperate lethargy is stealing over me … Not for me the labours of jolly old Hercules! I'll get my minions to pick up the pieces, don't you know…'

Phoning his office, he requested that 'two of our young gentlemen toddle over', and that they buy en route a complete set of Accountancy Books: 'Meanwhile, Phyllis my lovey dovey, where can we shimmy out to a life-saver cognac.

On their arrival — 'do your darndest old eggs however longey-oh it takes!' — he hugged me goodbye with valedictory: 'Before I swan in to weigh up their Trial Balance, those poor coves of mine'll have weeks sifting through your primaeval mess…'

'What's "Trial Balance?"' I called after him…

Within a few days, Miss Hemelryk rebelled. Against Harry's "young gentlemen"; and to them: 'I'm a secretary … Not a maid of all work! Either you clear up your own mess, and make your own tea, or else…'

'We're not used to slumming …' retorted the immaculate senior; but henceforth complied — marching down to our Napier House ground floor cafe with his junior for sacrosanct tea breaks and luncheon.

Sticklers for status were new to me. Not so alas were alcoholics. As was the ex-vicar engaged as trade rep by papa. A sullen fellow whose acceptable orders at the start of between ten and twenty orders a day, soon dwindled via ten a week to nil; and his appearances at the office from daily to pay-day only. Asked why, he fulminated: 'I knew you disliked me from the start … I knew you would take the first opportunity to sack me. That's what comes of working for a female … my wife warned me … I should have listened to her…'

Bleary-eyed and slumped in his chair, he waited for his basic wage which papa — always impressed by scholarship and professional background — had agreed to pay him irrespective of commission earned.

'Would you prefer another chance?' I asked: 'or two week's salary in lieu?'

'I opt for the latter!' — he smirked, kissing the bank notes, and decamping at speed: 'That'll pay for a hair of the dog that bit me.'

Sadder was the arrival late one morning of a distraught gin-reeking woman in transparent negligée, her ringlets of hair still tightly rolled in overnight cotton strips.

'Where are you Patrick bloody Nolan?' she shrieked through door after door: Where's that bastard skulking? … Call the police! … He's stolen my gold wrist watch ... the fine Swiss watch my father, a Church of England Rector — no Irish Papist he! — gave me for my twenty-first ... Are you his boss Mrs Pearsall? ... I know where the spalpeen's lurking ... At Uncle's. Hocking my watch ... to splurge every penny down his own hatch, never mind yours truly.'

My suggestion that he might be planning 'another party for the two of you tonight' calmed her: 'You could be right ... he's the most good-natured man I've ever met ... not a real soaker ... goes on the binge for a week or so once or twice a year ... I with him, I must confess ... And now I've libelled him to you ... Please oh please God I haven't jeopardised his job ... He does admire you so...'

Wrapping her in my coat — 'How long since you've eaten, Mrs Nolan?' — I led her downstairs for, as she put it, 'a good tuck-in'.

On parting she kissed me: 'You won't peach on me will you there's a dear? He'd kill me if he knew.'

In September 1938, papa once again, but this time unannounced, stormed across the Atlantic, into London and into the office: 'What's this I hear from your Uncle Frank! That you arrived too late at the bank to cash the pay cheque! ... I can't imagine worse! ... And why on earth isn't he here?'

'His heart ...'

'And I suppose you're still paying him! ... But to return to that pay cheque. Explain!'

'That must have been in June, papa ... the month for roses...'

'Don't tell me!' he groaned; but I did.

On commission to paint Holland House, — I had become too absorbed with its magnificent red brick Tudor facade to notice time: 'Until, papa, Lady Ilchester brought me some cheese and biscuits. Worried, she told me, that I'd been working there with nothing to eat since 4.30 in the morning till three in the afternoon.'

Entranced as ever by aristocrats, his scowl relaxed into self-deprecating smile: 'A Countess! Why didn't you tell me ... One of the great Whig families ... You should take your father to meet her ... Do you remember the Countess I used to dance with at the Cecil...'

Still beaming, he asked me to introduce him to Harry's young gentlemen — by now apparently rooted with us forever: 'Who are they?'

'Accountants from B.H.'s office ... You remember papa he vouched...'

Indiscretion, he cut short on the brink. In sonorous greeting: 'How kind of my good friend Mr Binder! Sparing you both from more important concerns — and properly run ones — to deal with my daughter's inefficiency!'

'We've nearly wrapped 1936/37 up now Sir ... What nominal salary and director's fee would you propose for Mrs Pearsall?'

'None.'

'Not even nominal? To increase the 37/38 Loss to carry forward for 38/39?'

'You have a point there', conceded papa: 'So I'll agree to Directors' fees ... for my artist son as well!'

Acknowledging that despite their kind attempts to enlighten me I couldn't understand what auditing had to do with common sense, I added: 'Isn't it fun though papa that they keep a "JOURNAL" and a "SUSPENSE ACCOUNT"'!'

'When oh when Phyllis will you learn to take business seriously! It's eighteen months now since I showed you the ropes. And what for goodness sake have you done since then? Apart from painting Holland House...?'

'Tenby Bay with the Lifeboat Slip', I began: 'View of Amroth — where Nelson spent a night with Lady Hamilton; and in London, from behind the Banqueting Hall, a water colour of the Ministry of Transport, commissioned by the Under Secretary ... for whom at present I've started on a detailed drawing from the roof...'

'Don't tell me ... I meant, what have you done businesswise?'

'Another lovely Americanism papa...'

'Don't try to mollify me ... Hardly a new publication ... Only the Authentic I initiated, a Thirty Five Miles Round London and a London to the South East Coast! ... What's Fountain working on now?'

'London to the South Coast, stretching West as far as Swanage; followed by a London to the Sea combining the two coastal maps reduced to the size of one...'

'Rehashes!'

'No papa! With latest road information. My Ministry of Transport client has given me permanent entrée to his Surveyor and District Road Engineers...'

'And what's this paltry Ideal Guide ... Didn't I warn you against light coloured covers...'

'I'd already published it when you were here last. You must have forgotten...'

'I never forget! But now I've a real London Guide ready to publish. Compiled by a professional — he worked for me in the old days. He's calling at 9 tomorrow morning with his Ms ... Get our paper suppliers and printers here too. Then I'll teach you how to publish!'

On my early arrival at the office a phenomenon awaited me. Elderly, bald, corkscrew-shaped and almost toothless wearing elbow-length black lace gloves over tatty shirt-sleeves.

'Have I come to the right place?' he asked (for it was a man): 'I've brought the finished manuscript Mr Alexander Gross ordered from New York ... His Famous Guide to London...'

Papa joining us, beat him down on price. As he beat down Mr Hayes for two tons of Art paper, and Mr Short — handed the MS — for setting it up — 'Let my daughter have proofs by Friday ... Confirm agreed price in writing for runs of 5,000, 10,000 and 20,000. Similarly for a 6d SOUVENIR

LONDON VIEWS which I'll have ready for your blockmaker Monday 8 a.m. sharp ... Goodday...'

A stop-watch conduct of affairs for my edification: 'You see how much can be done in a quarter of an hour, Phyllis! ... Now, off to Photographic Agencies!'

Of those we visited, Reuters and The Illustrated London News had the widest selection: 'Pick out the tourist venues, Phyllis — Big Ben, Tower Bridge, The Tower of London, Horse Guards, Westminster Abbey, St Paul's ... and of course the Zoo with the cuddliest inmate ... I'll need those for both guides...'

'But they're so hackneyed, papa!'

'The more hackneyed they are, the better they'll sell! ... Will I never hear the end of your artistic snobism! ... And NO! None with people in winter coats! Never but never! Too gloomy ... Springtime's best ... like this one of Buckingham Palace with daffodils and flower!'

Inclusions of mine he approved 'as topical' were the new Battersea Power Station, and an architect's plan of the Waterloo Bridge under construction to replace Rennie's: 'I've started to draw it, papa, from the top of the Shot Tower, with a panoramic sweep of London from Highgate Hill to Tower Bridge...'

'Can't you ever give me your full attention!' he complained; and sent me off — with notes of book and type space measurements — for reductions of the Souvenir photographs: 'Two to a page, Phyllis, and bring them to me to paste up.' For the Famous, he instructed me: 'Fit each photograph to its descriptive paragraph, and have reductions made to gauged size...'

On Sunday, as arranged, we met again.

'Look at my Souvenir maquette Phyllis!' enthused papa: 'Quite marvellous don't you agree? ... I've left you to write a caption for each photograph ... you know the kind of thing: "BANK of ENGLAND popularly known as The Old Lady of Threadneedle Street" ... So much for the paper cover edition ... But now look at this! My half-a-crown de Luxe edition! Case-bound. With oval cut-out on front cover framing Big Ben on the title page. And what do you think of my brilliant finishing touch! This scarlet silk cord along the spine, ending in dangling tassle! ... Now show me your famous mock-up!'

'I'm sorry to disappoint you papa ... I've nothing to show...'

'Out painting I suppose...'

'Sadly, no! At the public library. Re-compiling the Famous. We can't possibly use your compiler's inaccurate mish-mash ferreted out of competitors' guides!'

'Good Lord! The cost! It's already been set-up! For goodness sake there must be something you can rescue!...'

'I've tried, and I can't. It's all out-of-date. Including long obsolete cinemas, theatres, clubs, Sports Stadiums — with pre-war Entrance Fees and Opening Times ... And all the new, omitted! Besides, howler after howler from start to finish! So at a bob for each author's correction it'll be cheaper to start afresh.'

'Whoever's heard of such a thing! So what now, Phyllis?'

'When we meet on Monday I'll ask Mr Short to scrap it; to set mine up instead...'

Which I did; and the Famous and Souvenir technicalities settled, papa produced a small EVER READY Guide to New York. Nearly as small as my Ideal, it opened at it's pin-bound centre to bold headings one beneath the other.

'Can you step-bind, Mr Short?' asked papa.

'No, Sir. But I know where to put it out...'

Said papa: 'My daughter'll let you have the copy by tomorrow'; and to me: 'Decide on the most useful headings, and list the relevant information — to fit into the space at your disposal ... It shouldn't take you a minute ... Print 50,000 at least. Taxi driver will use it for quick reference ... instead of Tuckers.'

'But how am I to pay for all this, papa? The terrifyingly expensive Art Paper, and equally terrifying long runs!

'That's your look-out! Have you never heard of cause and effect?! I thought you studied philosophy at the Sorbonne! Can't you see that long runs are so much cheaper; and the profit therefore greater!'

'But if they don't sell papa?'

'You'd have your own lack of gumption to blame!...'

Thus, after enabling me by his 18 months absence to achieve a comfortable harmony between MONEY IN and MONEY OUT, did papa — prior to his early departure for New York — fling me once again from Micawber caution into entrepreneuarial debt.

Mr Hayes and Caroline Moore pressed for payment; so did Gordon & Kerensky via apologetic Mr Short. Not so, Mr Brydone — though himself in the throes of buying out his partner — 'Pay when convenient, my dear...'

Papa's new guides ready, I called first at Woolworth — my quickest payers. And received the initial try-out order for all three. Though, leafing through the 6d Souvenir, Mr Prescott jibed: 'You got that Battersea Power Station wrong, Sister! ... It's white "vapour", not white "smoke" streaming from the chimneys! ... Didn't no one tell you! Smoke abatement's the coming thing. To put paid to your darned pea-soupers!'

On my taking the sample from him — 'You won't want it then! — he tugged it back: 'You didn't have my street in the A to Z and it's selling isn't it! No need to apologise for being alive, honey! ... Just get yourself a better idea of yourself right quick!'

Wider distribution orders for the Famous and Souvenir poured in; followed by repeats. But not for the EverReady. As Miss Wilson had foretold: 'It's only for taxi-drivers.'

With increased sales through tireless effort, and Lester's willing and efficient aid in delivery, I once again climbed from paying papa's creditors in dribs and drabs to the haven of cash balance.

B. H. Binder, having asked me to come early before a dinner party — 'to discuss your accounts,' — rejoiced. For on Harry's say-so — 'Phyllis hasn't the foggiest' — he had feared the Company might have to be wound-up, he told me: 'But it's Harry who hasn't the foggiest. He can't see further than accounts — which took him years to learn. Nothing he likes better than to find mistakes in my arithmetic ... and they're legion. Outside of rules and regulations he's a moron. Not a spot of the vision you and I are blessed with ... You're doing well, my dear. Don't let anyone drag you out of your depth or pattern, and you'll succeed...

'How much do I owe you, B.H.?'

'I wouldn't dream of charging you until you make a profit ... and are liquid...'

'Liquid?'

'Cash in the bank ...' he smiled.

# PART II
## 1938/39 to 1945/6

# RUMOURS of WAR and WAR

# CHAPTER II

AMONGST my fellow guests at a dinner with B.H. and Amy were a Jewish Czecho-Slovakian couple — clients of his: 'Over here to ask my advice... They've lost their nerve...'

It was June 1938. Less than a week ago Britain had appeared to be on the eve of war. Treaty-bound as joint guarantor with France, Italy and pre-Nazi Germany of Czecho-Slovakia's Independence to come to her defence against Hitler's threat of annexing Sudetenland; on which Czech military defence depended. The Fuhrer's pretext that German nationals (topped-up by machiavellian infiltration) were suffering under foreign yoke had just been accepted at Berchtesgarten by 'PEACE IN OUR TIME' Neville Chamberlain.

'Is it safe for us to remain in Prague, Mr Binder?' nervously asked the Jewess: 'or should we sell out and emigrate ... with all our family? As you know we have ample resources in Swiss and American banks...'

'You've absolutely nothing to worry about, dear friend. Our Prime Minister has personally assured me that Hitler has no territorial ambitions...'

'Vansittart and Winston Churchill fear the worst', I ventured; and despite a brush-off from B.H. — 'Two disgruntled has-beens!' — I passionately warned: 'If I were you dear Sir and Madam, I'd get out! My Yugoslav relatives have already skedaddled to the States or South America...'

But compared to counsel from the corridors of power, my burbling went unheeded. Besides, those who think themselves important tend to listen only to their ilk.

Harry, steering the conversation away — 'bad form, ole gal' — to lighter touch, said: 'How me in my Bugatti'll be scorching along those top-hole autoroads to your factory the moment my minions have your '37/38 Balance Sheets tied up and hunky-dory for me to finalise!'

While Amy flirted with the Argentinian diplomat on her right: 'Do intelligent women attract you Don Pedro?' And he replied: 'Like any self-respecting macho, my lovely hostess, I prefer pretty heads without a single thought!'

Mr Fountain also refused to contemplate the imminence of war; and treated with scorn — 'What are you panicking for?' — my request for him to start on a map of Europe: 'Anyway that Hitler's made good roads and has trains running to time ... We could do with him here...'

Mr Scowen though agreed with me: 'My son, the Major's ready for a scrap

... all hush-hush of course ... He says Bosche trouble's brewing ... What do I use as base?'

At Foyle's I procured a Stiehlers Handatlas, tore out the relevant pages and mailed them to him.

As to U.K. publications, I halved all printing and paper orders: 'I'm marking time...'

Soo too did Miss Hemelryk, like many Britons, prepare for war: 'I've joined the Terriers ... It'll mean leaving the office every evening at 4 for training ... and of course, week-ends.'

But even the April '39 Anglo-French pact with Poland 'to come to her aid if attacked', failed to shake Mr Fountain: 'Who's going to risk his neck for them dratted Poles? ... As you've got Scowen wasting his time on Europe, fetch his Birmingham so I can get that out of the way and start on Manchester ... You've finished compiling it for me I hope?

'*War is inevitable,*' wrote papa: '*What are you going to do about it?*'

Instructions followed. Couched of course in diatribe:

'*Months ago Fountain should have prepared a Map of Europe for the Daily Telegraph. As I did in 1913. Tell the present Lord Burnham that I initiated the sponsoring of maps by newspapers. By offering The Balkans War Map in 1912 to the first Lord Burnham. And that I personally formed the connection with the D.T. He's honour-bound to listen to the daughter of Alexander Gross! Why do I always have to explain the self-evident?! That painting nonsense again, I presume!...*'

His letter forwarded by Miss Hemelryk to me in Pembrokeshire (where I was painting a view of Saundersfoot) arrived at the same time as a telegram:

A TO Z STOCK LOW SHALL I REPRINT TEN THOUSAND

The ambiguity of my reply — 'GO AHEAD STOP' — prevented her placing any order. Fortunately. For, under threat of war, wholesalers and retailers alike cut the risk of being stuck with unsaleable stock; and our sales dwindled to almost nil.

On my return to London, Lord Burnham greeted me courteously: 'So you're Mr Alexander Gross's daughter! ...' and on being told of the past relationship between papa and *The Daily Telegraph*: 'So what are you going to ask us to sponsor now?'

'This Map of Europe! ... Wouldn't it be lovely to resurrect an old tradition?'

'You must meet my editor, Mr Pulvermacher ... He'll look after you...'

Mr Pulvermacher, tall, formal in black jacket and striped trousers, led me to his spacious office overlooking Fleet Street. Aware that in his heyday papa had been persona grata here, I felt his nostalgia for past greatness flood into me, and asked: 'Was this Mr Richardson's office?' and at his nod: 'and the furniture?'

'Unchanged...'

'I only knew him, as a staid old gentleman', I said: 'But, on hearing from my father that the Balkan War was imminent, he leapt onto his desk — yours now, Mr Pulvermacher — danced the Highland Fling and hollered: "War!!! For a newspaper war is wonderful! Nothing boosts the circulation like war!'

Mr Pulvermacher smiled wanly: 'We don't do that kind of thing nowadays ... But for me time is the essence. Let me see your map.' Again I unrolled it, pointed out its superiority over all others: 'German autobahns and railways — strategically planned wouldn't you agree for troop and arms movements ... to frontiers, to the Channel coast ... Aerodromes too are detailed — both civil and *Luftwaffe*...'

One of his many telephones rang. A call from Rome. 'How could you let the *Daily Express* get in first!' he bawled. A pause, then: 'You have the audacity to say you don't know what I'm talking about! Their front page headline: "ITALIAN MOB ATTACKS BRITISH EMBASSY"! ... You're fired! ... What's that? ... Speak up can't you. You're trying to tell me it didn't happen?... No. I won't call the Foreign Office. Your word's good enough for me. So it's the D.E. who've made a balls up. Not us! ... Good fellow! You're re-instated!'

To me he apologised. 'Sorry to keep you waiting ... Got to keep our reporters up to scratch ... Let me know when you're ready with a dummy: paper, cover paper, map folded and tipped in. Quote for runs of a 100,000, 250,000, half a million and a million. Good day...'

Within a week, back with sample and estimates, I asked for his decision.

'Specifications have been slightly changed', he said: 'Quote for self-cover, and bring a sample round!'

Prelude to other pettier variations. Over several weeks. With final shamefaced admission from Mr Pulvermacher: 'I've been stringing you along'.

Spread out on his desk was a *Daily Telegraph* War Map of Europe published by papa's old firm: 'I'm afraid it'll be on sale tomorrow', he said.

'My fault for being such a sucker!' said I.

'You're heaping coals of fire on my head ... Let me try to explain. We couldn't let you cream off the market ... We had to be first out ... But nor could we publish without the additional information you'd got on yours. So it took longer than anticipated...'

After a pause he laid his hand on my shoulder: 'I feel an awful heel ... You were so trusting ... Is there anything ... anything I could do for you to ease my conscience?'

Informed of my failure, papa cabled:

*'TRY THE DAILY EXPRESS...'*

But that paper's policy being 'There'll be no war', their editor declined to see me.

On the 15th of March 1939, from his Sudetenland base, Hitler launched his invasion into dismembered, disarmed Czecho-Slovakia. Harry Binder — auditing the business accounts of his father's friends in Prague — escaped, he told us: 'by the skin of my teeth, gee whiz! As those Storm Troopers zoomed in, yours truly zoomed out! But not before I'd jolly well wrung our fees out of their Company Secretary, dad. And what's more in gold Swiss Francs ... At revolver point!'

B.H. flinched: 'Stop bragging, Rupert of Hentzau! ... I gave those dear Czech friends of mine fatal advice. As Jews under Hitler they can't survive ... We'll never see them again ... And all due to our British head in the sand optimism against unpleasantness.

'Don't be so gloomy B.H.' chided Amy: 'You'll take me to visit the darlings in beautiful Prague when things have settled down.'

'It'll mean war ...' said B.H.

*'It'll be Poland next!'* wrote a Warsaw friend of my Paris student days: *'How could honourable nations like Britain and France betray their duty! As guarantors — under the Treaty of Versailles — of Masaryk's newly created State?'*

Even Mr Fountain, his bigotry shaken, agreed to draw a large scale map of the Western Front — 'just in case' — highlighting the Maginot and Siegfried Lines, with semi-underground forts and passages, gun emplacements, anti-tank defences: 'The French forts are larger, he mused; and I: 'Strange ... None at Sedan where the Germans broke through in 1870 ... Nothing along the Franco-Belgian frontier...'

On completion of the black, I phoned Mr Pulvermarcher: 'Did you really mean you wanted to do something for me?'

'Kind of you to give me a chance. Come round right away.' At sight of the map, he warned: 'You realise we can't sponsor it ... We're tied to your father's old firm. A pity though as you have the ideas and clear new drawings — and that's not flannel. For they stick to their 1914/18 base.'

'I'd like you to reproduce it in the *Daily Telegraph*' I said; and he: 'A scoop for us! Thank you. I'll give it Saturday's half back page.'

Thus, seeing me backed by the *Daily Telegraph,* Mr Hayes and Caroline Moore ceased dunning me. Mr Brydone, though I owed him £2,000, never had: 'What can I do for you?' he asked; and I: 'If you'd take the risk of printing this Western Front map, I might be able to pay you what I owe you in one fell swoop...'

'We'll get straight on to it and supply the paper too. We've plenty of M.G. ... and empty Order Books. Not that I worry. War puts life into perspective...'

*The Daily Express* editor phoned me: 'We're interested in that Western Front of yours'; and made an appointment for me to see him at his office: '9 a.m. sharp, Friday the 1st of September.'

On the 24th of August Ribbentrop and Molotov signed a non-agression pact between Germany and the U.S.S.R. Sandbags, barbed wire and sentries frantically burgeoned beyond Whitehall. So — to prevent dangerous glass splinters should bombs explode nearby — did strips from sticky brown rolls of paper criss-cross window panes in offices and homes. Furthermore, in readiness for enforced black-out, we Londoners were busy lining curtains. While to confirm our fears of blanket bombing, up went the balloon barrage.

Miss Hemelryk, now a Major resplendent in khaki serge, gave notice: 'I'm a full-time soldier now.' Less glamorously Mr Arnold and Mr Nolan joined up as privates. Our poet had long since drifted away.

Uncle Frank bustled up with Auntie Peg to say goodbye:

'Farewell Isabel, I've got to leave you' he sang: 'I've got to go. My King and my Country both need me so...'

'Called up? The R.A.F.? On your R.F.C. record in the First World War?'

'Clerk at the Board of Trade in Hove — so I'll be with my Peg should danger threaten — To release a younger man for the Forces isn't too bad for an old gaffer like me ... Besides it means a regular weekly wage for the first time in my whole nat-puff...'

Gordon Lester's attempts to enlist, thwarted by the medicos — he told me: "No go", they says as I walks in: "Next!"' — alone remained to sell and deliver our street maps and atlases. Former orders for a gross or more, or dozens, reduced to ones, two and threes: 'So they pays on the spot.'

Nonagenarian Mrs Burgess side-stepped my request for payment of six months' arrears: 'Pay? Why should I? I shan't be wanting any more of your goods ... My lads are already off to work in factories. To make a fortune, they think ... But that kind o' work don't suit 'em. Nothing like clocking-in and boring routine to get the poor buggers down. So back they'll come to work for Ma Burgess ... to earn a bob or two for the geegees, for a pint of beer and a bite to eat ... Hear that machine in the basement?' (The whole decrepit building was palsied by it): 'Well that's Old Moore's Almanack's I'm printing ready for them. Them kind of things sells like hot cakes in wars ... wives and mothers of our fighting men turning to the Stars for comfort, bless their hearts...'

Her peacetime 'novelty' display in the glass cabinets, I noticed, had been replaced by a multitude of almanacs — some open at the 3rd of September prophecy: 'Look, Missie, War!'

'Wars!' she continued a little later as we sipped cups of strong sweet tea: 'I've knowed any number of wars. The Crimea War — as a nipper of five sittin beside my mum I sewed beads onto soldiers' bonnets ... The Zulu War ... The Boer War — the dancing in the streets at the Relief of Mafeking ... The Kaiser's War — the War to end Wars, my eye! — My twin brother was killed at Loos. More fool he for volunteering under age; but they'd have got him in the end with conscription.'

German troops were massing on the Polish frontier.

Our map originals and A to Z index stereos, a priceless spring-board for a future beyond the black clouds of war, I decided to move out of London.

From a safe deposit in the High Holborn branch of the Midland Bank — (reduced to rubble by a direct hit in the winter of 1941); from Mr Fountain, printers, finishers, I hired a car and drove them to Peasmarsh, near Rye. Where a friend helped me fit them into the steel-lined safe he had built under his garage floor to protect his cello and his wife's viola.

Arriving five minutes late for my *Daily Express* appointment, I apologised to the editor: 'I've just returned from Sussex ... From taking my map originals for safe keeping...'

'So you're a jitterbug!' he jibed. They alone in Fleet Street had taken no sandbag or window precautions: 'Now about our possible sponsorship of your Western Front ...' he began; and his voice suddenly drowned by shouts and running feet inside and outside the building, stood up angrily: 'What's this! What's this!'

Without knocking, a distraught journalist burst into the office: 'Hitler's invaded Poland!'

'Sandbags! shrieked the editor: 'Rolls of strong sticky paper! Get everybody onto protecting our premises! ... Our policy's changed to WAR and to the Solidarity of the British Empire!' Unnoticed I slipped away.

On Sunday the 3rd of September, Britain declared war on Germany. As announced in the House of Commons by the Prime Minister. A few moments later, bloodcurdling Air Raid sirens shrilled long and almost simultaneously throughout London. But the sky, instead of black with enemy planes as expected — for it was a false alarm — remained serenely sunny, serenely blue. Wherein lolled silver barrage balloons like ethereal elephant playthings of some Indian princess.

On the 27th of September Poland's resistance collapsed; on the 28th the German/Soviet Treaty partitioned that martyr nation. Sales of our Western Front map rocketed. Throughout the United Kingdom. Orders and re-orders avalanched in. By wire, telephone and mail. Day and night I invoiced, packed, while Lester set off at dawn to deliver, returning evenings to help me pack and label.

'Like a newspaper office!' exclaimed Mr Brown of Dickinson's: 'You need more clerical help! I've got the very woman for you. Honest, efficient, trained ... She left my department because — and this is confidential — too embarrassing for her to stay on ... May I use your phone?'

Told the job might only be temporary, she arrived with a tearful: 'Thankful for small mercies' took off hat, coat, gloves; and invoices, delivery notes, labels proceeded at top speed from my mother's old Corona portable typewriter. Even so we needed extra part-time aid. Provided by Lucy Freud (a friend through my painting a portrait of her architect husband Ernst — Sigmund Freud's son), who had asked me for paid work. Never without them could I have kept up. For even after their 5 p.m. departure, snowed under with orders still to process and still more flowing in, I worked on through the night. Pandemonium, in the midst of which one evening at 9, I received a shrill phone call from a furious woman: 'I'm speaking from the phone box nearest you! Six weeks ago you made an appointment for me to dine with you at your studio!'

I remembered now. At some pre-war party a woman MP had asked to see my paintings, but so full was her politico-social diary, that this was the earliest date convenient to her.

'The war since then's put it clean out of my mind!' I fruitlessly apologised; and continued entering Money In ...

Nevertheless, war like a great rift across the earth's crust, sliced through the frail continuity of life.

With Gordon Lester's help I had moved my New Street studio furniture to Napier House. For, to escape the centre of London and to keep a friend company — in her husband's absence with his regiment — I moved to their home in Golders Green.

Company books and relevant files, Lester carried there: 'Your Head Office now ...', he beamed: 'For me to bring you Orders, delivery notes etcetera ...' Brushing aside my: 'Too far for you ...' with 'Far?!! Not for Gordon Lester. You ask my Auntie, Vesta Tilley ... ''Gordon never stands still!'' she says: ''Not since he took his very first step!'' '

Towards the end of April 1940, with Lowe & Brydone printing ever longer runs of our Western front to keep up with demand, I received a letter from Woolworth Head Office directing me to hold a million for future delivery.

But hardly had I phoned Dickinson's for the tons of paper needed for so marvellous an order; and Lowe & Brydone to print it, when Mr Prescott rang: 'I'm speaking off the record Phyllis. Whatever you do don't mistake that stock letter for an ORDER. Our Company's policy on Best-Sellers is never to risk running out of stock. It's up to the supplier to guage the risk. I remembered hearing of over enthusiastic company's bankrupting themselves by producing goods to meet such requests from large firms.

I thanked him for the warning and dropped the letter into the waste paper basket.

Lowe & Brydone cancelled my order without demur; whereas Mr Brown of Dickinsons prevaricated for my sake: 'I was in the last War. When all seemed lost, we held the line. I'll deliver the M.G. to Lowe & Brydone just in case you need it ... but on Sale or Return...'

Mr Prescott's warning was timely. For on the 9th of April, Germany invaded Denmark.

In my penniless student days in Paris, I had spent long winter evenings in the Bibliotheque Sainte Genevieve huddled amongst other XV Arondissement paupers near the radiators for warmth. There, knowing German, I had read German High Command apologias for losing the 1914-18 war. The fault lay not in the Schilieffen Plan, they asserted, but in the encircling movement starting too far South … it should have been well North of Belgium. Strategy, I now believed, Hitler's Council was bound to advocate.

So it was not on hunch that during the phoney war I instructed Mr Fountain to produce a large-scale war map of each menaced area — based on my Stiehler's Handatlas map pages: Scandinavia, The Low Countries, Northern France: 'If Paris goes, so will the rest of France, Mr Fountain; so please don't go on drawing the whole country on the smaller scale …' Warning knelled by an elderly French survivor of Napolean III's defeat at Sedan: 'This smells of 1870'.

'You must be in Hitler's confidence' laughed Norton & Gregory's young lady in charge of our preparatory work;

Thus in grievous turn as history unrolled, I published them. Denmark — fifth columnist Quisling rotten — capitulated the first day. Norway resisted. Backed by French and British troops heroically landed at strategic points by both navies — (and in June, alas, even more heroically withdrawn.) Three months of bumper sales for my War Map of Scandinavia: 'I hate making money out of slaughter' I lamented to Mr Prescott.'

'Sentimental rubbish!' snorted Miss Wilson: 'Think of the comfort your maps are giving to thousands — able to pinpoint where their loved ones are … Beside serving public need to follow events.'

On May the 15th the Netherlands capitulated — after five appalling days for its hitherto prosperous and neutral citizens.

On the 28th Belgium. After the German panzer break-through at Sedan and their race to the Coast. Compelling the Allied troops, cut off there, to fall back on Dunkirk; whence 337,131 men were heroically rescued.

On the 22nd June — (twelve days after Italy's Declaration of War against the Western Allies) — France signed an armistice with Hitler.

'Thank God we're on our own at last!' rejoiced Mr Fountain: 'Now we can get down to winning the war!'

Whereas my friend Arnot Robertson dubbing as 'prophets of doom' the international journalists skedaddling to our besieged island, enquired what map I was drawing next. And at my answer: 'The British Isles,' ordered me to desist. 'You Cassandra you!'; and thereafter claimed credit for Britain's survival and ultimate victory.

While Miss Wilson declared: 'What we need now is a Map of the World!'

Encumbering the Napier House office were 3,000 flat sheets of them. On Field Staff Evensyde paper. Caroline Moore agreed to fold the thick 54 inch by 40 sheets down to a bulky 10″ x 3¾″; and tip them into covers.

Entitled ''WAR MAP OF THE WORLD'' and retailing at 6d, it intoxicated Mr Prescott and Miss Wilson. Embracing her and me, he charlestoned round his office: 'Dandy! Dandy! Dandy!' and ordered the lot: 'Right, Miss Wilson? Right!'

'What about the delivery routine you've taught me?' I asked her; but he replied: 'Are you crazy sister? You bring us the best value ever! And you don't even know it! ... You'll deliver right here PRONTO! ... We'll process the branches: Right Miss Wilson?'

Within two days, telegrams from every branch poured in, clamouring for repeats.

'Reprint!' shouted Mr Prescott down the phone.

'I can't! ... 6d is miles below cost!'

Any experienced publisher — as papa was to chastise me — would have reduced the original, and produced a trade edition on cheap paper (which he had done with the black copies originally sent him). Nor stupidly did I publish a Mr Scowen's Europe unsponsored.

Steady, if much reduced, income from the A to Z, Premier and Authentic ceased on July the 4th 1940. Under an EMERGENCY POWERS (DEFENCE) Statutory Order prohibiting sale or purchase of 'any map of any part of the United Kingdom ... drawn to a scale exceeding one mile to one inch...'

Straightaway Lester and I — by tram, bus, Underground and train — retrieved our banned publication from every wholesaler and retailer. Either paying them back or issuing Credit Notes. One Authentic Map of London, however, having evaded our net, was bought by a detective; and I received a plea from W. H. Smith & Son's Chairman:

*'Rather than break a single regulation, we'd prefer to do no business at all...'*

I received a written apology, though. For a Main Line bookstall manager blamed himself in a letter: 'It must have slipped from the pile when I returned the stock to Mrs Pearsall; and was sold by my inexperienced wartime assistant.'

But our War Map sales were unexpectedly bumped up. By a New Zealand cousin, just escaped from Swiss military service (his father being Swiss) — 'I saw your pa's name and the firm's address on a map at Woolworth. — He needed a job, he told me while waiting for General Freyberg to take on volunteers: 'I'll put my hand to anything ... Have you thought of selling your excellent series of War Maps to Gordon & Gotch for the Antipodes?...'

'Here's another that ought to go well there', I said (For Winston Churchill, Prime Minister since May the 10th, was sending troops and tanks to Egypt): 'Our WAR MAP of the MEDITERRANEAN.

# CHAPTER 12

THOUGH the rest of the war is history, it did impinge on me; and indirectly as well as directly on the business.

The first stage of Hitler's threatened invasion "Sea-lion" began in August 1940 with the bombing of shipping and South Coast ports. Followed by dive-bombing of our airfields, massive daylight raids on London, blitz by night, sustained for over ten months. Apart from the drone of planes, whistle of descending bombs and roaring din of anti-aircraft guns, most able-bodied Londoners lacked sleep; enrolled as we were several nights a week for Civil Defence duty — I, tin-hatted, for fire-watching.

Direct hits on the Underground which surfaced between Hampstead and Golders Green forced Lester and me to carry my account books and stationery back to Napier House, and clear a space for me to work. For, Lester continued to sell our unproscribed U.K. maps such as the '35 Miles Round London' even though often — on delivering a yesterday's order — he found his customer's premises destroyed. As with war maps. Though these now sold more sporadically. The Mediterranean map for instance, peaking at naval engagements between British and Italian fleets; at General Wavell's thrusts into the desert from Egypt; again in October 1940 at Mussolini's attack on Greece, when our Forces were sent in; and in April '41, after the Germans bombed Belgrade, swept through Yugoslavia and Greece; and our ultimate evacuation of Crete a month later.

And on the 22nd of June, my No. 4 War Map of Finland. Drawn when a German despatch of rolling stock from West to East was rumoured; with military build-up along the Soviet frontier. On the eve of printing, proffered to the *Daily Express* editor, he jeered: 'Finland! Nobody in England gives two hoots for Finland...'

'But they did when Russia attacked her in November 1939!' I reminded him: 'the cat lovers who named their Toms "Mannerheim" after his David and Goliath stand ... the shoal of Communists who left the Party!'

After a pitying silence from him, I got up to leave: 'Very well then, I'll back my own judgement.'

'My dear young lady', he coaxed: 'for your own sake, don't! You'd be throwing good money away.' But his next remark — 'Call back with it on Thursday. Meanwhile I'll discuss your proposal with Lord Beaverbrook ...' reeked of Pulvermacher tactics.

'I'm printing today', I said.

At Lowe & Brydone, during make-ready, a last minute hitch.

Spotted by Mr Williams: 'Am I wrong in thinking that the capital of Finland's Helsinki ... Not Helisinki as you've got it here ...' Alterations to the black plate too 'dicey' for any but an expert, I phoned Mr Fountain to take a taxi here at once.'

Denying responsibility — 'Never could I of let that "i" creep in. Somebody's tampered ...' he deleted the offending letter, re-spaced the remainder and, still mumbling self-exculpating accusations, departed.

The map was ready for Lester by the 22nd of June (1941) when Germany with Finland, Hungary and Rumania invaded Russia. Three weeks later — after we'd creamed the market — out, as suspected, came the *Daily Express* with theirs.


War Map No. 5 — 'THE ALL IN ONE' — comprised five adaptations of existing originals. A large scale but truncated Europe entitled LONDON PARIS BERLIN; and, on a much smaller scale, The World, Europe, the Western Front expanded south to Toulon; and Finland. Since the outbreak of war I had sent papa good black copies of every war map — from which without telling me he was reaping a fortune in America. Nor did he even acknowledge them until receipt of this one. Which by return, he lambasted: 'Who in his right mind would buy such a jumble? Are you mad?!!!' and never mentioned it again. Though, containing an inset of RUSSIA TO IRAQ IRAN AND INDIA, it gave him another best-seller.

A War Map of Russia completed, I rang the Soviet Embassy for an appointment 'to check its accuracy'.

'No!' replied the official; but when I specified a new canal, told me to hang on. Whereupon a different and authoritative voice commanded me to call there 'at once!'

The Embassy's formidable doors in Kensington Palace Gardens opened to my ring; but were immediately shut and bolted behind me.

Pushed rather than ushered into an anteroom, I was soon joined by a giant of a thickset official: 'What's this about a canal?' he without preamble growled.

Pointed it out to him on my sun-copy: 'running South, Sir, from the Baltic, you see ...' he barked: 'Who supplied this information?' and locked the room's two doors.

'I haven't the faintest idea...'

'Of course you know!'

'From some geographic journal, perhaps?' I suggested.

'Which? Where?'

I shook my head: 'Perhaps my draughtsman might remember...'

'Send for him. What's his phone number? I'll dial it.'

On being handed the earpiece, I asked Mr Fountain if he remembered how we knew about the canal. He did: 'From the Russky Embassy ... It was on the map they sent us...'

My interrogator, listening at my elbow spluttered: 'Ask him who?'

Mr Fountain for a moment could not speak for laughing; then: '... as if I could pronounce them outlandish bolshie names ...'

'Tell that idiot to come here! We've got to know the name of the informer in our midst.'

Congratulating him on his English, I wondered how I was ever to get out. Siberia and salt mines loomed sinisterly close. Looking at my watch, I realised I would be late for lunch with a friend at the Foreign Office; and told him so. Adding, 'He knows where I am.'

'What's his name?'

'Roger Allen...'

Corroborated on the phone by the Foreign Office, my would-be gaoler contorted his face into a smile: 'Why did you not mention that your friend is a Senior official?' and let me go.

Outside those great doors, the free world smiled on me. 'Thank God for you!' I said to Roger; and he 'Thank God Hitler's making Napoleon's mistakes...'

Due to the sinking of timber-laden merchantmen by Nazi submarines and Luftwaffe, paper was rationed and so costly that Dickinson's had withdrawn the tons sold me on Sale or Return. Nor had Lowe & Brydone any.

Thus when Miss Wilson phoned to ask — 'Where's your War Map of Russia Phyllis? You're usually on the dot! — I replied: 'The maps drawn, but I haven't any paper.'

'Don't let that worry you', she said: 'You're allowed to buy in the free market ... And I've got a chap right here landed with wrong sizes ... Julius Veil, a Greetings Card tycoon ... Since I introduced him to Harry Williams, he places all his printing with Lowe & Brydone ... I'll put him onto you...'

Invited to lunch with him at Bentley's, I asked 'Where's that?' 'Where've you been all your life!' laughed the fruity voice: Everybody who is anybody knows Bentley's in Swallow Street! I'll be waiting outside.'

Saville Row his suit, Turnbull & Asher shirted, Bond Street groomed and manicured, Mr Veil did not at first sight inspire confidence. Nor, as we were ushered to the best table, did his hail-fellow show-off with manager and waiters.

Two bottles of Bollinger already reclined on ice.

'Eighteen of your best Colchesters for my honoured guest and me, he said: 'and versez le bubbly!'

A clear mind essential, I covered my glass: 'Please tell me about the paper you want to sell ... Where does it come from?'

'Competitors nuzzled in on my Greetings Card market. So, my dear, I've overbought...'

'Sheet size?' I asked; and on being told, demurred: 'It would mean too much wastage...'

'You're not going to let a little thing like that stop you! Surely a business woman like you recognises a sellers' market! Don't tell me Muriel's led me up the garden path ... Now change your mind and join me in a glass or two...'

For two hours he tried to persuade me to buy — 'What a fascinating woman you are! I've fallen head over heals in love with you!' — but always side-stepped my queries about the source of his paper. Something fishy, I thought; and rising to go — 'so much to do at the office' — said: And when there's something I don't understand — often due to my own stupidity — I don't touch it...'

Before long, Miss Wilson, called on me at the office: 'Too dangerous to phone, Phyllis; it might be tapped' Her usually proud and impassive bearing in shreds; hair, make-up, clothing untidy, this battleship of a woman, gasped: 'Get Harry Williams to come here! Tell him he's got to get Julius to pay Lowe & Brydone at once, or he won't get a penny. And whatever he does, not to contact me. Or we'll all get our fingers burnt ... Harry'll understand. I introduced them Phyllis, so I don't want to let him down ... Call it honour amongst thieves ... What am I saying ... Then there's you to think of. How much paper did you buy from him? At Bentleys or after?'

'None.'

'Thank God for that!'

Soon after Julius Veil was arrested; appeared in Court; sentenced to 18 months. The paper offered me plus tons more had allegedly been stolen from the British Council. Simply loaded onto lorries in their own warehouses and driven away to his. 'A brick, though' according to Miss Wilson: 'Not a single accomplice or crony did he implicate! So's his wife a brick. I wouldn't have thought it of her. Before this blew up she'd started divorce proceedings ... "Now hubby's in trouble", she told me, "I'm standing by him. At least until he's released from jug." And that despite her jewellery gone, their mansion gone, several acres of land ... They lived it up Phyllis! Deep pile carpets; William & Mary furniture, Chippendale, Sheraton; Spode dinner services, Waterford glass ... The whole fantastic lot gone! ... Phew!' she concluded in relief: 'A close shave for me, I can tell you...'

One of the nearest-to-death shaves for me was from a bomb dropped on High Holborn, slightly east of Napier House. Fire Watching on the roof with the caretaker's wife since an 'enemy planes overhead' alert, we were blown down the stairs by the blast. 'Never again' she laughed picking herself up, 'Will I stand near the stairs when I'm fire-watching!'

But on the road, slaughter. A direct hit on a crowded bus.

Again attending to business at the office through the night, I also witnessed the devastating Gray's Inn conflagration.

And another morning, too absorbed in entering Lester's sales, I failed to hear a police order by megaphone to vacate buildings in our area. Until an exploded bomb was diffused. The alarm over, the caretaker finding me there on his return, apologised: 'We didn't realise you were here! ... And by the way, a man was asking about you yesterday ... A plain clothes cop if ever I saw one! ... He wouldn't leave me his name ...' A similar visit to Corringham Road followed. At last he caught up with me.

During lulls in business, ever since the fall of France, I had been drawing women at work. With relevant permits, where necessary. As I also had for drawing or painting other sensitive subjects, such as merchant vessels gathering for convoy at the mouth of Milford Haven. I had started on a water colour of a recent wreck there, when a young naval officer asked for my permit.

All my papers in order, I thought the incident closed. Until the detective caught up with me at the office: 'Sorry to interrupt you Mrs Pearsall. But we've been looking into your credentials ... At the request of Naval Intelligence ... A map publisher with a Hungarian born father drawing shipping ... airfields ... Army, Navy and Air Force establishments ... top-secret munition factories ... Rather suspicious, don't you think? How do you account for it?'

'Women personnel, not establishments', I said: 'A Ministry of Labour chap wants them as illustrations for a leaflet preparing woman for conscription...'

'And what's that got to do with your activities near Dale?'

'The Admiralty gave me a pass...'

'Are there responsible people who'd be willing to vouch for you?'

'Would Sir Jonah Walker Smith MP do? We play tiddlywinks together some evenings when he gets back from the House...'

'And?' he asked unsmiling.

'Sir Andrew and Lady McFadyean...'

'Sounds a bit like name-dropping, doesn't it...'

'I'll phone them if you like...'

'Oh no you don't!'

On guard at last, I stopped myself from saying 'This begins to feel like the Soviet Embassy'; and proffered: 'Kathleen Davis, a Principal at the Home Office...'

'Now that does give me something to bite on...'

Kathleen phoned next day to tell me she had cleared me: 'You won't be bothered any more.' Nor was I.


Not till 1943 was actual conscription for women decreed; when, objecting to the levity of my 'Foot Inspection', the Chief Controller of the A.T.S. — her rank equivalent to Major General — vetoed my drawings.

But already in March '41, girls of 20 to 21 were asked to register; and some months later, women from 18 to 50 — my age group. Joining a long queue slowly moving towards a Nissen hut, I eventually reached it; was asked the stock question — 'What can you do? — by a women clerical officer.

'I'm a map publisher.'

'I didn't ask you what you are but what you can do', she snapped.

'Maps are important in war...'

'They're not on my list. Can you type, what's your speed?'

'Only with two fingers...'

'Languages?'

'A few...'

'Stop being funny, will you! I haven't got all day! French? German?'

'And Spanish and Venetian.'

'You mean Italian...'

'They're not the same...'

'It's the Censorship for you', she concluded: 'Next...'

A daily commuter now, I joined the general early morning trek — after night-long bombing — across the Heath to Hampstead's deepest of all London tube stations. For Holborn; and thence to pick my way along pot-holed High Holborn littered with broken glass, fire hoses, rubble, masonry. And, in the evening, to the wail of air raid sirens, leaving the Prudential (and then Napier House — so conveniently near — after dealing with Lester's work) back to a transformed Holborn tube station. Seething now with families either bombed-out of their homes or just seeking safety under ground. Already on my Edgware line platform, many were *in situ* on their pitch; settling down for the night with bedclothes, thermos flasks of tea and the victuals rationing allowed. After such hubbub and stench (of unwashed humanity, urine and disinfectant), how welcome was the good air over Hampstead Heath, and the hope of hot soup — if the gas mains had been mended.

Enshrouded now within the Kafka world of the Civil Service, I daily sniffed the sheltered outlook of red-taped bureaucrats. (Leavened by a few selfless devoted individuals — as in church, law, medicine, armed forces, police, trade unions, journalism, art and other cast systems.) Here, they were so Pension targeted in their 'dead man's boots' hierarchy, that keeping the rules voided them of all responsibility. Members of the public were a nuisance; and — more than Germany — other government departments, the enemy. So that, they allowed people to be killed, rather than intervene, and, after a Peak District cloudburst, would, had they not been disobeyed, have left them to starve and freeze: 'Take no action! It concerns the Ministry of Health and the Board of Trade!'.

Undermining forever my youthful, New Statesman-like, solution — planned production and distribution — to world problems and injustice. For self-perpetuating administrators in self-perpetuating administrative blocks bog down the lot, and themselves consume their *raison d'etre* funds.

Thus, every government in thrall to them, I became apolitical; and vowed to cultivate my garden *a la* Voltaire; lay down no rules in the business; give increased duty to others — not status — on promotion.

On the 7th of December 1941, Japan attacked America's naval base at Pearl Harbour; and declared war on Britain and the U.S.A. Four days later, Germany and Italy also declared war on America; and, from behind the scenes supporter, she blossomed into a purposeful and powerful ally.

But resented by Mr Fountain as he worked on a post-war World Atlas: 'Come to our rescue, my eye! When we've done all the fighting, in come the Yanks like last time as if they'd won the war! You mark my words!'

By which time, I'd been moved to the Home Intelligence Department at the Ministry of Information. Amongst the clear endeavour and fun of other temporaries: E. Arnot Robertson, cartoonist Nicolas Bentley and tempera painter Eliot Hodgkin. Where I remained until D.E. Day (Peace in Europe).

Our remit was to compile a weekly report for the Cabinet. From reports sent to us from the thirteen Regions. On how people were reacting to the bombing — 'All hell let loose but dad's cutting his toe-nails in the kitchen' —; enemy victories at sea and on land; Lord Haw Haw induced rumours of disasters; personal tragedies; and, increasingly our province, the adverse effect on individuals of Government restrictions.

Further away from Napier House, and no longer working nine to five but often late into the night, I obtained a pass for Lester — so that we could keep the business embers flickering — though at a loss. Some papers he brought me evenings I entered in the Company Books and filed; others — for his deliveries — I would have ready for him next morning.

# CHAPTER 13

ON the 13th January 1944, a Control of Maps Order revoked the restrictions on the sale and purchase of maps.

In a London seething with American and Dominion forces; Norwegian,
Dutch, Polish, Belgian ... as well as British, our liberated A to Zs, and our large
scale maps sold out immediately. Mr Brydone supplied the paper — 'the most
I can obtain' — for 50,000 copies of each, and photolithoed them ... including
the A to Z index, (having made good black copies from my stereos) and did
the binding.

From the firm who undertook the 'finishing' of the sheet maps, stemmed
another warm and lasting friendship. With Sid Wells ... Who worked for his
jobbing printer father at Camberwell New Road; found by Lester in 1942 —
Caroline Moore having left London — to 'finish' our War Map sheets, and
supply and print the covers. Called on one Sunday night, Sid welcomed more
work: 'Tell L & B to send the flat sheets here. I'll get the whole family on the
folding; it'll take gran's mind off those blasted bombs!' After a beer together
he tentatively suggested printing my Ideal Guide: 'I know our quality's not
good enough yet — dad likes to stick to visiting cards, local leaflets, small cinema
posters and our Boxing News — but I've done my apprenticeship, am a fully
fledged printer and would like to have a go ... At your A to Z in the end...'

His lean little father having lurked behind him, sneered: 'Listen to 'im!
Wants to ruin me with new fangled machinery! I've run this business for years
and know 'ow.'

'Don't worry dad', sighed Sidney.

'See wot I mean?' he said; and using Cockney rhyming slang: 'The trouble
with Steak and Kidney is 'e's SOFT! ... My other son — Edward Wells and
Sons with an ''s'' see — 'e's a man! ...'

But out of earshot, Sid, accompanying me along the road towards the Oval
confided: 'Not a printer, my brother. Never does a stroke of work ... oozes
charm and lives off us ... But there! He's dad and mum's favourite...'

The Ideal Guide came out skew-whiff. No matter. Every copy sold out at
once; and I ordered another 50,000. 'It'll be better next time round', Sid
promised. While his father did all he could to thwart him. Never would he call
him to the phone: 'So you want to talk to Steak and Kidney. 'E''ll be back in
'alf an hour. I'll get 'im to ring you, OK?' Which he never did. Nor did letters
addressed to Sid reach Sid. Communication impasse, Sid — 'once the penny
dropped — overcame by ringing me daily from a call-box.

When the pre-war stock of the Famous Guide also sold out, I called on Mr Gorden of Gordon & Kerensky [the original printers of the A to Z index] for a 100,000 reprint: 'If you have the necessary Art paper?'

'Paper be blowed!' he said: 'Your metal, stereos and blocks are all destroyed.'

'Destroyed?'

'Non est! Don't you understand plain English!'

'In the air raids, I suppose. I do hope you didn't lose too much ...' I commiserated. Red-faced, he bundled me out of his office, shrieked: Never do we want to have anything to do with you or your father again!'

Compensation refused, I approached a solicitor. Whose fee plus cost for wrenching £100 from them totted up to £75.

Mr Brydone and Mr Williams pondered on how to get the Famous on the market again: 'If you have any good black pulls as you had of the A to Z index, we could print it litho. Of course it won't be up to scratch, but in this sellers' market it's no good being too fussy...'

Ferreting them out at Napier House we also found good black pulls of the Standard Street Guide. Both publications rapidly reprinted rapidly sold. Chiefly to Mr Cruise of W. H. Smith & Son, and Mr Prescott of Woolworth. As the latter laughed: 'With this darned shortage of print, even Telphone Directories would sell!' and handed me a plump and oven-ready capon from his Selsey Bill farm: Didn't I say to you, Miss Wilson, that as we're having to bribe most suppliers with gifts, why not one for Phyllis ... Particularly as I took a shine to her innocence from the start ... Right Miss Wilson? Right!...'

'Not only for her innocence, you naughty man', quipped Miss Wilson, restored to pre-Julius Veil aplomb; and explained: 'You've no idea how other suppliers badger us. Their only aim in life is to sell. Can you imagine anything more boring!'

Even Mrs Burgess wooed me: 'I'll pay C.O.D. right and proper-like ...' Nearing her century — 'I'm getting on a little. It's me breathing' — she was, she told me, coaching her nephew John Collins, demobbed on health grounds, to take over from her: 'The only one of me family that's done his bit. Fought for his country in Egypt he did ... I intend to make 'him my heir!'

But in the hawker trade John faced competition.

Not too seriously from Arthur who had tried to buy direct from me before the war: 'I'm a half a day a week worker', he told me: 'Saturday mornings at the Caledonian Market — now a gonner — where a lady's crocodile 'andbag I paid five bob for I sells for two hundred and fifty bangers to some toff with 'is fancy girl prowling round for bargains. Bargains! That's a laugh!'

'And the rest of the time?' I asked.

'Drinks with me mates ... plays the 'osses ... Wot else!'

But about 'Erb, John did worry: 'He's fly.'

'Erb at his licensed hawker stall on Charing Cross Embankment offered to buy from me direct 'for cash'; and giving me a verbal order 'for goods at wholesale discount', counted out £100 in £1 banknotes at lightning speed: 'Nothing in writing. No invoices nor that sort o' lark neither. Understand?'

On my handing him an invoice — 'My auditors go through my accounts with a fine tooth-comb' — he wrapped it round a stone and threw it over the wall into the river: 'See?' and, prefaced by salacious wink and tap on his long nose, suggested I abet him in another fiddle: 'If you was to publish a book of photographs ... now that would bring in the doh-re-mi! ... You know what I mean. Saucy ladies with nothing on, or just black stockings with *oh la la garters* or black corset. A French caption under each — don't matter wot so long it's French. Chaps on leave'll pay the earth for that kind o' thing ... Wot abaht it? ... It'd sell like wildfire...'

Lester revelled in his now multifarious activities: 'Keeps me on me toes! ...' Armed with his pass to the MOI, he daily brought me increasing masses of paper work. (To be attended to through the night — beside resultant increased Book entries to be made). Such as Orders to invoice, signed Delivery Notes to file, correspondence flooding into the office to answer, Bank Pay-In book to prepare — with cheques, Postal Orders, cash tucked in. Ready for him to take to the Bedford Row branch of the Midland Bank (to which — after their High Holborn one was bombed — I transferred our business account): 'The manager there' — reported tirelessly galloping, efficient, loyal Lester, 'keeps atelling me he wants to meet you. His wife he ses, knowed you from school...'

Not even VI flying bombs stopped him; though his customers' shops — particularly in South London — were once again bombed wholly or in part by the time he came to deliver an order taken that morning: '... but he's OK. Him and his wife got to the shelter before the engine stopped ...' The customer according to Lester, then voiced a general view: "In the blitz it was men bombing us ... Not spooky things like these ...'" Many people, including a woman assistant Eliot and I had engaged after Arnot left for the Film Division, admitted to being scared: 'I'm going down to the shelter, whatever you two say: I can't bear pretending to be indifferent any more. When I hear the sirens followed by that spluttering engine I'm frightened out of my wits; and worse when its engine shuts off ... Is it going to fall on me?'

She was in the shelter when some of us in the Senate House grounds, hearing a fast approaching VI cut out, looked up. The grey monster broke through the clouds immediately overhead. We gazed awestruck. 'My God! It's going to hit the Middlesex Hospital!' somebody groaned — expressing the horror in our every heart. Instead, it exploded between the hospital and us. A thickly populated area. Instantly, American troops — before our own Civil Defence came into action — were on the spot; digging dead and injured from the fallen masonry; ferrying them in jeeps to the hospital: 'The lives they've saved!' exclaimed a surgeon friend to me later: 'Quick on the draw, those Americans! They've got a thing or two to teach us slow coaches.'

The VIs over Britain, defeated by our anti-aircraft gunners and fighter pilots,

Winston Churchill's future son-in-law — a junior Government Minister — publicised the triumph. (Unwisely. For a map showing where and when each had fallen, enabled German calculators more accurately to pin-point and harass our troops at Antwerp after D Day.)

Good news at which a woman friend, having kept her children in London, raised her arms and voice in thanksgiving: 'Nothing more to fear now!' Whereupon we heard the dull distant thud of the first V2.

The unlikely harbinger of peace was 'Erb. In 1945. When, absent from his stall for a few days, I asked him why.

'I can smell the end of the war ... So it'll be Union Jacks I need, won't I. 'Cos every Tom, Dick and Harry's going to celebrate. The kiddies too ... And as everbody knows, St Albans the place for Union Jacks. So off I goes...

'First thing they asks me is "Wot abaht these new plastic ones?" But 'Erb 'ere wasn't born yesterday, and I asks: "Wot if the sun shines?" So I holds it behind me back to the gas fire. It curled. "Wot if it rains?" I asks. "Them colours is fast!" the woman answers; and 'ands me another. But accidental-like I drops it into the bowl of water at my feet marked DOG. Off comes the red, white an' blue ... clean off:

' "I'll stick to the ole fashioned contraptions", ses I; and bought a couple o' thou' ... At 7d each...'

In time for VE Day. May the 8th, 1945. As, on my return from a short visit to New York, he expatiated: 'Didn't I tell you I smelt victory — we gipsies have the Nose ... So there I was with Union Jacks bought at 7d each ... Wot you think I sells them for outside Buckingham Palace at midnight that night? ... Guess ... 'Ave a try ducks ... No? ... Well I'll tell you then. One guinea a piece. Ain't that a decent profit margin! ... Better than your stuff; though I do mark your prices up with a sticker week-ends, public holidays and daily after shop-closing-hours; and of course to foreigners who don't know better ... Never more than 100%, though ...' He paused; ruminated: 'I should of bought more at that St Albans place.

My own transition to peace in Europe grew apace.

Firstly, a precipitate move from Golders Green to Central London. For, amongst my specially mourned 'killed in action' was the owner of my wartime home.

Having stayed on with his inconsolable widow until she sold it, I told Eliot next morning as we sat down to work: 'Her purchaser wants immediate possession'; and while we wondered how accommodation could be procured in over-populated, bomb devastated London, his phone rang.

'Do you believe in miracles?' he asked on putting the receiver down. For the caller, wanting a Colonel Hodson in the Ministry had been put through to Eliot Hodgkin: 'Can't trace no Colonel Hodson!' said the girl at the switchboard.

'I can't trace him either', Eliot had told the caller.

'What a pity', she said: 'It's about a flat he wanted.'

'My colleague needs one ...' said Eliot; and jotting down her name and address made an appointment for me to see her. Thus I moved to an attic flatlet at 9 Robert Adam Street off Portman Square. £5 a week the rent.

Leaving the M.O.I., and refusing a Board of Trade Senior Civil Servant post, I threw myself back into business. Office space the priority, I tried to rent the rest of our Napier House suite. 'Nothing available at present', replied the landlord; 'and to continue in your present office you must sign this 24 year lease.' Which I did — with less trepidation than the original two year one.

An ultimatum from Mr Fountain — 'I'm not going to work at home any more!' led me to rent a rickety top floor at 21 Gray's Inn Road — shaky survivor between bomb pulverised numbers 19 and 23; at a £1 a week from The Prudential: 'without a lease as it's been declared structurally unsound ... condemned in fact.'

Together Lester and I scrubbed the rotten floorboards clean, put down lino; moved in our office furniture, the Chubb safe and oursleves.

By glass partitioning the Napier House office, we formed a stock and packing room; leaving the light larger area for Mr Fountain: 'Let me know when you've got it ready. With a work-bench from wall to wall along the windows for me and an apprentice. I'll tell you for why. I'm sick to death of mixing my own stick ink, fetching and carrying, thank you.'

Soon installed, and with a school-leaver alongside, he asked: 'What am I to start on?'

'Up-date the Pictorial. Renamed the Souvenir Pictorial it could sell as a separate publication.'

'And after that?'

'Finish the World Atlas you've been on...'

'It'd take years ...' The undertaking, already spread over three had been beyond his ability and vision: continents and many countries begun; none finished; non co-related; and I suggested he start bringing our A to Z up-to-date.

For book-keeping, correspondence and attending to Lester's orders, Mrs Ford returned. Transformed from bone-thin scarecrow to barely recognisable fat-embedded. Due, she explained, 'to shock altering my metabolism, the doctor says ... That VI cutting out, zooming down and exploding in my garden. Luckily the blast hurled me right out of my house as it collapsed. Or I wouldn't be alive to tell the tale...'

Taken round to 21, she did not blench: 'Worry about little things like creaking uneven floor boards and three flights down to the outside lavatory! Not after what I've been through!'

Mr Fountain complained about my absences, about Lester, and bitterly about the apprentice: 'Impertinent! No-good!' We adults could disregard his sarcasms, moods, blind fury. Not so a boy just out of school subject to vicious raps on the knuckles with steel rulers; and now dismissal.

'Give Tom another chance ...' I pleaded.

'So you take the little bounder's side against me! ... Any old how you're too late. I gave him his cards last Friday.'

Changing tack, I reminded him 'We're behind with updating London. You can't do everything yourself!'

'About time you acknowledged that! ...' And we agreed to advertise for a map draughtsman.

Many ex-servicemen applied. But their mapping ability as they themselves sadly admitted fell far short of our commercial standard.

However, one journeyman — unhappy in his firm — did apply. Wally Cooper. And with Mr Fountain's approval, I engaged him.

Routine safe, I left for New York. In answer to an urgent letter from my father:

> *I was found unconscious at the corner of Fifth Avenue and 57th, by a policeman and brought to my office, where I came to. I'm all right now, but want to familiarise you with my business and main customers.'*

Exit Permits still required for travelling abroad, mine was granted by the Ministry of Transport and Shipping; who also booked me on the Port Line freighter Port Chalmers. Sailing for the Far East war zone from Tilbury, her single cabins squeezed in four. But, after five beleagured years, no hardship. Laughter. Treat upon treat.

The appetising smell, for a start, of frizzling bacon wafted on the Thames breeze; and then the taste: 'Eggs and Bacon! Haven't seen them for years!' I drooled to the steward, whose reply: 'No variety!' underlined the rationing we civilians had taken for granted during hostilities — rationing that still continued ... My father, quite recovered, was busy at his office in the Chase Manhattan building.

'Are you still neglecting the London business?' he asked. My suggestion that he send me paper from New York; or print a large run of the A to Z and despatch it to me, he turned down: 'International trade's too complicated, costly and risky ... But Mr Sellers here of *American News* has a proposition for you...'

'We wouldn't touch that kind of thing ourselves', hesitantly began his visitor: 'But if you'd do the distribution in the United Kingdom there's a fortune in it ...' and he gave me the name and address of a man to contact on my return.

But it was the 6th of August 1945. The atom bomb dropped on Hiroshima, and three days later on Nagasaki, brought Emperor Hirohito's acceptance of Allied terms on the 14th; and formal surrender on 2nd September.

I flew back by Constellation. Bearing gifts unobtainable at home: a pair of chamois leather gloves for Mr Cruise's wife — he had given me her size — nylons and perfumes for my women friends, shirts, ties, socks for men, blankets, and not just food, but delicacies galore ... realising that after years of accepted restraints only luxury — as the French say — was necessary. (*Il n'y a que le luxe qui est necessaire!*)

And bearing with me too, an astrology publication of papa's called Horoscope that could apply equally to British aficionados. New companies allowed to buy paper in the open market, I formed The Authentic Co. Ltd., had Sid produce it; sold 20,000 copies, reprinted 50,000 — which, the public maw for print insatiable, were soon swallowed up...

Meanwhile, as cautiously mooted by Mr Sellers, I phoned a London firm: 'I hear you may want us to distribute for you...'

At his 'Come round to my warehouse, dearie,' I did so. Helping me off with my coat was near rape. Befitting — 'Titillating, eh?' — the Sex Comics he showed me: 'In the States they're a Wow! Particularly with University students ... Give them the outlets you've got for your A to Z and by golly we'll both make millions!' — he urged.

'I couldn't bear to unload such prurience on the British market ... I'm afraid I'm a bit of a prude ...' I recoiled, warding off his wandering hands; and incidentally saving Britain from this sleazy erotica for two years.

'An attractive girlie like you! Never! What about dining with me tonight at ...' and he named a restaurant notorious for Private Rooms.

On the 31st of December 1945, Mrs Burgess died peacefully in her bed. Leaving mayhem. As John Collins lamented: 'She promised that on the 1st of January she'd sign her Will leaving me the business. Now the family want to sell and I ain't got the dough to buy it. No charity please Missus. But could you help?'

'How much are they asking?'

'£50...'

'I'm short of storage space. Are you going to need your basement for printing Old Moore? ... No? ... Would you let me rent it for £1 a week ... A year's payment in advance?'

'I'll let you off two week's rent!' he laughed; and we shook hands on 'our arrangement to mutual benefit.'

A terrible blow to 'Erb. Next time I called on him, he cut me dead. As I waited on the pavement watching the traffic flow by, he suddenly capitulated. An open truck, empty except for a straw encased jeroboam bouncing about in the back, was just rattling by: 'See that bloke! ...' he pointed: 'Well, before the war was over 'e asked if I'd like five gallons of lemonade powder 'e couldn't shift. "Ow much?" I asks; and after a little argy bargy got 'im down to 'alf a crown: "OK!' I ses. Now wot you think I made on that little lot on VJ Day? Give in? Three thousand quid. And I'd have made more if I 'adn't 'ad to pay boys to pour the water into glasses an' take them round. 'Ot as 'ell it was! Them sweating crowds tightly packed along the Thames for the river celebrations hours afore the show begun 'ad their tongues 'anging out with thirst. They'd of died if it 'adn't been for all that lemonade!'

Angry again, he drew himself up: 'Never wanted to talk to you again!'

'What's wrong?' I asked.

'You've got a nerve! Wot you mean buying Ma Burgess's place for John Collins ... I'd 'ave given a four figure sum for it!'

'I didn't buy ... I'm renting it', I said; and: 'When did you know?'

'Last week.'

'You're slipping, Herb! It happened over a month ago. On New Year's Day!'

He took my hand: 'Shike! You're one of us!'

# CHAPTER 14

EXPANSION continued to be hampered by paper shortage. Restricted to a small percentage of publishers' 1938 consumption it was impossible to meet demand. An impasse from which my M.O.I. friend Eliot released me.

'There's a gentleman to see you', announced Mrs Ford: 'And I mean a real gentleman.'

In he walked — we had not met since our Home Intelligence days — and laying a large mock-up of a book on my desk, asked me to publish it: 'On every left page, a New Testament story; facing it on the right an Old Master painting illustrating it ... Not stereotyped ones ... A careful personal choice ... The reproductions to be in colour of course.'

'You'd do better with a Fine Art publisher ...' I advised: 'I've no colour block experience.'

'Don't worry about that. I've brought an expert with me. The British agent for an Amsterdam firm. I'll fetch him up.'

The unprepossessing agent's first words — 'By special arrangement with the British Government everything we at Van Leer print can be imported here' — brought me to my feet: 'If that's so, maps are my priority! I'm off to the Board of Trade for confirmation! Please leave your card...'

'My book?' asked Eliot running down the stairs after me. Agreeing to publish it — 'it touches an aesthetic chord' — we planned to meet again when he had copy ready, and copyrights cleared.

At The Board of Trade, the official in charge of Imports, reclining in his chair, feet on desk, savoured the rare treat (under rationing) of a ginger biscuit with his cup of tea: 'What can I do for you?'

'Don't let me spoil your pleasure. I'll wait.'

'Sorry I can't offer you one' he smiled hospitably: 'But I've only got two...'

His eleveneses over, he lapsed into Civil Servant arbiter of fate: 'Now what's your problem?' Told it, he replied: 'That agent's got it wrong, of course. We are helping the Netherlands to recover, it's true. But only by permitting our paper dealers to export to them.'

I rose to go: 'Silly of me to have believed something so unlikely...'

'Wait my dear', he refrained me — human again: 'I'll eat my hat if there isn't some kind of exemption for maps ... I seem to remember a darned funny one ... Half a mo'. I'll go look see...'

He returned laughing. Brandishing a dog-eared age-yellowed Leaflet: 'What did I tell you! You're in luck! An Open General Licence ha ha would you believe it for Gold Nuggets, Winkles, Maps!'

An Open Sesame, in fact. But I demurred: 'Does it really allow me to import maps of London by the hundred thousands ... I don't want to take advantage of a loophole...'

'Stuff and nonsense! Your competitors can! So why not you?'

Amsterdam. Ravaged. Inhabitants haggard. Children pathetically so, with rickets distorted limbs. The only form of transport bicycles, their wheels without tyres rasping bumpety bump over cobbles. Myriads of them. Swirling, intertwining, miraculously eluding collision. Circus agile, the riders balance baths on shoulder and handlebars, wardrobes, gigantic bundles; and young lovers from bicycle to bicycle embraced without falling off.

Meeting my train from the Hook of Holland, a young Mr Van Leer guided me to his bomb damaged factory. Within, vast emptiness: 'Before retreating, those Bosch devils in vindictive jackboot kick, threw all our machines into the Gulf of Ij. At first, dismantled; in final panic, intact. As you see, we're hoisting them out, derusting, reassembling ... That's my brother over there. Bosses and workers together, day and night. Till we've got things going. For our own sakes as well as in memory of my father ... brutally herded into a deportation train ... exterminated with other jews in the gas chamber at Auschwitz ...' Gulping down sorrow and rage, he led me to the only printing press in working order: 'Our 20 x 30 Mann — ready for your three colour Pictorial London ... The 100,000 run we quoted for ... Have you the 36½ x 29½ plates?'

'You've been carrying them for me...'

Plates supplied by Mr Williams. After Mr Fountain's alterations to our black, blue and yellow originals; highlighting the bombed-out areas, particularly around St Paul's. (Vainly I hoped that Wren's plan for a spacious approach and surround to his Cathedral would be at last, two and a half centuries later, be implemented.)

'Paper?' I asked.

'Ready hung at home in my kitchen. Our Government let me import it for export.'

'Would the same apply to my far more important A to Z?'

'We aren't letterpress printers. I've asked a Mr Groen to quote. He's joining us for lunch at your hotel.'

The maitre d'hotel placed a Union Jack on my table: 'We love the British. Every day during the horror of Nazi Occupation we listened to the BBC. It gave us hope. And now you've liberated us! ... We've only one thing against you. Why didn't you allow our Queen Wilhelmina to be the first to enter Amsterdam? Instead of Montgomery? ... After all, you allowed General de Gaulle to enter Paris first!'

Mr Groen, a six foot five inch bear of a man inspired immediate confidence.

Though his estimate was double that of Antwerp and a third more than I had obtained in Paris I gave him the order for 250,000 copies: 'The demand's so great.'

'I've included paper cost', he said: 'but please arrange for it to be exported to us.'

'Mr Van Leer had no difficulty...'

'It would speed things up.'

Back at Gray's Inn Road, a phone call: 'Customs and Excise here. London Docks. There's a consignment for you from Holland. Pictorial Maps of London...'

'Open General Licence ... Board of Trade ...' I burbled.

'Don't talk to me about that perishin' lot sitting on their behinds all day long ... You can't have the maps and that's that!'

'I'll come straight down to see you...'

'What good'll that do? ... Without the country of origin no print is allowed into the UK ... Got to be destroyed...'

'We could overprint ...' I thought aloud.

'Ah! Now that's another story!' he relented, giving me his name, phone and extension numbers: 'Put your printer in touch with me.'

As Sid Wells recounted: "At the docks, blue, white, yellow, pink and God knows papers to sign! Then they let me load the packages. But would you believe! Suspicious lot down there! One of their blokes had to drive back with me on the pick-up van to my works and sits beside the press until the last "Printed in Holland" sheets come off.'

Immediately I called on Mr Cruise to ask if 'Printed in Holland' would adversely affect sales — particularly of the A to Z.

'Of course not! People's tongues are hanging out for it. Good for you if you can put them on the market! ... And good for us.'

Henceforth Van Leer and Mr Groen added a corrected version of the imprint — 'Printed in the Netherlands' — to every publication.

Papa had been right about the complications of international trade.

Bad enough to transport paper from Liverpool Street station to Harwich, to ship's hold, to the Hook Customs. Export and Import papers queried at ports of departure and arrival. And worse: the tons of Mechanical Newsprint (paper) for the A to Z — ordered to Mr Groen's specified size and weight — were compulsorily held at the Hook. Without it, I entrained for Nijmegen, reached his office, told him.

'Stoopid bureacrats!' He shrugged, and phoned them: 'Despatch my paper forthwith! Or are you going to stop our nation's recovery?' And then to me: 'They think they're still under the Nazis! ... But there's a favour I want to ask you ... 'Could you reduce your A to Z trimmed size by an 1/8th of an inch?'

'The maps are already small to read', I refused.

'Very well,' he agreed. So resignedly that I asked: 'Is it possible you underestimated?'

'Yes. But that's my funeral. You gave me the correct specifications. What's more, a copy of the A to Z for my estimators to work on!'

'So the paper I brought over's no good! ... wrong size ... after all that trouble with your Customs! ... and now it's going to be wasted!'

'My fault entirely ... My responsibility', acknowledged Mr Groen: 'But don't worry about the paper I've got. No problem. I can use it for some other publication...'

'Let me phone my paper supplier for immediate correct replacement.'

Asked how much he would lose by the error, he told me; and I suggested we halve the sum.

'You don't need to...'

Tearing up his estimate, I requested the new.

'That's very generous ...' he said; and shaking my hand, sealed lifelong friendship.


Less generous had I been to Gordon Lester, whose vital contribution to the business deserved reward. Paying myself nothing while re-establishing the business, it did not occur to my henceforth troubled conscience to give him the substantial rise he deserved, instead of waiting until future A to Z sales restored our liquidity. And lost him. To Kangeroo Books: 'He didn't approach us. We kept seeing him at bookstalls and shops. A live wire if ever there was one. You wouldn't stand in his way?' Sadly I let him go. Nor could such a paragon ever be replaced. But quickly somebody had to be found. For by now I was flying to Schiphol and back once or twice a week — in war-time Dakotas still unadapted to civilian flights. My greengrocer in Chancery Lane, kind supplier of used wicker boxes and wrapping paper for the ever increasingly large orders I had to pack, introduced me to a man of about 24 — 'Canadian or American, I think, by his accent. I never can tell the difference' — keen for a job.

His first morning, he arrived briskly before time. In clean white overalls, pencil behind ear, notebook in hand: 'rarin' to go. But nothing done by the evening — 'How could I know where to start Ma'am?' — we worked together to get each order packed and despatched that night. Returning unexpectedly from Northolt a couple of days later, I found him fondling a prostitute — most uncomfortably on the stock-piled floor. Giggling alto, she skedaddled. He, feet apart, hands clenched confronted me: 'She tripped on this darn box ... I gotten her up ...' and, shoving a small parcel under his arm — 'I've promised Larby's immediate delivery ...' hurriedly left me.

Within the hour, Guy's Hospital called me round: 'Your warehouseman collapsed on Holborn Viaduct ... He's recovering here.'

The doctor in charge of Accidents and Emergency diagnosed a malingerer: 'Though he complains that you gave him far too heavy a load to carry, I can find nothing wrong with him.'

'He's trying to avoid dismissal!' I said; and two days later invited the now menacing fellow into my office: 'I'm sorry to say we'll have to part.' Shutting the door I had purposely left open, he locked it; put the key in his pocket; and after a feint or two to right and left he threw his whole weight behind a lunge at me across the desk. Before he could recover balance I hurled myself through the bomb-weakened door, shouting to Mrs Ford in the next room to call the police. Before they arrived, he bolted.

'He's sworn to kill you!' warned our Napier House caretaker: 'My sons told me. They've seen him prowling around waiting for you. Whenever you leave here or 21 Gray's Inn Road, they follow you in case he should attack.' Finally, the Canadian Military Police caught up with him: 'He's a murderer as well as deserter ... You've been lucky, Ma'am...'

The packing and delivery problem came to a head with a mammoth one: Forty six 35" x 45" bundles from Holland to be picked up before midday from East London Wharf, Bow', and forced a solution. The hire of a van and driver. From Rapid Van Service down the road. From then on, tri-weekly, the same driver, Mr Noakes, helped me deliver parcels stacked ready in areas, and to pick up new orders as we tore through London. Soon, he helped pack stack and deliver; drove me to and from Northolt. 'Why don't you take me on full time?' he asked: 'Then I could do the lot whether you're here or in Holland.'

His old lag physiognomy caused me to hesitate; but doubting my discrimination since the Canadian murderer's pleasanter one, I engaged him.

'Let's hope he's a diamond. He's certainly rough', commented Mrs Ford.

An arrangement his employer blessed; with the suggestion: 'It'd come cheaper for you in the end to buy the van from me instead of hiring it ... Fully overhauled like new ... And your Company's name on it to your design.'

Thus on the 1st of July 1947 did we acquire our first vehicle — proudly blazoning on white ground, our cobalt blue insignia. Of vital use too became Mr Noakes. Nothing too much for him, he handled large zinc plates of our various maps from Lowe & Brydone for Holland; a heavy 50 by 40 inch plate-glass sheet 5/16 inch thick on which the positives had been stripped (substitute for an unusable zinc). And black plate and transfers made by Van Leer, back from Northolt to London Bridge for Mr Fountain and Mr Cooper to draw the three colours. Rapidly completed — though the two draughtsmen were by now no longer on speaking terms — and back I flew to Amsterdam. Where the Van Leer brothers, less eager for our work since the lifting of the wartime ban on book imports to Britain, were falling behind on completion dates.

For the benefit of a posher new customer extolled by Mr Van Leer: 'Chairman and founder of a Bloomsbury book publishing company ... His initials printing and binding orders top hundreds of thousands of pounds sterling ... He and his Szasza Gabor attractive wife — both Hungarian born — have invited you and our families to a fabulous dinner tonight ...'

Half Hungarian myself, and immune to the fascination they exert on intellectuals and Anglo-Saxons, I knew that my inclusion as guest must stem from some arriere pensee. In true Magyar style it started with attack: 'The Van Leers tell me you are too preoccupied with costs.'

'How else can we produce publications cheap enough for the general public?'

'Listen, my dear lady. It's not cheapness but imagination you need ... I intend the books I publish to do a great social good. I intend to educate the British public ... widen their horizons ...' As I thanked him for the feast provided: that delicacy of delicacies Dutch smoked eel, beef fillet bearing two fried eggs on it, and now Rum Baba, he beamed at me over his horn-rimmed spectacles: 'Ah! You like the good things of life! Why don't you join my firm. A little matter of a few hundred thou' and I bestow on you a seat on my Board...'

'I'm not ambitious' I refused: 'just an artist avid for time to paint...'

Neither was his next request unexpected: 'You were in the Civil Service, I understand ... My naturalisation papers seem to have floundered in your Home Office ...' So eighteen months later did he flounder out of publishing.

But now, with an addenda of last minute LCC street name changes for the A to Z, I took the train on to Nijmegen. Also, aware that books could henceforth be imported into Britain, I gave Mr Groen the specifications for Eliot's book. But on him asking me 'How many colours for the Old Master reproductions?' I pleaded total ignorance: 'It's got to be top quality Fine Art. What do you suggest?'

'We at the Drikkerij Thieme are Fine Art printers ... Leave it to us.'

Armed with his estimate for 100,000 copies, I went straight from London to Boots' head office at Nottingham; where the buyer, Mr English, gave me an order for 50,000, retailing at 30/-. (Which, by meeting the cost, eliminated risk).

'We'll want them ASP' he added.

'What's ASP?'

'As soon as possible and sooner ... You've somehow got the IN for post-war paper and print. What we're really short of is a child's ABC. Here's my written order for 100,000 copies ... Also of course ASP! ...'

'I've given that conceited ass Cooper notice!' Mr Fountain greeted me on the doorstep of Napier House: 'And I'll tell you for why. He defied me. I said "do it this way" and the impudent so and so answered: ''Well that's what I'm doing!"'' Suggesting he have a quiet cup of tea at the cafe next door, I took the lift up to the drawing office.

'I've had about enough of that Fountain. Silly grumpy old sod. I've given him my notice and applied for my old job back ... I'm sorry Mrs Pearsall. Mind you I've got nothing against you. I don't like leaving you in the lurch neither ... I like working with you.'

Which I told him he could continue to do at Gray's Inn Road — 'while I sort things out ...' Like most map draughtsmen he was also an artist; and happily agreed to start on drawings next day for the child's ABC. Meanwhile, child-psychologist friend, Anna Freud, advised: 'For each letter of the alphabet show a picture of something a child delights in. "B" for Birthday Cake, for instance; "E" for Elephant; "I" for Ice Cream; "M" for Me; "W" for Wellingtons. And Mr Cooper aided by pictorial reference books 'got stuck in.'

Then, before I had time (or perhaps, courage) to confront Mr Fountain, I recognised his measured tread mounting the ramshackle stairs. Withering me with a glance at sight of Mr Cooper, he snarled: 'I smelt a rat. So that's it! Either he goes or I go!'

My trilemma — shame at this apparent deceit; our six year working friendship; and his drawing of all our maps — contended in my mind and heart with the cul de sac into which his incapacity to work with any other draughtsman, boy or man, was forcing the business. At length I suggested: 'Wouldn't you be much happier working snugly at home?'

'After all I've done for you! Worked myself to the bone! I am the business. You won't be able to manage without me! Either I work here or not at all.'

'But it would be a solution ...' I ventured; unaware that against hurt pride one pleads in vain.

'Solution! If you're going to back that ninny against me, I'll tell you the only solution. That I never have anything to do with you again!' And out he stalked. Leaving me trembling, conscience-stricken. First Lester, now Mr Fountain. The two corner stones. The true founders. Was I misusing power by severing their connection with what they had so devotedly built? Was my belief that they were endangering or paralysing the business merely self-justification? How right they were to feel betrayed by me. Nevertheless, what a relief it was to be free of Mr Fountain's carping ... free to engage the extra draughtsmen needed.

Soon Mr Cooper's staff grew to six. An apprentice and five journeymen including an acquaintance of Mrs Ford's: 'He's a good worker, though a Communist...'

Another applicant arrived in knee-high tightly laced leather boots over army ducks, and dictatorial bearing: 'I've just been demobbed and am choosy. I'm very ambitious. I want the best niche for my talents. I want the chance of becoming Chief Draughtsman ... I want to become a Director...'

'He's a good draughtsman,' said Mr Cooper; and engaged him. So that made eight altogether, immersed in the revision and expansion of the A to Z.

For indexing, two demobbed applicants seemed almost equally meticulous. The one I engaged, phoned next day to ask me to release him: 'My brother wants me to join his business ...' Whereupon George Elston, pre-war taxi driver, accepted the post; and remained with us for the rest of his working life.

Of the Field Staff, only Mr Nolan returned — on honourable discharge from the Army: 'I've had a lovely war ... As Mess Steward ... Just my line ... Now down to the grindstone! What have you got for me?'

The Premier London, 35 Miles Round London, London to the South and London to the Sea, all revised, Mr Nolan's orders exceeded 100 a week. But the mounters lacked cloth and wooden rollers for them.

A Board of Trade Application Form for linen filled in by me and sent as directed to their Manchester Sub-Division, received no answer; and their telephone number forever engaged, I took the train there. But before I could put my case to the harrassed official, he handed me the requisite Licence: 'If you've taken the trouble to come up here, that's good enough for me.'

Sufficient rollers, Sid Wells tracked down in Highgate at a timber merchants behind Archway Road.

Hardings grown too busy with government contracts, Bliss & Son in Cursitor Street just of Chancery Lane, eagerly undertook our work, soon cleared up arrears and thenceforth kept pace with Mr Nolan's increasing orders.

'I just don't know how you do it all!' Mrs Ford complained: 'I find it difficult to keep up. That Noakes and that Nolan always hanging over me with their own commission calculations chivvying me to pay before I've had time to check! ... "I won't be rushed!" I tell them ... By the way, Mrs Pearsall, the safe was broken into again last night ... That's the third time. Lucky you told me to keep nothing in it ... It's when you're not there, and they don't see the light on...'

Most evenings when in London I stayed late finishing off the days' work left over on her 5 pm departure for home.

In the peace that settled on Gray's Inn Road after the evening rush hour, much could be accomplished. Time sped. It was about midnight, that a creak of the decrepit front door broke my concentration. As of being prised open. Then all was still. For a few moments. Followed by muffled footsteps on the stairs slow and with pauses. Stopping at each landing; on the floor below. Then up to ours.

'Who's there?' I called out. Silence. Except for heavy breathing. Again I called out: 'Who are you looking for? Perhaps I can help you?'

In shambled a man in greasy mackintosh and Homburg — its brim pulled low over his face, a chisel in his hand.

'Who are you looking for?' I asked; and on his mumbling the name of some firm, said: 'You must have the wrong address ... Can't you see I'm busy ... all these papers to finish. Please let me get on.'

But he stood there cogitating. So did I cogitate.

My only weapon, the Company Seal, I decided not to use — 'He's stronger than I' —

'Get out! I ordered. A moment's hesitation, and then to my surprise he shuffled away. But I did not hear him descend. 'He's lurking for me in the shadows', I quailed.

Thus fearfully half an hour later in total blackness I expected at every turn on that perilous staircase for him to spring out at me. But he did not; nor from other buildings as I hurried to the safety of lighted and more populated High Holborn.

Before leaving for Amsterdam on Monday the 4th of November, I phoned Mrs Ford: 'I'm catching the first plane to Schiphol. Will be back tomorrow!... Please have Mr Noakes meet the evening plane at Croydon.'

Thus, in the exhilaration of energy, endeavour, purpose, did I refer to future plans with a certainty never to be presumed again.

I did not return on Guy Fawkes Day. Nor to the office for weeks thereafter.

PART III
1946 to 1963

WHEN THE CAT'S AWAY

# CHAPTER 15

IT was a beautiful starlit sky in Amsterdam after a clear sunlit day. But my flight home was first delayed; then cancelled: 'Fog at English aerodromes', explained the BOAC representative to waiting passengers: 'If you hurry you can catch the boat train to the Hook for the night boat for Harwich! The coach is waiting for you outside.'

The majority darted off. Not I. The printing plates I had come to Amsterdam to fetch, some of them 50 x 40 inches, were bound to be damaged by the multiple handling such a journey entailed. In and out of coach, train, ship and finally train to Liverpool Street station. Put up at a hotel for the night by BOAC, the remaining six of us dined together; became friends.

Fog still persistent over Britain at dawn, our BOAC flight was again cancelled. But the same helpful representative had transferred us: 'to that KLM Dakota out there on the runway already revving up ...' He wired Mr Noakes the new scheduled arrival time at Northolt.

Out of a cold blue winter sky the sun shone on the sparkling Hobbema landscape beneath us. Happily we congratulated ourselves on the comfort of our journey compared with those who opted for the ship last night; chatted about world affairs, about war experiences — all the way across the North Sea and its toy-size boats, their white wake clearly defined — to the English coast. The cloud delineating it stretched far inland. A dense black pall. Though, as we flew above it in the sun, we marvelled at the magic carpet of billowing snow beneath us. Which as we entered was ominously transformed into impenetrable swirling white fog. The plane bucked. Wallowed. Increasingly bucked. Our sense of direction totally lost, we seemed to rise, fall, shudder, regain height, hang motionless. Chat and laughter spasmodically started, stopped.

Until at last — to a general sigh of relief felt rather than heard through the loud reverberating throb of the engines — the mist thinned, gradually shredded.

To the terrifying sight of treetops rushing up towards us at lightning speed; followed by a tearing impact ... a battering through twigs and late autumnal foliage — 'Shrubbery along the edge of our landing strip ...' — someone hoped aloud as great timbers fell about us. Then a staccato series of buffeting bangs ... and a final ear-splitting crash.

Total stillness. Blackness. I had been thrown backwards and forwards in my seat like a rubber doll. A woman screamed. Ceaselessly: 'Poor woman! I must help her!' I thought. But still unable to see — 'the lights have gone out!' — I put my hands up to my eyes. I had no nose. A sticky liquid poured through my fingers. Blood. 'I'm blind', I thought.

'Fire!' shouted an authoritative male voice: 'Get out of the wreck! Everyone OUT!'

Drifting in and out of consciousness, I remember being carried at a run through frozen grasses; laid down in scrub; a man's thick overcoat tucked gently round me against a bitter wind; and trying to gasp: 'Your coat ... it'll be ruined by my blood ... clothes coupons...'

'Hush', said a woman; and gently wiping my face, lifted up my head: 'Oh God! What a terrible gash! ... Blood gushing from it!'

A Dutch doctor among the uninjured passengers ministered to me. 'If that blow on the back of her head had been a fraction lower', I heard him say: 'she'd have been a gonner — as you say in English, no?'

'Is her poor face mangled for ever, doctor?' commiserated the woman. He laughed: 'It'll be better than before!'

'What happened, pilot?' I heard a stewardess ask in Dutch.

'I haven't any idea', he answered: 'I knew nothing till we hit...'

'Where are we?'

'How should I know.'

The ex-RAF passenger who had extinguished the fire fetched help from a distant farm: 'We've phoned the ambulance. They'll soon be here.'

The farmer and neighbours murmured offers of help: 'Brandy? Hot coffee?'

'Don't give her any liquid!' forbade the doctor.

In moments of consciousness, the cold wind bit my wounds: 'When will we be rescued?' I repeatedly thought or said.

Hours later, through the mist of my mind, I heard a new voice apologise: 'Sorry for the delay ... first we had to get everybody together from their jobs ... then to man-handle the ambulances up this steep hill through the dense copse ... Even so we've only been able to get one through. So please, those who can possibly walk, please do...'

I tried in vain to get up.

'No, not you!' laughed a kind voluntary St John's man, lifting me expertly onto a stretcher: 'It's good experience for my mate here ... His wife's expecting their first baby...'

The woman's screams seemed never to have stopped: 'Poor woman ... ' I said, consciousness turning on and off like an electric light: 'She must be terribly hurt...

'More like shock', said the doctor, as he helped slide the stretcher into the ambulance.

'It won't be long now ...' murmured the attendant inside; holding me steady as the vehicle lurched through tangled undergrowth.

'Look after that poor lady ...' I managed to say; and fainted. Consiousness, regained on an X-ray table, faded, returned. 'Sorry we can't give you an anaesthetic', said a doctor behind me: 'I've got to stitch the back of your head. You've sustained a fractured skull, nose, cheekbones, and injured spine. You're lucky to be alive...'

'I've got to get to my office', I said. He laughed: 'Matron's holding your hand...'

'Everybody's so kind ...' I thought or said through dry lips.

'She can't take any more ...' I heard matron say; and woke up in bed.

'What happened?' asked my neighbour in the ward — echoed by multiple voices. I told them: 'The pilot must have hit a wooded hill in the fog.'

A giant Dutchman towered over me; coldly asked: 'How are you?'

'A fractured skull ...' I began.

'Where did you get that idea?' he boomed: 'you're fine.'

'Who's that unpleasant man?' my bedside neighbour asked a nurse.

'The K.L.M. doctor', she replied.

It was night by the time I revived again.

'You were wrong blaming the pilot!' said a patient: 'Here's the headlines in my evening paper: 'Pilot's skill saves passengers!'

My friends, Arnot and her husband Henry Turner took me to Guyon House, their Hampstead home, where — friends indeed — they looked after me.

(At the Board of Inquiry a year later it transpired that the pilot had miscalculated his height as over sea instead of over land; and, completely off-course for Croydon, had flown into a Surrey hill near Shere. The resultant compulsory regulation that all passenger planes had henceforth to carry a navigator, comforted me. At least some good came out of bad.)

Through ferocious headache as I lay inert, my injured brain groped for the business threads so suddenly sliced through. Intermittently. Threads it took a timeless fortnight to piece together. In mind and by phone.

The printing plates carried on the ill-fated plane (despite a label VERY FRAGILE irretrievably damaged like me) had to be replaced by Lowe & Brydone, and sent back to Van Leer for urgent printing. All done by Mr Harry Williams. Sid Wells took over the printing of sheet map covers, map folding and tipping in: 'I'll take that off you ...' he commiserated; adding: 'I've brought you some ducks eggs and a goose. My mum plucked it ready.' To Arnot's delight: 'What a feast! Almost worth your crash!'

Amongst many other gifts received were butter and tea from 'Erb — now cafe owner instead of hawker — 'You can make a fortune if you're careful with the tea ... One teaspoon for the urn lasts you all day!' — Parma violets and muscatel grapes from my solicitor friend Humphrey Thackrah: 'I've become a contemplative, Phyllis, and am hoping to be accepted by the Carthusians ...' Bouquets of flowers. Long stemmed white lilac from Andrew McFadyean — a surrealist confusion for my unfocusing eyes of his feet on chest and flowers as face: 'Never forget you're a painter!' he sympathised. As did Eliot, despite disappointment when I stammered: 'I ... won't ... able ... produce ... book'.

He clasped my hand: 'Just get well...'

'I ... can ... see ... speck of De Vinci ... blue ... through the cloud ...' I tried to reassure; but, aware within my blurred mind of the opposite effect, thought: 'They're acting normally. Out of kindness. So must I ...' and managed not to cry out or wince at the eye piercing pain of a chink of light as he drew the drawn curtains aside to see for himself: 'It's bucketing down!' he sadly said: 'Don't worry about my book or anything ...' Mr Bowman, my Bedford Row bank manager, also told me not to worry: 'We'll allow you an overdraft of up to £8,000 should you need it...'

Mr Duncan Porteous, his joyous pre-war bulk reduced to shadow since his only son was killed at Tobruk, warned my hosts and me against Insurance personnel: 'Whatever you do don't let them into the house or see them. But if they do force their way in, as is their viper wont, refuse to settle!'

But hammering incessantly at my pain-suffused cotton wool brain was the need to deliver the new A to Z copy to Mr Groen by the 13th February 1947. The maps would be ready by then, promised Mr Cooper in December: 'What about the Index?'

The name "Zoar Street, SE1" floated into my consciousness: 'Is it the last entry?' I asked. He nodded.

'Then before I pranged I did finish the index cards and the alphabeticising ... For both the A to Z and The Standard Street Guide.'

And on the 11th of February, my will power clenched on this new A to Z, I set off — despite shattered body and doctor's protest — for Nijmegen. Still unable to dress myself, with corduroys pulled over pyjama trousers and cardigan over the jacket, I let Mr Noakes help me down the stairs, into the van; and, arrived at Liverpool Street station, into the Harwich/Hook of Holland night boat-train with the precious originals and four heavy packages of index cards.

A nightmare journey. Headache still held me in a twenty four hour vice. If I did not move my head, the pain accumulated to even more unbearable pitch. If I did move it, the slight respite brought worse upon itself. The ordinary noise of train and voices crescendoed into Niebelungen foundry. Only the recollection of Apsley Cherry-Garrard's *Worst Journey in the World* tempered self pity. He and his team must in the black Arctic winter have been more bitterly cold even than I. At least, my purpose might succeed; not fail, as did his, after impossible odds, with a broken Emperor Penguin egg. (After procuring it at embryo stage for scientists seeking the evolutionary process from scales to feathers).

At Harwich a kindly fellow passenger, before dashing off to the ship with the others, helped me out of the compartment with my packages. The emptying platform stretched out ahead of me to infinity. After a first few dizzy steps I swayed to the ground. Cheery sailor voices broke my reverie or faint: 'A gentleman told us you were in a spot of bother. So we're carrying you aboard ...' and as I protested, added: 'Light as a feather you are. Nothing like the seventeen and twenty stone we usually get...'

Compounding my plight, there was nobody to meet me at Nijmegen station, and amidst my packages I sagged to the ground on the arrival platform.

When I regained consciousness, I was tucked up in bed. To the rowdy pandemonium of a drinking saloon reverberating from the floor beneath.

'The only hotel not bombed', gently explained a woman beside me: 'I'm Mrs Groen ... Gerritt and I came to meet several trains. Forgive us for being a little late for yours. Every room is occupied at home — my daughter and two sons ... impossible to look after you there...'

'My A to Z maps and index cards?' I asked.

'My husband has driven the parcels to his office...'

I must have told her that a great aunt of mine, now in her nineties, had been a nun since eighteen in an Ursuline convent at Roermond. For next morning she drove me to a peaceful convent in snow-mantled countryside: '... where your Aunt's Mother Superior has arranged for you to stay.'

Mother Bernharda, a tall ageless nun, showed me to my room: 'As long as the English lady will wear a skirt over her trousers, we shall be happy to welcome her, and profit by speaking my rusty English with her ... How long dear Mrs Pearsall will you be staying?'

'It depends on how soon Mr Groen my printer lets me have proofs...'

'I must leave you now. My lay sisters and I are off to the woods to gather twigs for cooking. As you know the Waal is frozen and the coal barges are caught in the ice ... What a winter! Did you see the poor seagulls caught in the frozen sea? Everything's being done to rescue them...'

My eyes unable to focus on the proof corrections, Mr Groen engaged a bilingual part-timer: 'His mother's English. He wants the money; he's always done a good job for me ...' As with the original cards, these served the dual purpose of indexing the A to Z and providing copy for the Standard Street Guide. To settle queries took ten days. A restful stay which recharged me in strength and courage to face the dreaded journey home.

Alleviated by Mr Groen: 'I'll drive you to the Hoek and will see you onto the boat ... I've arranged for your office to pick you up at Harwich.' Kindness maintained with a weekly parcel of cheese, butter, cookies...

In writing, Mrs Ford confirmed my verbal order to him for 250,000 A to Zs — 'What a risk, Mrs Pearsall!' — but over-impressed by so many noughts, ordered 100,000 Street Guides instead of the intended 50,000. For a public trained by war to maps, too many anyway — and warehoused without charge for years by uncomplaining Sid Wells — lumbering his home, garage, garden sheds.

# CHAPTER 16

'WHERE'S the money for wages coming from?' panicked Mrs Ford. Mr Duncan's unexpected cheque for injuries — 'I thought you'd only insured me for death' — staunched the gap until the new A to Zs arrived from Holland. Which by mercurial sales paid for themselves, the overheads; and for an increased reprint. But suspended though I was in barbiturate zombie-land — (prescribed by the medical profession, and its after effects diagnosed as multiple sclerosis) — I began increasingly to attend to business. Only to find that my pre-accident £10,000 bank balance had slid to nil. For, intimidated by threatening demands from Mr Nolan, Mrs Ford had paid him huge sums in commission — whether due or not. Abuse I stopped forthwith. And, canalising my frail energy, restored simple housekeeping methods to ensure more money In than Out.

Next, resurrecting a pre-war project, I entrusted Mr Cooper with the planning and production of a hard case London Street Atlas covering a larger area than the A to Z.

'All them built-up additions to draw ...' he mused fascinated: 'the long-winded fudging of our old perimeter — distorted by that so and so Fountain to match with the new...

'Pressed for an early date for completion: to pay salaries and overtime', he responded: 'I'll stick my neck out and plump for eighteen months to see it out of the way ... if I can get another draughtsman ... By gum yes we'll do it! But not if my draughtsman's got to traipse round the boroughs for up-dating...'

'George Elston will love to', I said; tactlessly adding: 'He's always longed for the chance to rid our maps of error.'

'Who does he think he is!'

'Anyway he's accurate ... I persisted; unaware of the extent to which trained map draughtsmen tend to resent interference, however helpful, from anybody else.

Pernickety Percy's what we call him ... If you don't shift him from our drawing office, he'll send us round the bend!'

We compromised. Mr Elston moved out of Napier House; but undertook the compilation.

As to an additional draughtsman, Mr Connor suggested Fred Bond: 'We were apprentices together. In 1939, before I joined up. He's not very happy at the old firm.'

Tall, fair, handsome, Mr Bond told me that though entrusted with more responsible work, his salary and prospects had not been improved. We liked each other; and I sent him a written offer. But at sight of it, his boss Mr Thorpe immediately raised his salary, promised greater consideration in the future and persuaded him to stay.

'The bastard's let me down!' shouted Mr Connor: 'He's made me look a right Charlie! I'll never forgive him!'

Increased turnover and costs, compelling me to abandon my 'One Man Business' outlook, I suggested to Mrs Ford that we needed a manager: 'My energy's so sporadic...'

'I've got the very man! My husband!'

'Qualified?'

'John Dickinson's Chief Accountant for years!'

Recalling Mr Brown's recommendation: 'a skeleton in the cupboard, poor woman!' I phoned him for advice.

'I wouldn't touch him with a barge-pole! ... an infatuation with racing cars, it came out in Court. An expensive hobby ... for us at Dickinsons!...

On being refused, Mrs Ford tearfully confessed: 'John wants the chance to prove he's a reformed character ... To prove it to me — he thinks the world of me — and above all to himself ... Please Mrs Pearsall.'

I steeled my heart; and at my 'I'm sorry, no', she resentfully withdrew ... But next morning returned to her desk.

Pleasanter possibility was a young fighter pilot friend — (his face a Mackindoe miracle of plastic surgery after rescue from his Spitfire shot down in flames over the West African coast): 'My pre-war Building Society job's been filled, and adding insult to injury they've given me a junior post at lower wage...'

His blue eyes still those of the enthusiastic, reliable humorous Chippie I knew, I agreed to engage him: 'Though I must warn you that with me a physical wreck who knows whether the business will survive or go under...'

'That gives me qualms ...' dithered his blond slim fiancee: 'I won't marry him until we can afford a Silver Cross pram ... and please, Mrs Pearsall, would you stop calling my Mr Harold Smallwood by that vulgar nickname "Chippie".'

His employers, shown my written offer — as had been the case with Mr Bond — upped him in salary and status.

'I've agreed to go back to them', he came to tell me — with slight acquiescent gesture towards his Phoebe, and his aside to me: 'reluctantly...'

'So I should think! she snorted: 'I've made enough sacrifices. I get engaged to a handsome fellow ... and look what I've got now!' Thus was he denied an exciting fruitful life; and my firm a loyal manager.

So I fell back on asking Harry Binder. Who recommended a young clean-cut qualified accountant as Company Secretary; only to phone the moment I had engaged him: 'You wouldn't want to stand in his way, Phyllis ... He's been offered a better post with much safer prospects ... I've got an alternative for you though. You know that excellent fellow we send round to audit your accounts. You like him don't you? ... Too modest I expect to mention that he rose from the ranks to Captain in the Indian Army. A credit to us ... Gets on famously with everybody...'

Subservient, yet too 'hail fellow well met' was this Mr Swift with black toothbrush moustache; and wish — though denied — to be called Captain Swift.

'References?' I asked Harry.

'Trained at Binder Hamlyn's surely good enough for you! ... for anyone ... And time presses. We mustn't let your routine fall back into original chaos, eh? ... Anyway, he's waiting downstairs. I'll bring him up.'

Salary agreed, I detailed my requirements to Harry: 'daily, weekly, monthly and quarterly management accounts from you Mr Swift, my new accountant.'

'Accountant!' bridled the applicant; and with shuttered eyelid glance at Harry: 'You promised I'd be Company Secretary, Sir!'

'With you so ill Phyllis it's my duty to take any and every weight off your shoulders ...' wheedled Harry.

'I remain Company Secretary', I reaffirmed.

'Don't worry, Swift! You'll prove yourself ...', placated Harry.

'When do I start?'

Mrs Ford he won round with bouquets; with account book panache — such as writing headings on the last page alone after cutting the tops off the other pages: 'Like so, dear lady...'

'I objected to him coming here at all ...' she giggled: 'instead of my John ... To his usurping part of my job — though it's got too much for me ... But he's quite a card...'

A gem of an acquisition to the staff was Nigel Syrett. Directed to us by a strange concatenation of events. Triggered by Eliot Hodgkin — (as had been our Dutch connections). Having compiled a London Souvenir View Book for me to publish of 55 black and white photographs aesthetically chosen and arranged, he proposed 'they might make postcards as well'.

A cut-throat field from which postcard printer, Mr Cotmore of the Manton Press, dissuaded me: 'They'd undercut you! And when they'd knocked out your competition, up would go their prices again. I deal with them every day. You'd be a lamb to the slaughter ... Don't touch it!' On parting, I happened to mention my need for an office boy.

Some weeks later Nigel's father phoned me. Diffidently: 'I'm a neighbour of Mr Cotmore's ... The vacancy's probably filled by now? ... No? Well my son is 15 I'm afraid he's doing no good at school. Which is a great disappointment to me and his mother, I'd have liked to give him the education my parent's couldn't afford for me. All his time he spends playing his trumpet. Oh! The din! And the trouble with the neighbours...'

Next day he arrived with his son — a bright-eyed mercurial pencil-thin slither of a lad, energy sparking from him even when constrained by his father to stand still: 'Well here he is! He's no good. Don't pay him a wage ... don't give him a holiday. There must be no gap between his leaving school and coming to you...'

Memorably, on the 6th of April 1948, Nigel joined us at Gray's Inn Road. Mustard keen he darted through London's Underground with mounted Board maps larger than himself — dodging in and out of coaches — unloaded heavy Dutch consignments (chiefly of A to Zs and Eliot's '55 LONDON VIEWS'), carried them up and down the dicey office stairs, to and from the rat-infested Burgess Basement; and mission efficiently and promptly completed asked 'What next?'

As gipsy quick as Gordon Lester. But with grace and spontaneous wit; steady applied brain word and deed.

The fortnight trial over, I phoned his father: 'I don't know if you'll be pleased or sorry, but Nigel's the very person for us. Sunny, enthusiastic, practical and willing. We are paying him a salary ... and giving him a holiday!'

'Of course I'm delighted!' he replied; and to celebrate took Nigel to lunch at Gamage's — 'Eat up my boy! ... You must always be punctual. In my 33 years with my firm I've never been late or off ill ... — and, held up at the pay desk, made his son a few minutes late.

'I hope you're not starting as you mean to go on', reprimanded Mrs Ford. Whereas Mr Swift looked up from his books to say: 'Don't be too hard on the lad, there's a dear.' For, with a bodeful growing friendship between accountant and vanman, tension was building up against her. The real friend to Nigel — and protecting him from Mr Noakes's coarse trouncings — was Mr Elston, who on Waterloo Bridge would pick him up most mornings at about twenty past eight and drive him to the office.

Impressively too did Nigel carry out his first selling assignment. Based on my father's American Map of Palestine showing the proposed UN boundaries, we published our own in August 1948 for the Jewish Chronicle. But though British troops were out there fighting, sales — apart from the paper's readers — stagnated. Under pressure from owner Mr Kessler — 'Surely you could do better!' I asked Nigel to have a go.

'Off to Whitechapel!' he flashed. Returning hours later sweating profusely: 'I've sold the lot!'

(A subsequent Jewish Chronicle Map of Israel, Mr Kessler himself, by arrangement with me, published in December 1951.)

# CHAPTER 17

A T last Government restrictions on paper ceased.
Allowing me to transfer the printing of our sheet maps from Van Leer to Lowe & Brydone. The A to Z, however I left with Mr Groen. Out of appreciation; but also because Harry Williams saved me from divided loyalties: 'Your long runs are more than we can cope with ... Besides, your Dutchman's letterpress does a cleaner job than litho.'

Publishers again free-wheeling, printers, as in the pre-war days, began to compete for work. Cowells of Ipswich I turned down despite their four colour presses; but with our Greater London Atlas on the stocks, mentioned that in a few months time we would like them to quote for setting and printing a 30 to 40,000 word index; accept maps printed by Lowe & Brydone to Cowell's imposition; and bind 10,000 copies into 'stiff case binding.'

'Hard case binding', their rep, Mr Campion, apologetically corrected me: 'A gentleman should never contradict a lady ... Can you give me a more precise date?'

Mr Cooper refused to commit himself: 'Best not to tie me down till nearer the time.'

Paper merchants also flocked. Amongst them, Mr Bould: 'I've left Walter Makin and have struck out on my own ... Here's my card.'

'I stick by Mr Makin ... He generously gave me credit in the early days ... I'll continue to buy from him...'

'Please call me Ted ... He's agreed to me keeping my own customers ... Honest! If you don't believe me, phone him.'

Mr Makin himself answered: 'You know what reps are! ... They think they are the business ... Give Ted a chance. But watch him ...'

'See!' triumphed Mr Bould, taking out his order book: 'So how many tons of mechanical for the A to Z?'

'None. I'm continuing to put the job in Holland...'

White to the gills, Ted Bould stood up: 'You can't do that to me! ... I counted on your A to Z! ... Or I'd never've left Walter Makin!'

'I'm sorry that my plans don't coincide with yours ...' I said. While he in quick-change to nonchalance, sat down again:

'Never mind. I'll call every week. Even if only for cover board and other dribs and drabs.'

On perpetual look-out for map draughtsmen, Mr Cooper handed me several long letters from one man: 'I'm getting about three a week. Corrections to errors in our A to Z. The more complicated areas drawn for us on a separate sheet ... Obviously by a properly trained draughtsman ... Should I offer him a job?'

'He'll be coming to you for it ...' I mused: 'Let me know when he does. There's something strange about his cramped handwriting...'

Shortly after, Mr Cooper asked me to pop round: 'You were right about those letters. The fellow's in my office now.'

A replica of Van Gogh's San Remy self-portrait, stood stiffly to attention as I entered — red-headed, chin and cheeks orange stubbled.

Mr Cooper introduced him as Mr Mottram: 'He's asked me to employ him ... What do you say Mrs Pearsall?'

Side-stepping, I asked the applicant if he could work for us at home: 'on a trial basis?'

His voice hoarse as if with long disuse, he hesitated: 'That would be difficult ... I'd have to ascertain.'

'References?...

'On both counts I'll have to arrange for them to get in touch with you ... I can do the work, you know...'

'It's up to our standard', agreed Mr Cooper ... 'Where were you trained?'

'That they'll also tell you...'

'Who are "they"' I asked.

"They" were Father Joseph at St Edward's House, College Street, Westminster.

'Thank you for the offer' he said on leaving: 'You'll be hearing from them...'

Within two hours I did: 'Could you come straight round.'

Tall, black cassocked, Father Joseph reproved me for my lack of faith — 'Mottram's a first-class map draughtsman, you admit. Why be so pedantic about dotting "i's and crossing "t"'s?' — and with cold academic smile, added: 'Talking of map-making, rather neat that, don't you think!'

'Would you let him work here?' I asked.

'Despite the inconvenience to us, yes. Temporarily. In his room ... What we couldn't allow is for your people to bring or collect copy...'

'If he's to come to our office I must have references.'

'But I'll vouch for him...'

'How long have you known him?'

'Six months ... Long enough to size him up. I'm a good judge of character.'

'Where did he live and work before?'

'I'm not used to such an inquisition, Mrs er ... forgive me, your name's just slipped my memory ... Have you young men working for you?'

'Several. Why?'

'That'll be good for him.'

'I'm sorry, but I'm responsible for them. That's why I need a reference prior to yours. He's middle-aged ... What did he do? What are you hiding?'

'If you insist — and I have to say this is hardly Christian on your part — he'll have to tell you himself ... The poor chap's waiting downstairs to know the outcome...'

Poor chap indeed. In prison for five years. My shamed apology — 'there's no criticism in me' — unleashed a full confession. After 25 years in the County Surveyor's Department of the LCC, his paedophilia had been discovered; and 'the second chance generously granted, I forfeited ... By compulsion ... two irresistible youngsters. But I'm cured ... Converted by the prison chaplain. I'd welcome the opportunity to prove I can resist temptation.'

Not on our lads, I intimated; and arranged for Mr Elston to deliver and fetch the work Mr Cooper allotted him. But his ability to concentrate impaired by five years hard labour, he produced less and less until finally nothing.

(Some years on, the verger, sweeping the aisle of St Pancras Church, asked if I remembered him: 'Thank you for helping me, Mrs Pearsall. God be praised for letting me express my gratitude ... My work here isn't so demanding ... You're wondering about the choir boys ... Yes! I am able to resist temptation ... or is it just that with age the urge weakens ...')

Sad I did feel. But not conscience-stricken. As I now for my lifetime became. In acceding to an ultimatum from Mr Swift: 'It's either Mrs Ford or me!'

He could no longer work with her, he explained: 'What I need is an assistant with a proper understanding of accounts ... Not just an old bossy bag ... who, crams her vicegenerency down my throat!' Recalling, in self-justification, her attempt to foist her husband on me and her expensive knuckling under to salesmen bullying, I ashamedly, nay heinously, gave her notice.

'Not me!' she wailed: 'Not your Mrs Ford!'

Mr Swift replaced her with David Hetherington — 'Not qualified, but with sufficient accountancy experience to do the donkey-work.' A small bouncy fellow full of cricket and rugger talk — chiefly of after match 'booze-ups ha! ha!', though not to me — and, handshake limp and damp, looked from under lashes unblinkingly into my eyes and everybody else's.

My excursions into one-shot book publishing — such as *Horoscope, Guide to Income Tax* and children's *ABC* — had been devoid of competition due to national paper shortage. But I now again excursioned into this diversionary field. For friend Alfred Read, MBE., FCIS, Secretary and Past President of the Chartered Institute of Secretaries. Following his request to read through his draft manuscript on Company Law: 'Because as an artist you know nothing about it ... Blue-pencil everything you don't understand, so I can clarify it for the layman. It's the simple story of an imaginary Company from its inception...'

The publication of his 1944 lectures on Company Law and Practice delivered to Technical students of the University of Wales, had been held up originally, he told me, by post-war restrictions; and now further delayed by himself 'to allow the inclusion of the new Company Law legislation resulting from the

Companies Act of 1947 and the Companies Consolidation Bill of 1948.'

How we wrestled during several week-ends — his dear wife Kitty keeping us deliciously fed — to integrate my stupid queries with his expertise. Co-operation which sparked his title: *ABC of LIMITED LIABILITY COMPANIES.* (Stupidly I did not suggest A to Z) 'I'd like you to publish it Phyllis...'

'Pitman's?' I demurred.

'They're preparing their own professional one. You know what its like with long-established publishers. It'll take them years to bring out.'

Mr Cotmore set and printed the fifty two page book and bound it into grey paper cover. Issued in July 1948 it sold by the thousands. To Pitman's. Wholesale for retail resale. Until their own more complicated tome came onto the market; when Alfred and I let ours sell out.

# CHAPTER 18

OCTOBER 1948. My father arrived in England on his first visit since the war. Despite the plastic surgery on my face to remove keloid scars, he flinched at sight of me: 'Good Lord! What a fright you look!' and chafed at my exhaustion during a late dinner at Frascatis: 'How dull you've become! Your mother never bored me!

At the office, worse.

Flicking through files, he rasped: 'What's this ... and this! Declining to quote for ICI! For Shell! For Courtaulds! ... Call yourself a business woman!'

'I agree with you Sir!' intervened Mr Swift.

'We can't fritter away draughtsman's time from our own vital programme...' I protested.

'But you did do one for your friend Alfred Reed when one of Powell Duffryn's directors flew to Australia on mining research...' said Mr Swift.

'A plan I drew myself ... But before reaching his destination the plane crashed. All lives lost. Better for them I know from my plane crash than to suffer years of pain and impotence.'

'Do you think that's any comfort to me!' said papa: 'Now back to brass tacks, for goodness sake. Never but never turn down an order!'

'I agree Sir ... I'm always telling Mrs Pearsall that a business should never refuse good money!'

My next fault — letting a Government Inspector take our books into the back office and study them alone — caused papa anxiety rather than wrath: 'I've never heard of such a thing! Go into him, Phyllis! You can't leave him like that ... He'll find discrepancies. That's his job!'

'I agree with you, Sir', again sucked up Mr Swift, while I tried to reassure papa: 'It's only a routine call on importers to check whether we've spent controlled Sterling illegally abroad ... which I haven't done ... We've nothing to hide papa!...'

In vain. Until half an hour later, the Inspector rejoined us: 'As usual here, eveything clean and in the clear.'

'Yes Sir', smiled papa: 'We have nothing to hide.'

'I assure you Sir nothing to hide!' echoed Mr Swift. To papa's admiration. As he expatiated to me over a drink alone together at Henekeys: 'You're very lucky to have a gentleman of his stature working for you Phyllis! ... Without him you'd never have got away so easily with that Inspector. Phew!' and he mopped his brow: 'How I needed this double Scotch and could do with another!'

It was this fear of officials — legacy of Austro-Hungarian heritage and youth — which in a convoluted way was to cripple the Company's renewed steady progress.

Though living and working in the States for a quarter of a century, papa had never applied for a Residents' Visa: 'I prefer to be irregular than to be refused.' Nor had he taken up his chance of post-war U.S. Residentship granted to all immigrants domiciled there for five or more years.

He had booked his return passage for the 20th November. On the 18th, he called at the U.S. Consulate to renew his Visitors' Visa.

The day Amy and B.H. were giving an evening cocktail party in his honour. For my friends, and customers — including Mr Cruise, Mr Prescott and flamboyant Miss Wilson ('Who is that lovely dynamite?' asked B.H.) — and suppliers. Though not Sid Wells who phoned from hospital: 'I've had to rush my little daughter here. She's swallowed a mustard spoon. Thank God, they think she'll be all right.'

By 6.30 papa — due at 6 — had not arrived. Nor by 7.

'Where can he be, Phyllis?' asked Amy.

At 7.30, the butler announced him.

Tense, grey-faced he walked in without apology; without acknowledgement when Amy toasted him in champagne; nor courteous smile as I introduced him to my guests. However, when clients of mine invited me to drive with them to Italy — 'for a painting holiday, Mr Gross' — he reacted violently: 'Impossible! I need her in New York!'

Alone together in my flat, I poured him a stiff brandy.

'Disaster!' he exclaimed: 'Flagellated by my lifelong fear!' On the point of receiving his Visitor's Visa from a smiling young women Consul he told me: 'I signed my own death warrant. By a stupid unnecessary remark: "I'm thinking of applying for American citizenship on my return to New York..."'

The dialogue that followed, he frenziedly poured out: '"In that case I cannot grant a Visitor's Visa ..." she said; and I: "An immigrant's? ... As a British subject..."'

'"You're not British born ... It says here you're naturalised..."

'"Long ago. In the first decade of this century..."

'"Your passport stated Hungary as your birthplace ... The Hungarian quota's full."

'"Yugoslavia? Since the 1918 dismemberment of the Austro-Hungarian Empire, Csurog, where I was born is in Yugoslavia..."

'"The Yugoslav quota is also filled for years."'

'"But I'm a substantial taxpayer ... My pre-war Visa allows me to travel on map publishing business between our two countries..."

'"Next please" said the Consul, 'and handed me back my passport. So

Phyllis', he concluded: 'There's only one alternative. You go in my place. The Queen Mary leaves from Liverpool the day after tomorrow. Your brother and I will come to see you off on the boat-train ... Here's my State Room ticket — there isn't time to get you something cheaper ... Now listen carefully to what you're to do on reaching New York. Take the first train to Washington D.C.; and a taxi from the station to the Immigration and Naturalisation Department. There you induce them to cable their London Consul to grant me a Visa forthwith.'

'And if they don't?'

'You'll take care of my New York business until I come.'

'Who'll look after the London one?'

'Do you think I can't do it better than you!...'

'The Greater London Atlas! ... Double Elephant paper ordered for it ... binding cloth from Scotland to be sent by passenger train to Cowells ... A big mounting order of maps on blinds to be fitted to a Slough boardroom wall...'

'Swift will attend to it all more efficiently than you. You're lucky to have such a first class executive! ... It's time you learnt not to bark yourself when you've got a dog (I like that English saying)...'

'At least make sure papa that he sends me the daily, weekly, monthly and quarterly accounts, and the first bound copy of the Greater London Atlas...'

Understandably, his own preoccupation blotted out all else: 'Most important of all, Phyllis! Never but never mention my immigration difficulty to anybody. Not to my staff, business acquaintances nor above all to my so-called Hungarian friends — however much the Hungarians with their love of gossip grill you. The reason you'll give for my not returning to New York on schedule is a sudden illness. From which on doctor's instructions I'm convalescing in Europe ... Anyway, it shouldn't be for long ... It's not as if you're going to be away for a year!...'

It was.


A woman senior official at Washington, received me in her vast office, and having listened sympathetically to papa's predicament, sadly shook her head: 'I'm afraid we cannot override London ... Unless there's some family reason for his sudden departure from the States?'

'I was severely injured in a plane crash...'

'Ah! Good! When was that?'

'November 1946...'

'And we're now November 1948 ... Hardly a distraught father rushing to his dying daughter's bedside! ... Tell him to return to our London Consulate in twelve months time. I'll arrange he'll be given a Visa then ... It's the best I can do.'

'What about his business?...'

'On his return here he'll need a special Senator's Bill giving him permission to work while his Residentship's being processed ... which could take five years.

Nor can he leave the States until it's granted … Perhaps you'd better let me help you word the letter to him…'

'Meanwhile I suppose I'll have to run his New York business …'

'Which you cannot do on your Visitor's Visa! … But the British quota's wide open; so fly to Canada and re-enter on a Resident's.'

Health regulations, though, prolonged my stay in Quebec. Firstly because my blood for the statutory VD test froze en route to some distant laboratory, and had to be taken again; and more seriously when the French Canadian doctor on examining my eyes found trouble: 'You've had serious head injuries, *non?* I cannot pass you.' But relented on hearing my urgent need to get to New York: 'I like that. A daughter helping her papa … Come back to me in two weeks time and I'll see what I can do … A rest, meanwhile, is medically indicated. At Montmerency Falls, I suggest … In a quiet hotel where your Queen Victoria's father lived happily for years with his French mistress. You can go by horse sleigh…'

Papa, purporting not to have received my letter from Washington wrote angrily:

> *'Can't you attend to MY affairs instead of harping on your convenient ill health. Gallivanting around Canada at my expense! … As you'll see from the postmark I'm staying in Nice to recuperate…'*

On my arrival at his 57th Street office between 6th and 7th, the young ladies on his staff greeted me with genuine concern: 'How is dear Mr Gross? Is he seriously sick or really convalescing? … Is he just saying so to stop us worrying. Such a wonderful guy!'

The Washington official kept her word. A year to the day, papa — having left Nice and left behind the courtisane with whom he had set up home — obtained his Visitor's Visa in London; and took ship for New York. Where, as I joined him at his apartment he lashed into me: 'Why didn't you meet me at the Cunard pier?…'

'An appointment at your office with the City official to pass the Visitors Map we won Bid and Award for…'

'Will I never hear the end of that City rigmarole! … I'd have won it on the dot — I like that English expression — And what do you mean by paying yourself that excessive salary … I'm not a millionaire!'

'You told me to…'

'I feel differently now … A thousand dollars for hospitalisation! Five hundred to a doctor! Another five hundred for aureomycin! Have you become a hypochondriac?'

My reason — virus pneumonia — rather than mollify, exacerbated him: 'And how do you think I liked hearing from Mr Cruise that my daughter produced better quality maps than I did?!'

Even then, aware of my own failings, I did not realise that jealousy lay at the heart of his tirade. Jealousy that a woman should have built a firm in England and understudied him successfully here. Instead, I attributed his venom to enforced exile — fanned in fact, unbeknown to me then — by his Riviera mistress — 'Betrayed by you own daughter! Oh *Mon pauvre* King Lear!' — and which exploded in final monstrous accusation: 'So you plotted to keep me out of the States for ever! To steal my business!'

'Papa! You know I've been doing my utmost to help you! You know very well that I did my best for you in Washington...'

'What proof have I?'

'You must have received that letter, papa ... A verbatim report of my interview with the Immigration official written on the spot...'

'So you say. I believe in cause and effect. You left me, your own father in the wilderness.'

'If you didn't receive it how did you know the exact date you had to re-apply for your present Visa in London? How did you know to write to Uncle Charlie for an introduction to his Senator friend about your U.S. Residentship?'

'So my own daughter's calling me a liar!'

'No papa. But you're treating me like a criminal...'

'You said it.'

It was difficult — ill and exhausted as I was — to remember that Hungarians revel in family quarrels; and that papa was only following his oft-reiterated policy of 'DENY! DENY! DENY!'

His complaint to my doctor — 'Why's my daughter always sick?' — brought the reply: 'If she doesn't get at least a year's rest I cannot answer for the consequences!'

# CHAPTER 19

**M**OMENTARILY restored by the sea voyage, I went straight to Napier House. Where Mr Cooper with justified pride showed me the Greater London Atlas.

At my delighted surprise, he exclaimed: 'But didn't you get it in New York? I packed the first bound copy from Cowells for Swift to send you ...' (To save cost, Mr Swift had mailed it surface mail instead of air ...). 'That Swift', continued Mr Cooper, 'Puts his nose in where it isn't wanted ... tries to run the whole bloomin, show! Not that I'll let him touch my drawing office, I can tell you ... And, changing the subject: 'I'm down in the dumps today. I've missed winning the pools by one point...'

'Asked what else had been published in my absence he showed me four sheet maps of London covering the Atlas area; England & Wales Road and County maps, a Premier Birmingham and Premier Leeds: 'We've just started on Manchester ... By the way, do you rememeber Fred Bond who applied for the job and didn't take it? He's applied again. Do see him. Just the kind of bloke I need.'

Mr Bond — sickened by Mr Thorpe's broken promises — gave a week's notice, and joined us in April 1950. Despite lower wage, no overtime, and a drawing office 'almost totally occupied by planning bench ... squeeze round and duck under shelf.'

From the start, as with Nigel Syrett, a golden acquisition.

As for Mr Swift's stewardship, it had been non est. To my first question 'after the first month or two you stopped your routine letters to me in New York, why?' He sullenly replied: 'With all the work you've left me with?' The phone rang: He snatched it up: 'Swift here.' Listening to the caller for a moment, he answered aggrieved: 'You insist on Mrs Pearsall. Well, here she is.'

It was my Slough client for a series of wall maps mounted on blinds: 'Thank God you're back. Ever since you went away that fellow of yours has been full of promises, and nothing done...' 'I'll call you back', I said; and to Mr Bliss: 'When will that Slough mounting be ready?'

'I'm glad you're back ... I've been waiting this ten months for that pompous ass of yours to pass the job ...' Which I did; and he delivered and installed the maps under the required canopy that day.

Mr Swift, indifferent to this and other past or present urgencies, was totally absorbed in his vendetta. Muttering, as he rifled through masses of delivery notes and invoice carbons: 'I'll nail that bastard Noakes ... I'll have him goaled if it's the last thing I do ... He was my only friend here ... and he's done me down...'

'Where is Mr Noakes?' I asked.

'I sacked the bloody man.

'Who's selling for us then?' I interrupted. Nobody was.

Straightaway I called on the main customers.

Back at Gray's Inn Road, I queried why a staff of five was now crammed into Mr Elston's office: The big London jobs are finished ... and you can easily manage to index and proof-read the sheet maps as they come along...'

'We're checking the A to Z index...'

'Why?' (and I felt as inquisitorial as papa with me!) 'Surely you know that every time one eradicates old mistakes, one creates as many new.'

'They're art students your brother asked me to give a job to...'

'Anyway we can't afford to pay them ... I'm awfully sorry ...' And sorrier still was I at their courteous acceptance of dismissal — 'We quite understand.'

Sales the priority, I took on a Yugoslav recommended by a publisher's representative; but entrepreneurially distracted from attending to our customers — 'I have many irons, as you English say, in the fire' — he brought excuses instead of orders: 'The buyer's on holiday' ... 'overstocked' ... or 'Too busy to see reps...'

Whereupon, I offered the job to Mr Elston; and he accepted: 'As ex-taxi driver I know my London well! I like the idea of getting out and about again!'

At Victoria Main bookstall where I introduced him as our new London representative, the manager whistled at Noakes' departure: 'Goodbye to what I loaned him', but refused my offer to refund: 'It's my own bloody fault! Never a lender nor a borrower be!...'

Similarly, most other managers and customers — though some of them for larger sums, welcomed Mr Elston. Not so the baddys who had shared the profit on stolen A to Zs: 'What about my "bunko"?' Thus did he find his niche; and we a perfect representative.

'How did you let Noakes get away with it, Mr Swift? Didn't our routine stock control alert you?'

'The cad pulled the wool over my eyes ... Convinced me that "thirteen to the dozen" is accepted trade practice ... I'll get him on that!'

Which Mr Elston, a devout Baptist, sternly opposed: 'Your unchristian resentment's not going to lose me a single customer — however shady! ... Judge not that ye be not judged! ... Who's going to look after the indexing, Mrs Pearsall?'

I did. From six every morning until Mr Swift's arrival at 9. When I enjoined him to make order out of chaos ... to 'get down to the details you despise ... That's our priority! Not your obsession with Noakes!' And for hours after his 5pm rapid departure, I immersed myself in indexing. To Mr Cooper's concern; and embarrassed suggestion: 'If you don't mind my Mary indexing at home, she could do it … She's sure to be accurate after years on telephone directories.'

'Your wife?'

'Not yet…'

Glamorous to crimson finger-nails, she took over.

Just in time before a broadside from papa put me out of action. A ten page letter to my brother filled with imaginary grievances against me:

> *'I advise you to look into Phyllis's accounts. I'm certain you'll find — as I have done here — unjustified withdrawals of money, and in the Minute Book, unjustified entries. She has to be watched. Show her this whole letter …'* And concluded: *'I have therefore no alternative but to give you the control of the London business; I shall issue further shares in your name…*
>
> > *Your loving father,*
> > *Sandor Gross'*
>
> *PS.*
> *On receipt of your Will, I'll take the necessary legal steps.*

The offer 'too good to be refused', and — notwithstanding the substantial monthly remittance I paid him, with additional financial help when required — my brother phoned to tell me he was accepting: 'It's all rather embarrassing … But what with the children's education and Daisy's threat of suicide if I don't get her a new car…'

That night I suffered a stroke.

Papa did not however implement his threat.

Firstly, as he later told me, because Tony in his Will left everything to Daisy, *'my bete noire.'* And secondly because my dear friend, Lady McFadyean, in no way blamed him in a commiserating letter she sent him immediately:

> *'… Due to Phyllis overworking since her air crash injuries, say her doctors. As a parent I know how anxious you must be. She's always talked so lovingly of you I feel you too are my friend … After ten days, God willing, I'll be sending you a happier report.'*

# CHAPTER 20

I N Cyprus, where, cut off from international phones (because of the — as yet non-violent — 'Enosis' movement for independence from Britain) I exiguously recuperated ... began to write again; and as my eyesight improved, to paint from my Kyrenia balcony. The many coloured sails on azure sea, golden headlands, golden islands lapped by white rim of gently breaking waves; a great mother turtle swimming just beneath the surface with her young ... After almost a year of slow recovery from my left-sided hemiplegia, a succinct postcard from Mr Cruise of W. H. Smith & Son Ltd. — 'It's high time you returned' — jerked me back to the tempestuous duties I had been tempted to discard for ever.

Urgently, for fear of losing my own incentive, I pressed Nicosia's travel agent to book me home.

'Siga, Siga ... Slowly, Slowly ...' he soothed. But in February 1951, leaving behind me peace and almond blossom, I sailed from palm tree graced Larnaca to the Venice I also loved to paint. Thence, across France and the Channel to Victoria Station. And trouble.

Harry Binder met me: 'Swift'll be cock-a-hoop you're back! He's been having a very difficult time. It's quite impossible, he complains, to have two people at the helm ... and I agree with him. You'll have to get rid of Cooper...'

'How's the business doing? Why hasn't he sent me the accounts as instructed? And why no 1950 Balance Sheet...'

'With all that work on his shoulders! Have a heart old girl...'

'What's our cash position?'

'In the red...'

'But we were liquid when I left ... with sales and map production increasing...'

'I'll phone him that we're on the way to River Plate House, and for him to meet us there.'

'No Harry, I'll go straight to the office by myself — and don't tell him I'm coming.'

Mr Swift was not at Gray's Inn Road. Nigel, lugging up a case of A to Zs — (only decades later did he refer to still recurring nightmares of falling through that tottery staircase) — directed me to Napier House: 'Mark Swift moved us there last winter. When I brought our stock here from the Burgess basement. Just in time! Before the Thames flooded it ... You'll find him in the small office that used to be the Women's Parliament.'

There sat Mr Swift posing for me; feet on desk, studying a large map held open like a newspaper before his face; and murmuring as if to himself: 'What a great day for us map-makers when names can be flashed onto originals!' and in mock surprise at my entry, added aloud: 'instead of all that tedious hand drawing...'

Though prophetic, irrelevant.

'Where have you put the draughtsmen?' I asked: 'the light's right for them here...'

Hasn't anyone told you of the great Thames flood?'

'You should have found somewhere else for the general office.'

'A business is judged by its administrative facade...'

'Where are the draughtsmen?'

'You'll be sorry to hear that your precious Mr Bond's a malingerer ... He says he's ill but the doctors can't find anything wrong with him...'

'Fred Bond! Never! ...' And, wresting their address from Mr Swift, I took a bus to London Bridge.

Adjacent to railway sidings a few tall Victorian buildings, condemned in a condemned area, had survived the bombing. Gaunt, stucco cracked, shrapnel-pitted, masonry crumbling. I entered the worst of the lot. Within, darkness. Hand on rail I hauled myself up steep unlit flights of wooden staircase; and limped into an enormous high ceilinged room. Dreary, derelict, dun coloured wallpaper peeling off in strips; rotten floor boards unevenly aslope; a bitter draught howling through rattling sash-windows.

'We're having our tea-break', said Mr Connor.

'How did you get your benches up here?' I asked, appalled: 'Your printing plates?'

Together but differently each recalled: 'The lorry carrying our gear arrived at rush hour' ... 'We thought we'd never get it up' ... 'Reams of quad crown hand-made paper must have weighed a ton...'

An impotent gas fire spluttered at the far end. Above it hung a new dartboard, at which Wally Cooper aimed his second dart.

'It's Mr Bond I'd like to talk to ... he's been seriously ill'; and to Mr Bond: 'How wretched for you ... Are you any better?'

'Fingers crossed and touch wood...'

With pang of sympathy from personal experience, I touched his sleeve: 'If you don't mind, tell me about it...'

'For months I've been in pain. I thought I'd die ... In and out of hospital, but no relief ... It started one night working overtime. Sitting on my stool, I crossed my legs under the bench. Awful pain. Right through my body ... Better now ... Could it be cancer...'

After the others left Fred admitted that since his illness the atmosphere had changed; with Mr Swift and Mr Cooper implying he was malingering: 'Not that I've got anything against Wally. He works us hard. But always a let-up between jobs — bending a six inch nail or some fun of that sort ... The day he ousted us from Napier House — the 16th of March this year — is a day engraved for ever on my memory! Any night I stay on late here, I feel pretty frightened coming down the last flight of the creaking stairs in the pitch dark unlocking the front door and wondering if someone's waiting outside ready to cosh me...'

'Why didn't you refuse to move?' I asked; and though no longer physically able to look for better accommodation, I determined to find it for them in the end.

'How's Mr Nolan doing, Mr Swift?' I enquired; and on being told 'Jolly well', asked to see his orders. Lethargically — 'If you must, you must I suppose' — he threw over to me rubber-banded roll after roll of them. Dating from my departure to New York — till now.

'Why aren't they filed with their delivery notes and invoice carbons?'

'Because they've not been delivered...'

'Why not?'

'Because there's a six week's delay at the mounters...'

'What commission have you been paying Mr Nolan?'

'£80 a week ... He earns it...'

'£80! And nothing coming in...'

Mr Elston popped his head into the room: 'We're out of 35 Miles as well, Mr Swift'; and seeing me: 'Thank God you're back. How can I keep sales figures up with less and less to sell!'

'Mr Elston! Leave my office at once!' roared his boss. 'And don't come barging in like this again!'

'So you've let us run out of stock!' I exclaimed. Blandly he riposted: 'If suppliers can't be paid ... Q.E.D.'; and to my query 'How do you see your duties with us?' crystal-gazed: 'Planning ahead ... Thinking — my brain's fizzing with great ideas ... The opportunities for expansion are here for the taking...'

'What have you actually done, Mr Swift?'

'Done! I've tracked Noakes down. Got him to Court.'

First I sent an apology to each of Mr Nolan's customers, 'for our unforgiveable failure to deliver'. Due, I explained to a stroke following plane crash injuries. Their sympathetic response immediate (only a few cancelled — 'We had to place our order elsewhere') — I appealed to Mr Bliss: 'Please give me delivery dates so I can let the purchasers know...'

'Six weeks to finish work in hand. After that we'll refuse all other work till we've cleared your backlog.' Norton & Gregory likewise, 'If you can supply rollers ...' Which Nigel ferreted out in North London — though of poorer quality and stained too black.

Next — 'I'm sorry I have to' — I slashed Mr Nolan's weekly drawing account to £10.

'I knew the pipe dream would have to end one day ...' he smiled. But on being told that he would receive commission on new orders, he sped to untapped Birmingham; from there sending us a phenomenal batch for the Premier.

Cancelled, before we could pay him, by a conscience telegram:

'DON'T PAY ME ORDERS PHONEY'

Thereafter, he did well. With new Premiers of Manchester, Coventry, Leeds, Glasgow, Wolverhampton, Walsall, Bradford, West Midlands, as they appeared; with Birmingham and London as stand-by during drawing and revision interludes).

Mr Elston's sales steadily escalated: 'To cover London properly, I need to hand over a third of my territory to another rep...'

Nigel, he agreed, often helped — 'A willing lad! — But I need a full-timer. There's a South London newsagent would like the opportunity. The hassle and sorting out the papers 5am every morning's too much for his wife...'

Confirmed by Reg Peters at an interview: 'It's the wife's dicky heart, the doctor says. Too much for her, that's the simple truth! The hassle of up at 4 or 5 every morning sorting the papers for delivery; and after a hard day in the shop, on till 7 or 8 stacking the unsold ones ready for Sale or Return van next am ... checking the day's takings...'

As to working for us, his words also came tumbling out single-heartedly: 'You can count on me ... I'll give my utmost for my good friend here. I know the publications and terms of sale through buying them from him ... which gives me a head start anyway ... I'd say...'

Which established a precedent for both of them, voluntarily to release territory for other reps as their turnover increased. Until finally Mr Elston narrowed his to Central London: 'In season got to call on some bookstalls and kiosks every day...'

And thus Jack Harris of Barnet came to look after North London starting from Paddington.

Amongst additional characters in the General Office was grizzled Mr Brown — Cash Book calligrapher. Bowler hatted for the street with neatly rolled umbrella on his arm; but beneath that deceptive exterior burnt a passionate pride. Twice taken prisoner by the Germans in the 1914/18 War, and twice escaped, he now twenty years later rented a Streatham bed-sitter from an exiled Polish couple he worshipped: 'He, a distinguished Colonel in General Sikorski's Second World War army ... You should see his medals! ... And his Countess of haunting beauty and fascinating accent, Mrs Pearsall ...' Ruled by their daily problems, his agitated tea-break soliloquy hung on their feuds with decorator, plumber, window cleaner, roof-tiler: 'The ladder broke imagine, but thank God the Count jumped clear!' To the exclusion not only of himself but of his favourite pastime: water-colouring black and white photographs: 'This one of a Cotswold cottage I'm giving to the Countess for her birthday.'

Then as office boy, John Lambton — taken on by me at his father's beseeching: 'He's a natural innocent ... They'd make mincemeat of him in any ordinary business!'

John, though a perpetual risk, entranced us. Artless in all he said and did. Given a packet of cut-to-fold Field Staff maps to deliver nearby, he returned a couple of hours later.

'What on earth have you been doing John?' asked Nigel.

'It's such a lovely day for Lincoln's Inn Fields.'

'And the maps? Delivered first?'

'Oh the maps. They were rather heavy. So I left them on a wall.'

'Take me there...'

The maps of course had gone. 'Must I pay for them', said John, reaching for his wallet in an inside pocket. Shaking his head, Nigel admired the lining: 'If I had that jacket, I'd wear it inside out...'

'Would you really...'

'Now I'm working in the City, I've been lucky to get a Mayfair flat at only £20 a week.'

'£20 a week John! But that's a fortune!'

'You can't get a flat under that...'

Off to lunch with his father, he asked Mr Brown: 'Do you prefer the Berkeley or the Savoy?' and on Mr Brown's pointing to Lyons across the road 'That's my Berkeley!' answered: 'I must try it one day...'

His favourite lunch, though, — when carrying and fetching took him there — was at the drawing office: 'Are you cooking your succulent sausages today, Mr Bond?'

Asked on the first occasion, to put the kettle on, he placed it on the gas ring. Not hearing it sing, Mr Bond guessed it had been put on empty: 'Better put water in...'

'Where from?'

'The tap.'

'Oh.' And on returning, he put the filled kettle back.

'Better put the gas on...' persisted Fred, absorbed in map drawing; and, alerted by a whiff of gas: 'Turn it off John.' Flash! Bang! 'You should've lighted it ... Here's a match...'

About horses, however, he left his colleagues standing: 'May I have this afternoon off please Mr Swift?'

'Why?'

'My horse is running...'

'A likely story ... as excuse it beats my grandmother's funeral...'

'In the Derby please Mr Swift ... My mother and I have half a share each...'

'Hope you have the front end then', said Nigel.

'It's fifty fifty as I said ... Perhaps you don't quite understand...'

From putting invoices into envelopes, he graduated — 'Thank you for promoting me' — to letters. And mix-ups. His nadir was to send a Life Insurance form for Mr Cooper — now married to Mary — to my father (fundementally opposed to employee benefits) in New York instead of to the Insurance Company.

But it was only on hearing John referred to as 'the finest gentleman of us all' that Mr Swift had taken umbrage — 'Enough is enough!' — and to our great sadness dismissed our beloved innocent.

'Thank you and your staff for putting up with him so long, Phyllis ... He's never been so happy!' wrote his father.

Meanwhile Binder Hamlyn's staff cleared up the neglected accounts. 'Tell Swift to vacate his office while we have a private talk old top', said Harry; and there explained: 'He left his former employer under a similar cloud.'

'That you didn't tell me, Harry...'

'I implied he needed watching...

'By you, I understood...'

'He'll have to go, Phyllis...'

'Who'll replace him?'

'David Hetherington, of course.'

'I don't quite trust him either...'

'You've no alternative. He knows the business ...' said Harry; and on leaving: 'I'll leave it to you to do the dirty on our Captain Swift ... But you can use my name, old dear. Toodleedoo...'

Mr Swift stormed in. 'Why did you prevent me seeing Mr Harry? Your father promised that if ever it came to a show-down between me and you, it's me he'd back...'

'I'm sorry, Mr Swift, but Mr Harry Binder and I have agreed you'll have to go...'

'How will you manage without me?'

'Better...'

Harry's accountancy bill for over £1,000, I refused to pay: 'If it weren't for your father's generous help in my early business days', I told him: 'I'd be sueing you for damages.'

'Let's call it quits, then, eh? ...' consented Harry.

But the Swift saga did not quite finish there. B.H.'s partner Ralph Hamlyn phoned to demand a reference: 'for my protegé...'

I refused: 'I can't tell or write a lie.'

'Do you know who I am?'

I did indeed; a socialite, powerful in the City, but of sinister repute; and rejoined: 'It doesn't matter two hoots to me who anybody is!'

# CHAPTER 21

TO face the Cash Balance plunge from £9,000 to £165 — I assessed Mr
Swift's disastrous legacy; and, in doing so unwittingly laid the foundation
for Management Accounts: 'Audited Accounts are only history' I realised: 'I
must have moment by moment figures to work by'; and devised a Stock Bible
in use ever since (though modified by events). With columns to each publication
headed 'Quantity Stock Held', 'Past Weekly Sales'; and 'Reprint' sub-titled
'Quantity', 'Date', 'Cost'.

'That's not the way to bookkeep!' sneered Mr Hetherington: 'And seeing as
how you can only pay when you've got the money to, what use is the list of
Creditors with amounts due that you've asked me for? And of Good Debtors?'

'Subtraction and addition, Mr Hetherington, will show a simple person like
me exactly where we stand!'

Daunting deficits I showed Barry Bowman. For the overdraft promised on
his sick-bed visit to me.

'But your air crash was long ago', he stalled: 'And when your account was
well managed ... Which it isn't now ... What sum had you in mind?'

'£8,000. To enable me to reprint every publication ... For one year, but
thereafter as you can see by these accounts gradually decreasing ... Any lesser
advance from you and it'd take much longer...'

Reluctantly he consented: 'After all like my wife you were at Roedean ... So
I can count on you as I do on her never to let anyone down ... to see
things through...'

More easily did he agree to a further £500 for a Famous Guide reprint I had
stupidly omitted from my list of publications.

'Shall I put it in writing?' I asked.

'No need. Your business is already showing good management; for instance
in raising your A to Z retail price from half a crown to 3/6d.'

But I should have confirmed it. For bank managers, outwardly such
confident dispensers and refusers of bounty, are scared stiff of their superiors.
(In addition to perpetual dread of a 'hand-over-the keys' Inspector arriving
unannounced.)

'What's this unauthorised extra £500 you've spent Phyllis?' phoned a
panicked Mr Bowman: 'Head Office want to know...'

'For our Famous Guide ... I rang to ask you, and you agreed ... Don't
you remember?'

Mr Ted Bould too turned shirty: 'No cheque for me, no paper for you!'

But Mr Brydone, Mr Groen and Sid Wells extended the credit denied to Mr
Swift: 'Take your time, my dear...'

# CHAPTER 22

B Y the end of 1952, months of sustained effort — turning annual losses since my accident to a £2,000 Net Profit before tax — had totally exhausted me. Two and a half stone lost in weight I was reduced to five stone; and hardly possessed the strength to eat. Nor, unaided, could I climb the stairs to the drawing office: 'Those awkward blooming stairs', laughed Mr Bond as he and Les Connor making a bandy chair carried me up.

But other friends — Dora McFadyean and Kay Robson: 'You can't go on like this, Phyllis' — combined to book me into a Sussex rest home: 'Mary Campion's on the Committee so it should be all right', said Kay: 'If not send me a postcard and I'll fetch you away...'

Peace. The only sounds: the cowherd's call at milking time, and the cook housekeeper — wholesome, buxom Mrs Scott — calling to the gardener: 'Cauliflower today Collins', or leeks, or sprouts; and only twenty minutes before lunch. Which, on a daintily laid tray, Olive brought to me in bed. A delicious roast and vegetables, castle or other pudding with lashings of cream — 'from our own herd', she gloried: 'You must see our new calf. A little heifer. Born out in the field last night. To Ruth...'

From my Tudor beamed room, three sky-bathed views (without a house in sight): rolling pasture where cherished Jerseys cropped, or chewed the cud; apple orchards beyond. And through another window, the flower and vegetable garden bounded by a copse of silver birch, larch, oak, beech and rhododendrons thick about a lake. An old gnarled ilex on the south side dappled the lawn it graced; revealing the summit of a gentle hill beyond crowned by a spinney of cherry trees.

Such was Backsettown, Henfield. My blessed haven at intervals for ten years to come.

Founded by Dr Octavia Wilberforce — direct descendant of Slave Emancipator, William —

'to supply a Rest Pause, under special conditions, to the efficient women in every class whose activities are threatened or impaired by the stress of modern life.'

Thankfully I complied with a message from her to stay in bed. On the third day, waking up from an afternoon nap, there she was sitting beside me. A massive woman in well-worn blue Harris tweed, with gold watch dangling from long gold chains: 'You're going to have to stay here much longer than a fortnight ...' she said quietly.

'Impossible! The man I've left in charge of my business is an unknown quantity.'

'Very well, go back to work as planned. But arrange from then on to spend long periods here at a stretch ... Now let me see you stand ... You'll need physiotherapy on that poor left side of yours. But, as you need rest without appointments, not till you come back. If you feel like a little walk in the garden, use this stick ... Most of our patients here are underfed. So eat well, weigh yourself on the reliable old-fashioned weighing machine in the upstairs bathroom, and let Mrs Scott know the result every morning ... Like the others you're also overdrugged — prescribed alas by my medical colleagues to ease pain.'

Shown my prescription, she shuddered: 'No wonder you're so poorly ... How long have you been on them?'

'Since a plane crash in 1946 ... I'll give them up. From now!'

Her warning, 'it has to be gradual', I ignored. But after three horrific nights — Wagnerian demons hammering myriads of tin cans within my head, and my whole self ashake — I admitted defeat: 'Help me doctor.'

'It'll take over two years for complete withdrawal to be accomplished ... But until you return here go back to your old dose.' Her regimen after that was: 'halve the dose one night only the first week. The week after back to usual dose. Then halve it for two nights, back to usual 'and so on and so forth: 'You'll succeeed because you want to. Unlike those unfortunates who use drugs as escape...'


Mr Cooper is dead!'

Thus did Mr Les Connor break the news to me. At Backsettown: 'Wally's the best friend I ever had ...' he sobbed; and — like Harold at the death of Edward the Confessor — offered himself as successor: 'He couldn't do without me ... I'm afraid there's nobody to take my place. Fred Bond couldn't ever be such a good Assistant Head Draughtsman to me as I was to him ...' Gulping down another bout of sobs, he blurted: 'Mary needs you. I'll drive you to her ... Flu killed him. Too much fat, too much swimming, his doctor said...'

Dr Wilberforce, light on her feet like many heavy people, had joined us unperceived; and — lung cancer and heart attacks not yet attributed to nicotine — with prescience asked: 'Was he a heavy smoker? ... Everybody should see X-rays of their filthy lungs ... They should be shown in schools...'

'We'd better be leaving, Mrs Pearsall,' said Mr Connor. Said the doctor: 'How old was he?'

'Mid-thirties, I should think...'

'Young to die of flu ... That germ must be a killer', she mused; and to me: 'You've no resistance ... You can do no good ... But if you insist on going, return here tonight. Phone me the train you're catching and I'll meet you at Brighton station ... Whatever you do, refuse to view his body...'

After a tearful embrace, Mrs Cooper, pasty-faced and already dressed in black, asked if she could continue to index for us: 'There's not a bean. Rent due ... Would you like to see him?'

'Doctor's orders no I'm sorry. Don't worry about money; and besides, you'll be getting a regular weekly income as I insured his life...'

Three days later, she sent me an S.O.S.:

> *'Mrs Watson your London Bridge office cleaner's just got this terrible letter (enclosed). Accusing her of stealing Wally's jacket hanging on his office door which I told her she could have.'*

Taking an early train, I was waiting there for Mr Connor when he arrived at 8; followed him into Mr Cooper's room and handed him the offending letter.

'What's wrong with it?' he snarled: 'I'm in charge here. Nobody but I can give permission for anything. I should have been asked. I call filching Wally's jacket stealing.'

'And you may have given poor Mrs Watson a stroke or heart attack! Accusing her of theft! How could you! ... Just look at what you wrote! How many times on this one page have you used the pronoun "I"?'

'I don't know what you mean ... She's only a char!'

'I'll save you the counting ... Thirty three I's!'

'I wanted that jacket.'

'Either you write a letter to Mrs Watson apologising ... or we'll have to part.'

'You can't do without me.'

'For you to decide ...' I said and left for Backsettown.

Apology beyond him, he did at least write to Mrs Watson. With valedictory: 'in the hope you're in good health as it leaves me.'

'Dr Wilberforce's prognosis proved true. I went down with Asian flu: 'Wasn't I right to get you back here where we can look after you!' she declared: 'Or I'd be arranging your funeral now!' It took me a month to recover.

In March 1953 a TO LET sign 'Whole or in Part' appeared outside a refurbished Edwardian office building, Number 24 Gray's Inn Road. Despite qualms at the tenfold jump in rent from a few pounds a week to £2,125 a year plus rates and maintenance, I signed the forty two year lease, starting Christmas Day. On my personal guarantee. To my naive exclamation. 'But I haven't a penny!' Mr Moss the landlord replied: 'We only need your commitment ... as proof of faith in the future of your business.'

The 1st of November arranged as Occupation Date, the draughtsmen at last moved from their decayed environment to salubrious quarters. Where, for better natural light, they were allotted the top floor.

On terminating the Gray's Inn Road weekly lease, and sub-letting our Napier House suite, the rest of us followed. On the first floor, Mr Hetherington, Mrs Cooper, Records and Boardroom — with a desk for me. On the second, the General Office for Nigel Syrett, Mr Brown, recently taken on, gentle scatter-brain John Sweetlove as Nigel's assistant; shyly beautiful young Doreen Eustace as secretary; and in charge of Mr Nolan's ever-increasing mounted map sales, Mr Westbury — retired colonial administrator, integrity incarnate, trainer of our respectful young — 'A lovely man' — whose English laced with Swahili, added some Kenyan words to Nigel's vocabulary.

All helped carry great loads of packaged and loose stock to our basement warehouse from 21 across the road. Prior to the arrival of the demolition squad. Who, at the touch of a broomstick brought the whole edifice crashing down.

'We seem to have got out just in time ...' sighed Nigel nostalgically as — from the new General Office window opposite — he watched his first working place disintegrate into dust-clouded rubble.

But Number 24 had a shop. With a bus stop right outside. 'Good for business', approved Mr Cruise on an advisory visit: 'Start with a maximum expenditure of £300 on other publishers' maps. Over-stocking's the devil. So any customer asking for what you haven't got, you promise it by 9 next morning ... No difficulty as the wholesalers open at 8. Now let's see your warehouse. Right. Erect a wall between bundle stock and daily draw ... to curb temptation.' And on parting, added, 'With the extra profit made by selling your own goods, you're bound to succeed ... as long as you remember "Shoemaker keep to your last."'

But Harry Binder disapproved: 'Take my word for it old dear this darned Gray's Inn white elephant's going to land you in Carey Street.'

The shop my sphere, I worked from early morning to late evening at making it look like one. The draughtsman arriving at 8am would wave encouragement as I demisted the large plate glass window. A Sisyphus task, and apparently like most manual labour alas, despised: 'Can I speak to somebody who matters?' callers asked ... and be directed upstairs. But a representative carrying a small world globe caught my attention: 'That interests me!', I said; and retail price and discount favourable: 'If you can deliver within the week I'll buy a couple of gross...'

'May I phone Birmingham Despatch to confirm?'

On Opening Day their cheap 3/7d price high-lighted, these miniature globes formed the leitmotiv of my shop window map display. Harry, arriving in black, gloomed: 'How do you know you'll sell anything at all?'

Whereupon my first customer entered. A Cockney lady from the slums nearby, the lost buttons of her old greenish black coat replaced by nappy safety pins strained askew by bulging bosom.

'Am I right for them 3/7d globes?' she asked: 'They caught me eye from the top of me bus. On my way to buy a pinny at Gamages for my friend. Her son's in the Navy. "Better than a pinny for Christmas", I thought: "She can follow 'im round the world."'

'As my first client you can have it for half a crown!' I said — if it hadn't been for Harry standing by I'd have given it to her for nothing.

'Thank you ducks ...' she embraced me; and happily wandered off.

'You won't get rich on that kind of custom', scoffed Harry. But by the end of the week we had clocked up £59.13.-d. More the next, and Christmas Eve a bonanza as last minute gift buyers splurged: 'Thank God you're open!'

I loved serving. To diverse and specific — 'My son's going to Spain on holiday. Can you suggest an unspoilt part?' Having spent eight years painting and writing there, I could: 'Estremadura' the Monastery of Guadalupe...' The holiday over the father brought his son to thank me: 'What a place! What an experience! To think that otherwise I was going to the Costa Brava with my pals!' — Followed by failure. Over a request for large scale Overseas Survey sheets covering a specified part of Nigeria. The 40 supplied me I sold unopened to the customer; most of which, as he showed me on returning them — merely stated UNEXPLORED.

Other justified complaints about map errors — 'It made me late for an important meeting!' or — with litigious hint — '...it made me lose a £1,000 order' or 'Matron wouldn't let me see my daughter after visiting hours!' — evaporated on being told the draughtsmen did their best to prevent 'errors creeping in.' As one young man said: 'I didn't realise a map went through human minds. I thought somehow that the information was just blown onto it straight from the ground.'

The majority were courteous, kind. One, on buying an A to Z, mentioned that he really wanted the G.L.A.: 'But I haven't a quid on me.' I handed him the Atlas: 'Settle when you're passing.' Two months later he popped in to pay: 'I hope my delay's taught you a lesson ... Never to trust strangers. Or you'll go broke.'

As customers continued to increase, Mr Nolan commented: 'You're lucky! They come in wanting to buy. Mine have to be talked into needing to!.'

The pace though, Dr Wilberforce decreed, was too much for my frail health. The hunt for a shop manager was on.

The woman deputy book buyer at Selfridge's proposed herself: 'I'm fed up to the teeth! Instead of promoting me to Book Buyer, when Mr Ellis retires, they're putting a man over my head. A man who knows less than me about the trade.' But her directors managed to persuade her to stay on, she told me: 'I'm so grateful to you, though, Mrs Pearsall. You restored my self-confidence. You made me feel that somebody thought me good enough to employ ...' and suggested I seek advice from the head of The Booksellers Association.'

In a large Westminster store, his office crammed with his own published classic on bookselling, he cut my request short: 'I get the gist ... Give up the whole idea. You can't run it. Nor could any woman. Women lack the necessary profundity, stamina and flair...'

'You must have eight sisters', I guessed right.

'How did you know that?'

'Whether it's a man or a woman doesn't matter ... as long as it's the best person for the job ...' I persisted.

'Only very few are given the double talent of looking after customers and not ruining business by overstocking ... As I said at the beginning, give it up!'

Our need however filtered round the trade. A Map House assistant arrived for an interview, but unimpressed by our empty shelves, joined Stanford at a lower salary and prospects: 'I've got to think of my future ...' While I turned down another because of his widely known hand-in-till tendency.

So we settled for inexperience. With a lot of come and go, until an efficient glamour girl took over; combining with our geographical tone a soupcon of Moulin Rouge. Allure enhanced by the chain-smoker cutie she took on as assistant. With men of all ages of every ilk returning not to buy (though the more timid might make some token purchase), but bearing bouquets, chocolates, trinkets — even jewels — and racy invitations. It was an interest in maps, though, and solving complicated problems put by some customers which enticed our packer Mat Harford.

Come and go too were warehouse characters — 'Trouble with my back', the excuse of an East-Ender for late arrival. 'What's the trouble?' asked Nigel; 'Can't get it off the bed!' came the quip. Until meticulous Mr Bob Penny took over; and extended his kingdom to a spacious lock-up garage in Long Yard for his assistant; whose complaint: 'But it hasn't got a toilet!' he silenced with: 'What you griping for? There's a public lavatory just round the corner in Guilford Street.' Though a passionate steam engine buff — fairground organs in particular — he suffered from recurrent mental depression; requring periods of voluntary hospitalisation. Attacks preceded by verbal diarrhoea; return to normality, by endless card tricks — 'Do you know this one?' — And the only time he left us for another job (nearer his wife's new place of work), he soon wanted to be reinstated: 'The doctor asked me where I'd ever felt happy' he explained: 'and I realised it was here.'

# CHAPTER 23

BEFORE leasing 24 Gray's Inn Road, I had asked Barry Bowman's advice. 'You must have the place surveyed', he said: 'Get in touch with John Rutter. He's top class.'

With him, I went over the building with Mr Moss, the owner.

'That's only a cosmetic job you've done!' said Mr Rutter: 'You've just papered over trouble!'

'Where for instance?'

Mr Rutter thumped one of the walls: 'A hollow sound! Something wrong with the brickwork...'

'We'll soon put that right ...' As he also did to a few other defects: and lulled me into confidence. Falsely. For early in our tenure, reality struck.

Every lavatory pan suddenly overflowed. And continued to. The plumber with his mate — still war-emergency triggered — arrived instanta; and crouching with Mr Hetherington and me under the basement stairs, at once diagnosed: 'Main drains blocked ... since the bombing they're any old how ... Turn out the light! With water about, no electrics for me!' and asked for candles.

Produced by Mr Hetherington. But the first one lit ignited a blue flicker along the exposed narrow gas pipe above our heads: 'Put out the candle! Call the gasmen! So's the gas any old how since the bombing.'

At a gallop two joined us in our stinking Hades; smeared the leaking pipe with some substance: 'Only temporary mind ... The whole bloody place needs re-piping ...' checked with lighted matches — and galloped off.

'Don't expect our rods'll get through the black muck ...' mused the plumber: 'It'll be shovels, hands and buckets...'

As indeed it proved. From 5pm to 3am they toiled — 'Man in his wholeness wholly attending', I quoted D. H. Lawrence — profusely sweating, red-faced, exhausted: 'We'll get it done if we bust!'

Mr Hetherington and I, sharing their vigil, plied our two zealots with sandwiches and tea fetched from an all-night cafe stand nearby. And — 'Our hands are too blinking dirty' — straight into their mouths: 'Ta! ... Eats and drinks like babies!'

At last — 'as usual, women to blame!' they removed the last impediment; and, overalls off and a good wash, accepted brimming tankards of beer: 'Cheers!'

The next mishap, — caused by a trained draughtsman and an apprentice — was water streaming down the stairs.

Tearfully ineffectual, our cleaner tried to mop it up. 'Somebody's left the tap on.' thought Mr Bond on early arrival: 'Crikey! It'll be pouring down to the basement!'

'I was there in a jiffy', he recounted: 'In pitch dark. The flood rapdily rising to the bottom shelf laden with Greater London Atlases. I tore off shoes and socks, rolled up trouser legs, paddled in, and shifted stock to higher shelves ... With the other draughtsmen arriving I soon got a chain going. We baled out the water with the office's tin filing tray ... emptying it out onto the garden at the back ... until the floor was reasonably dry ... 'It was only then the penny dropped. The previous evening, on coming out of the office for home I'd noticed water gushing into the street from a burst main ... I'd left Mike and Cliff at darts. When they turned on the water to wash, there wasn't any; and, stopper left in the basin and tap on, home they went. So, the main mended, on came the taps!'

These, at his suggestion were replaced with pressure taps — 'shutting the stable door after the horse has bolted, perhaps ... but it'll stop it happening again.'

Despite the culprits' confession — 'Sorry, we never thought!' — Mr Hetherington accused Nigel: 'When will you learn to become responsible!'

Nigel stayed mum. But thought: 'A fine one you are to talk about responsibility. Every evening when on leaving I say "goodnight", there you are play acting you're so busy ... and last out: "It's all right for some ..." Then, while I'm waiting for my 18b bus to London Bridge, out you skedaddle before you can say knife. Leaving everything open ... Nothing locked up ... Not even the safe! ... No flies on Mrs Luck about him! Next morning she says: "I see our little sirocco flew off as usual last night!"'

Slapdashery, which precipitated a drama. In 1955 — bumper year for our intake of school-leavers: Ken Palmer in General Office; Mike Manning as apprentice; David Churchill — turned down by Mr Connor as 'too old at 16' — on invoices. Shortly after David's promotion to accounts, Mr Hetherington phoned me to come: 'Old geyser Brown threatens to resign if he doesn't get a salary increase ... You'd better see him.'

Belligerently the ex-soldier marched into the Board Room: 'It just ain't right!'

'What isn't Mr Brown?'

'You're paying a Junior more than me...'

'How do you know we are?'

'From the Salaries Ledger...'

'Would you consider it ethical to rummage in confidential books?'

'Left out on His Lordship's desk, why shouldn't I, eh?'

Accusation, Mr Hetherington side-stepped: 'How often have you refused extra responsiblity Brown?!!! ... While David fields anything I throw at him...'

'Mrs. Pearsall, I herewith formally hand you my week's notice in writing', said Mr Brown.

'How sad. Why not stay with us until you find another job?' I suggested. He drew himself up: 'I'm worth my weight in gold to any firm ... My friend, the Count, assures me...'

'You'll be replaced', threatened Mr Hetherington — still seething at being faulted in front of me: 'I won't take you back ... If you hadn't given notice, I'd have sacked you!'

Donning his bowler and brandishing his rolled umbrella, Mr Brown made a grand exit: 'I shake the dust from my feet. Now. Today!' Alas, as we feared, to rebuffs and unemployment.

Soon he began to haunt the entrance to our office.

'Have you found a job yet?' asked sympathetic Nigel. Jauntily he at first replied: 'I'm on several short lists.'

Noticeably he grew shabbier. What could we do?

'Poor Brown! As usual Hetherington's to blame!' inveighed Nigel to John Sweetlove.

On his ceasing to appear, we grew anxious. Enquiry from his Polish landlord provoked a wigging: 'The Countess my wife and I settled in this country trusting in British Fair Play...'

At 6pm on a bitter November Monday, my bell rang. From my bedsitter on the top floor I looked down into darkness.

Blacker still loomed Mr Brown's unmistakable bowler and rolled umbrella. I let him in.

Shoe uppers torn from welt, coat threadbare, and shivering with cold, he loftily offered to help us again at Geographers': 'My friend the Count feels I should show magnanimity ...' But devouring the quickly prepared breakfast of eggs and bacon, toast, butter and marmalade, — 'Yes, coffee please; the Countess always pours me coffee' — he pathetically confessed: 'My rent's in arrears ... My friends are very kind ... I can't impose on them any longer. They can't afford to carry me ... And I'm too old, I'm told at every interview, to get work...'

Diffidently I asked: 'Would you perhaps allow me to help you personally?'

'Charity? I who escaped three times from the Boche! Never!.'

'How soon could you start with us, Mr Brown? ... Any advance you might find useful could be subtracted from your salary ... say at £1 a week so as not to inconvenience you ... I'd be so happy if you'd rejoin us today ... You'd make all of us at the office so very happy. How you've been missed! What a welcome you'll get! And with business steadily increasing your accountancy will be even more valuable than before.'

At 9am back he was at his old desk. Head down. He might never have been away. Except — as Nigel patted him affectionately on the shoulder — for a voiced criticism: 'What a mess you've made of my books.'

# CHAPTER 24

ONE morning at 3 the ringing of my telephone startled me awake. 'A terrible shock's sobered me up!' sobbed Mrs Nolan. But instead of the usual tirade against her husband through some tiff, only woe: 'I thought Patrick was stoned ... out for the count ... We've been on the binge for the last few days and nights. But he's not just dead drunk. He's stone cold dead. In the bed beside me ... I've never seen a dead body before. The doctor's been and gone. After pronouncing my darling Pat dead ... All right he did get sozzled off and on. But so do I ... We had our punch-ups ... All told though, he was a good husband ... Thought the world of me ... and of you Mrs Pearsall...'

Twenty years I had known him — my only pre-war colleague. And despite those unsmiling eyes in blarney smiling face, I liked him ... would miss his panache. Indeed my conscience lay heavy. Had I broken his spirit by slashing his income on my return from the States from £80 a week to £10?

A second funeral Dr Wilberforce forbade me to attend; and at which Mr Westbury represented us. 'A very good turn-out', he reported; and mourned: 'Where will we get another Mr Nolan, Mrs Pearsall?'

Waiting in the wings was Mr Karl Melene. Recommended by my landlady some time ago: 'A fine baritone. In our Cookham choir. But to make a living he sells Directories ... which means he can't call back on the same customer for years ... Being a friendly fellow this saddens him ... While with your new maps and up-dated old he could return ad infinitum.'

'Mr Nolan's territory is sacrosanct', I had told her. But now she arranged we meet. Perfect accord. Gregarious, relaxed in his large teddy bear coat, ten years my senior to the day and 6 foot tall, his answer to my query — 'When can you start?' was an immediate: 'A week next Monday...'

Mr Westbury approved: 'A gentleman'; and after six months: 'I don't want to be disloyal to Nolan's memory. But Melene's less aggressive selling, brings in more repeats ... and his orders are up because more consistent ... None of those stoppages for the Irishman's sprees ... Not that I mind a sundowner myself...'

Meanwhile trouble from the two managers persisted.

While I pondered, Mr Connor himself burst in: 'If you're not careful Fred and Dennis may be off to join Ron Davey!...

'Where?'

It was a newly formed company, Chislehurst Red Arrow, originators of ready mixed shandy. As drayman. At £1,000 a year. Ron had offered his two former colleagues similar jobs and pay. To Fred and Dennis, I said: 'If you'd told me about Ron's offer a year ago, I'd have advised you to accept it ... Things looked so dicey.'

'The thought of leaving never entered our heads', interposed Fred; and I continued: 'Now with the excellent maps you're turning out we're forging ahead ... Particularly your new Birmingham A to Z...'

'All we want to know is when we'll be earning £1,000 a year', said Dennis.

'I haven't the faintest idea. But you'd be bloody fools if you left...'

Convinced by my vehemence — never having heard me swear before — Mr Bond said: 'We'd better go and get on with it then...'

Mr Connor's misrepresentation I ascribed to pique. At his exclusion from Ron's offer.

After giving notice, our best apprentice wrote to me that he could no longer work under Mr Connor:

> '... He makes us all unhappy ... You'll lose Fred and Jimmy Mayo next if you don't get him off their backs. It's Mr Bond who's patiently taught me all I know ... I'd have liked to stay on. That's why I'm writing to you...'

Fred's six year old son, Allan, developed Perthés Disease: 'The surgeon says he's got to have his leg in irons for a year ... Imagine what Doris and I feel like', Fred confided.

Wanting to give Mr Connor credit for kindness, I asked him to give Fred all possible time off: 'and an extra two weeks during his son's school holidays.'

'I don't need telling. It's what I'd have done anyway!' came the reassuring response. So that when the surgeon ordered another year in irons for poor Allan, I said to Fred: 'Take all the time off you want with the lad ... Like last year, and not just a fortnight as before, but the whole of your son's school holidays.'

'Like last year? What do you mean by that! Nobody offered me even a day off!' he exclaimed incredulous: 'And crikey! So much for an extra holiday. I didn't even get my one week decent. Wouldn't like to go through that again! In Bognor with the family — Pauline in her pram. Allan beginning to walk on the irons but falling all over the place ... And down I went with Asian flu. "Bed for you!" ordered the doctor, putting me on M. & B. Awful! Talk of sweating! Doris had to change sheets day and night ... No extra week's holiday offered me, that's for sure!'

'Well for this year anyway and in front of you, Mr Bond, I definitely do!'

Allan's cure took three hard years. Whereafter the intrepid boy became an athlete.

But Mr Connor did show benevolence in September 1958. When Mr Mustafa Zihni applied for a job. As a Turk married to a Greek Orthodox wife in Cyprus, he and his family — in particular danger during the Greco-Turkish internecine fights — had to flee the country; and as British subjects found asylum in London.

Purchasing an A to Z to find his way about, and guided by our address on the cover, he called at Gray's Inn Road; where Mr Connor interviewing him, asked me to join them: 'He's been head of the Survey in Nicosia, he says ... I can't make out why he left; and why he's ready to work here as an ordinary draughtsman...'

My knowledge of Cyprus; of its political and religious conflicts confirmed Mr Zihni's bona fides, and we took this grateful gentleman on. But I was wrong in ascribing his drawn face and grey complexion to such traumatic events. He was suffering great pain from kidney stones.

Three months later, Mr Connor rang me: 'Mr Zihni's just been taken to Barts for an emergency operation! What do you want me to do?'

'Reassure him that his job's safe — However long it takes him to recover ... I'll go to the hospital tomorrow when he's over the anaesthetic ... And of course any of you in the drawing office may want to cheer him by a visit as he gets better...'

Mr Zihni praised our health service; but was even more impressed by the size of the extracted stones placed in a bottle on his bedside table: 'The surgeon told me he's never seen such large ones!'


On renewed complaints from Mr Elston of running out of stock, I went to see Mr Hetherington. Busy with some stranger (for acting as Supremo he never introduced me to anyone) he told me to wait outside.

'When can we expect the Premier and Ideal?' I asked.

'Held up by my suppliers...'

'Are you one of them?' I asked the pleasant man with him.

'I'm Roy Dewar. An artist. A commercial one. Dave and I are in the same cricket club ... He's our Treasurer ... and I've just dropped in about a query in our accounts.'

'We're needing a cover designer. Might you be interested?' I asked.

'Yes. Less stress than T.V.! We've got to make your A to Z stand out from other covers on the bookstalls! ... So long Dave!'

Each of our suppliers — whom I phoned in succession — denied having received orders from us. I turned to Mr Hetherington: 'You heard?'

'They're lying.'

'All of them?'

'Are you accusing me?' he challenged; looked at his watch, rustled his diary page: 'I'm already late for my next appointment...'

'Cancel it ... Instead, we'll go through your stock records, order what's urgent ... and four and six months ahead.'


He cast a shadow too on the growing romance between Doreen and Nigel. Their engagement announced, wedding day fixed, she invited me: 'But I don't want to invite Mr Hetherington ... Please talk to Nigel.'

Said Nigel: 'He's my boss. He'll take it out of me if I don't.'

'It's the bride's day' ... I persisted.

Nigel gave in. To be proved right. For a few months later Mr Hetherington struck. Through me: 'I'm afraid Nigel's let us down again ... Didn't come into work Saturday morning. Didn't let us know ... And this morning, no apology. We can't have that kind of thing can we? ... I've told him to come down to the Board Room in five minutes...'

Without giving me a chance to ask Nigel what had happened, Mr Hetherington mercilessly chided the unfortunate young man; who, flushed, fists clenched, apologised for 'giving you trouble, Mrs Pearsall ... The last thing I'd want to do ...' and left the room.

'You see ...' smirked his boss: 'He has no excuse.'

All lies, it ultimately transpired. Early that Saturday, Nigel had had to call the ambulance for Doreen. While waiting for it, he tied a dustbin lid to her door for her to rattle if she needed him so that he could pop out to the nearest call-box and phone Mr Hetherington: 'Sorry I can't get in today. I've got to rush my wife to hospital.'

To his confidant, John Sweetlove, Nigel went on to say: 'What riles me too is the way that bantam takes credit for everything ... Did you hear Mrs Pearsall say to me: "Nigel, how do you like Mr Hetherington's quicker way of tracking down your Control Balance?" Mr Hetherington be blowed! My idea, as you know. Not his. To divide the customers' accounts into batches like the London telephone directory: A to K, L to M, N to R, S to Z, But he's my boss. What could I say? So as usual I said nothing. Nor about the show he puts on for Mrs Pearsall when he hears her voice ... The novel he's reading quickly shoved into his desk drawer; account books galore spread out opened; and sham surprise at finding her standing beside him ... eyes lifted wearily from overwork ... All he lets us see. For he shuts the door on us so we won't hear his load of lies. His triumphs, my eye! ... And our mistakes ... When oh when will Mrs Pearsall find him out!'

I already had. From first sight. Suspicion corroborated by a stray remark from his wife: 'My parents opposed our marriage. Thought him too fly! Funny isn't it how wrong they were!'

Ever more frequent absences — when I called at the office or phoned — he explained away with some grandiose executive reason. Absences which began to form a pattern: Cricket at Lords, the Oval, Edgbaston ... And Rugger at Twickenham, Cardiff.

But Harry Binder insisted: 'Who else have you? Make him a director and he'll astonish you. At school they always made the bad boys prefects, and how right they were...'

'If only he'd attend to the accounts I could run the business from Backset-town ...' I uselessly bewailed.

# CHAPTER 25

'WHAT would you say if I asked to work for you?' asked Mr Stewart — who had kept in touch with me since 1935; and at whose request for an interview, Dr Wilberforce had allowed me to invite him to Backsettown. Where, sitting beside me on the bench in the walled garden, he continued: 'I've given Thorpe my notice.'

Mr Thorpe, clerk in my father's time, was now Geographia's Managing Director.

'Why?' I asked.

'On principle. They've brought in a Pension Scheme. Fine for the younger ones. But us old-timers are to get a measly £3 a week for life, and our widows half of that! I'm all right. I've always put something by ... It's the others I'm thinking of ... And when Thorpe announced: "It's The Board's decision ... You've not contributed anything", I spoke up for them: "Only our lives! And what thanks do we get for that!"'

Relief at so unexpected a solution to my managerial dilemmas enhanced the peace of this halcyon Spring morning; sweet wallflower scent on zephyr wings; full-throated blackbird aria from Bramley bough ... calves newly released from sheiling pen penumbra, skipped, cavorted, butted, nuzzled in sheer joy of sun-bejewelled grass under blue canopy of heaven.

'I'd appoint you Director', I said: 'But it'll be no sinecure. You'll be supervising two petty dictators ... Above all ensure that Mr Hetherington keeps the accounts as laid down; sends them to me regularly; and that neither he nor Mr Connor victimize their staff. They'll resent you.'

'What do I care? I'm a free man, aren't I? It's I who'll give them what for!.'

Pride reduced to terror a few mornings later — 'I'm phoning from the shop ... I've just seen Mr Thorpe peering through the plate glass window from the street ... and gone in a flash. He spotted me all right. The malevolence in his face gave that away. What'll he be thinking up?'

At the end of the week, Mr Stewart's usual pension cheque did not arrive.

Then another panic phone call: 'A letter from him you must see, Mrs Pearsall. Accusing me of a criminal offence. Please take the first train here.'

Mr Stewart, face grey, and hands trembling, had shrunk within his clothes. Mr Hetherington stood smiling beside him: 'It's scared the pants off him! I've told him there's nothing to worry about, and have drafted this reply...'

Crumpling it, I rejoined: 'Don't you realise that none of us know how to...'

For the letter, couched in legal terms — though signed by Mr Thorpe —

accused Mr Stewart of disclosing trade secrets to a competitor.

'We need a first-class lawyer ...' I said; and rang Mr Bowman. Told of our predicament, he made an appointment for us. With Mr Ffrench. Who, putting all else aside, saw us straight away: 'Is there any truth in their allegation?'

'Never did I ask for information, nor did Mr Stewart offer it.'

'So you've been meeting? Over how many years?'

'Since 1935 when I started our business.'

'Why, Stewart?'

'I've been drawing maps for Mrs Pearsall's father in New York. Out of working hours we draughtsmen are allowed to sell our skill wherever we can...'

'Common Law then ...' the solicitor approved; and for the first time smiled: 'It would be a Civil, not Criminal case, anyway...'

But for over an hour he grilled us as if under cross-examination in the Law Courts, and concluded: 'I have to think about it...'

But as Mr Stewart left the room, I stayed behind to plead: 'Can you tell us what our chances are? To put Mr Stewart's mind at rest...'

'Call him back.' And to Mr Stewart he said: 'They haven't anything against you. Or they wouldn't have sent that letter. They hoped to frighten you into incriminating yourself ... It'll take me a day or two to draft your reply ... Send it, and that should put an end to the matter ... Good day.'

At the office, a woman, neat in navy blue costume, hat and gloves, anxiously awaited our return.

'Mrs Stewart?' I enquired.

'No. That's why I'm here. I told Jimmy to make a clean breast of it. Of the skeleton in his cupboard ... He left his wife for me. Over a year ago. She treated him something terrible ... He's started divorce proceedings ...'

'Is your wife vindictive, Mr Stewart?' I asked.

'She always has been ...' he began.

'Poor Jimmy. He stuck it for his children's sake ... until they were grown-up.'

'What harm could she do, Mr Stewart?'

'The papers she's got.'

'What papers?'

'Your father's written instructions...'

'Then what's worrying you? We've done nothing wrong.'

'Given half a chance, God knows what that harpy I married would invent if it came to Court ... To get her own back on my Gladys here and me!'

Picking up the phone I said: 'I must let Mr Ffrench know at once.'

To be reassured by him: 'A wife can't give evidence against her husband ...' but voicing my own fear added: 'Let's hope the silly little man isn't hiding anything else...'

He was not.

A spin-off, however, was a report of the divorce proceedings in the early edition of the Evening Standard:

— *Mr James Stewart of Forest Hill seeking a divorce on the grounds of cruelty accuses wife of making him mow the lawn on his return exhausted from heavy day's work at Gilbert Whitehead.*

Which Mr Connor hastened to Backsettown to show me: 'Have you seen this? How can any of my draughtsmen respect him after that!'

'Mr Stewart's private life, or anybody else's for that matter, is no concern of ours ... When will the Premier Birmingham offsets be ready for Lowe & Brydone?'

Firmly, Mr Stewart took charge. And though Nigel dreaded being called to his office — 'I can hardly stay awake ... On he goes with reminiscences I've heard a hundred times' — and Fred Bond recalled unhappy days as his apprentice — 'even if I was naughty, I was only a boy ... he didn't need to be so harsh'; and added on a graver note: 'No man can serve two masters! Why didn't he join you outright from the start!'

But our other young men thought him kind, and trusted his advice to 'keep your nose clean ... It's the company you keep ... Your mother's your best friend'; and on their call-up to National Service: 'Keep your head down. Never volunteer.'

'But what does the man do?' asked Mr Bond.

The vital job (though I could not say so) of controlling Mr Hetherington. No longer did he play hookey; and the requisite accounts reached me on due dates. Allowing me to plan ahead; and to pick up and deal with problems they revealed.

Including a corker.

As usual with our new ventures it had taken time and failure to find the right representative for Birmingham — the interludes filled by Mr Elston, Nigel or me. In fact, unlike London, the Birmingham A to Z started off with quite a fanfare. A half page spread in the *Birmingham Weekly Post,* by Ellen Foxon, featuring it and me in an illustrated text: '... *the one and only woman publisher of maps* ...' And Mr Bond, while obtaining information at the Council Offices, being asked by the Borough Surveyor, Mr Bland, to let him use our original as base.

At last we thought we had engaged the right man. Intelligent, modest, with a slight stutter; and, judging by increasing orders, a good salesman. 'Almost too good to be true', we congratulated ourselves.

Then the orders decreased and continued to do so. Yet, according to my accounts our head office stocks were decreasing so fast that reprints had to be ordered ahead of schedule.

But first I queried a loan to him of £200: 'Why, Mr Hetherington?'

'Because he repaid a previous loan of £50...'

'That makes it worse', I said: 'Do a spot-check on the stock he's holding.'

'No need, We've just totally restocked his van this morning. So we know exactly where we are.'

'I hope nobody in the warehouse gave him prior warning...'

Excitedly, Mr Hetherington phoned me next morning: 'Bad news! The poor devil needs much more than a £200 advance. His van's gone up in flames ... Our new van, of course!...'

'And he?'

'Safe! ... Clothes singed, hands burnt trying to beat out the fire to save our publications ... Absolutely game, in fact. Which should put paid to your suspicions!'

Suspicion shared by the Insurance Company: 'We're paying. But we'd like to warn you to watch that man. We understand he'd been warned of a stock check ... He could have started the fire deliberately to hide the theft of all the A to Zs he carried. Inspection of the burnt out van points that way. Plenty of charred sheet maps but not a single A to Z! Books just don't consume that easily. We can't prove it...'

'Nevertheless, it's only fair we share part of the cost ... 'I offered; and they appreciatively accepted: 'You don't need to...'

We dismissed the rep — 'Not for theft', Mr Ffrench had advised: 'or he could sue you for libel' — but on the grounds of a drop in sales during his first year trial period.

An advertisement for his replacement, brought an applicant from Edgbaston attired in black, his black homburg pulled low over ashen face. El Greco's Conde Orgaz, I thought as he entered the Board Room — though not in armour, and upright instead of being tenderly laid in his tomb.

'I've reached the end of my tether ...' he began; and stopped.

'That's why your letter says you're willing to work for half your present earnings ...' I prompted: 'What's obsessing you?'

'Fifteen years of ever increasing sales for the firm I work for ... Yet never once have they invited me to their London Head Office.'

I pushed the phone towards him: 'Tell them you're in town ...'

Their delighted reaction: 'Come round at once. What about lunching with us!' thawed his whole being: 'How can I ever thank you?'

'Could you find us a representative in Birmingham ... as honest and dedicated as you are...'

'Gladly!'

Thus did Mr Harold join us. 'He'll never set the Thames on fire', rightly assessed Mr Hetherington: 'but steady, yes.'

Amongst other brief interventions Doctor Wilberforce permitted was with my nephew. Brought to the Boardroom by his French mother — 'Phyllis, I can already see my cher Jean-Pierre sitting at your desk, giving orders' — to work at A to Z for part of his school holidays. In the general office, and also to help Mrs Cooper compile our Famous Guide extension into outer London, we decided. But nobody liked having a close relative to the boss around; nor a public schoolboy — though a scholarship one — nor, worst of all, Jean Pierre himself. Particularly his flamboyant farewell on departure: 'I'm off to the South of France!'

'South of France!' muttered a clerk, voicing the general exasperation: 'With all of us overworked and underpaid!'

Henry Turner, however, although a friend of mine, everybody liked and respected. Founder of the Empire Press Union shortly after the 1914/18 War — its name after the Second World War changed to The Commonwealth Press Union — he was reeling from dismissal by the Chairman he had himself appointed.

'Could you find him a job in your firm, Phyllis?' appealed Arnot: 'to help him regain self-respect after Lord Astor's shabby treatment ... Whatever you do don't let him know I've asked you ... Find some excuse to need him.'

A conscientious indexer a perpetual need (since Wally Cooper's widow had left us to remarry) I offered him the post, and he accepted — Sir Henry now, as Lord Astor's conscience sop. Though too intellectual for the concentration demanded — 'Sir Harry sometimes nods off to sleep' — Mr Stewart commiserated — he cut through bureacratic red tape for us; such as obtaining official supplies of petrol during a tanker strike. Particularly did he savour writing a thank you letter to Lord Astor for an eighteenth century firescreen donated for his services to the Union: '... *How I enjoy business integrity after a lifetime in the dog eat dog world of journalism...*'

Dr Wilberforce's command to rest at home by early afternoon — frequently frittered — reached nadir one dark torrential night. Alone upstairs in the tall office building, I struggled to collate Mr Hetherington's sheaves of paper crammed with his cramped sloping figures. At 11pm the vital reprint records extracted, I was preparing to leave when the phone rang. Obscene calls prevalent, I hesitated before replying. It was Sid Wells. In distress: 'I'm up against a brick wall. You're the only person I can speak to without feeling a disloyal heel ... Can I come round?'

'Now?'

'I'll be with you in ten minutes.'

At the roar of his old Bugatti and squeal of brakes, I unlocked, unbolted the door to him; and he began: 'When your father was here from America I saw him and your brother lam into you ... But couldn't speak up for you as I knew they'd only turn on you worse ... Just as my dad does! ... Why do you and I go on? ... Ted Bould tells me I'm a fool not to pack up: ''*The Daily Express* are crying out for skilled printers. Offering four times your wage ...'' So all right. I am a fool. But it's like Edward Wells & Sons was my child ... I've seen it through the doldrums ... worked at it day and night, still do ... Hard to swallow, Mrs Pearsall, that our dads would rather see us dead than see us go one better than what they have.'

'And the last straw?' I asked.

'Two years ago you'll remember I ordered the machine we needed to take on your black and white maps. No delivery. Dad kept saying 'no news, son'', or "yes they've rung and apologised for the delay..." So this a.m. I finally got on to them myself: 'When can I expect delivery?'' You could have knocked me down with a feather when the bloke ses: "What you talking about? You cancelled the order!'' ... ''I never did'', ses I. Ses he: "You personally did Sid Wells. Ten months ago. On the phone.'' That tore it! To think my dad actually mimicked my voice to kybosh my hopes of growing with your Company...

'My father at least, thank God, can't mimic mine', I chuckled. So did he: 'Are we suckers to go on?'

'Probably...'

He drove me home; on parting, warned: 'I mentioned Ted Bould. He and David Hetherington are getting a bit too thick...'

Next morning Dr Wilberforce — impressive in manner and tailor-made immensity — descended on me at Robert Adam Street: 'On and off I phoned you yesterday evening from 7 to well past midnight! How often have I got to tell you your health won't stand up to any social life?...'

'It was business...'

'I don't care what you're up to! If you kill yourself what good will you be to anyone? ... Arrange your affairs so that you can take off several months at a stretch. Of complete rest at Backsettown. Or I'll wash my hands of you!'

At last I could. After a late breakfast, stroll to the copse, the spinney; gradually further afield to the village, the Common, the windmill and the Lyddes nestling in the Downs. And after lunch snooze in the Tudor inglenook where a log fire melodiously crackled; while beside me Timo — named after Timoshenko, the Finnish hero against Russia — the farm cat lazily purred. Then, strength regained, I could paint again. Paint the myriad beauties beckoning me — tree reflections in pond and lake, acacia in white bloom against blue sky, an early spring apple orchard with a blackbird singing to me from a bough ... Or, confined indoors by cold, rain or some only too frequent infection, I wrote again — a Spanish story and later a Cyprus one to be published in *The New Yorker*. To Arnot's delight — '*The New Yorker!* The most sought after literary accolade!' — as she and Henry partook of a scrumptious scone tea with me having driven down from London: 'What a heavenly place!'

Under Dr Wilberforce's regimen, I had totally kicked the barbiturate habit; and, blessed by a Damascus Road conversion, totally kicked my humanist agnosticism. From naive belief of knowing how to live to good effect, to the 'I know nothing' of *le milieu divin* where grace and purpose abound.

So that instead of blaming papa — 'Father forgive him, for he knows not what he does' — I blamed myself: 'Father forgive me for I know not what I do' and looked forward to papa's arrival after five years separation — the time needed to process his Resident's Visa — at long last achieved.

At his greeting: 'If you're an enemy of mine, I'll smash you', I kissed him, hugged him, said 'Don't be silly papa!' Some hours later, walking me home arm in arm from dinner at Pruniers, he referred to his indictment of me to Tony: 'I should never have sent that letter ... I didn't think you'd care so much...'

Moved to tears by my old father's repentance, I answered: 'I'm grateful you did, papa ... You taught me to harm or hurt nobody, instead of caring what others did to me ... And after betrayal in the twenties by your friends, employees, brothers-in-law and even my mother, how could you ever trust anyone again?...'

'That's very generous of you', he murmured.

Reconciliation with a father, with which Sid was also blessed. But alas 'on my dad's deathbed' as he told me: "You've got a lot to thank me for son, my dear Steak and Kidney." ... "Yes dad I know. I do thank you." ... "You don't know. Not what I'm trying to say, son. If I'd 'a' spoilt you like I spoilt that selfish brother of yours, you wouldn't be the fine man your mum and I are grateful to ... and pretty proud of..." '

At the office too, papa was benign ... for him: 'A whole building Phyllis? What's your rent? How many vans did you say you have? You'll go bankrupt!' And to Mr Stewart: 'I see my daughter has made you a Director Stewart. Do you think you can earn your salary in that capacity?'

'It's my endeavour to do so, Mr Gross ... 'What the father promised all those years ago, his daughter has fulfilled ...'

His interest in the rest of the staff pleased them; though Ken Palmer never lived down papa's affectionate stroke on the head and spontaneous: 'What a pretty little boy!'

On papa's next visit, I met his ship at Southampton. To his delight. He looked ill, I feared; and ghastly on receipt of a disturbing letter from his New York office: 'I've got to go back. American News have switched from the distribution of publications to bowling alleys ... Two directors have committed suicide ... Our friends, Mr King and Mr Sellers have had heart attacks ...' Neither did papa recover from this loss of the only reliable distributor covering the whole United States; and he too suffered a minor heart attack. I sailed to spend Christmas with him. After a happy two weeks reminiscence, he said: 'I know you're religious ... So do I have my transcendental moments ... when I feel my mother and your mother watching me lovingly...'

In March 1958, leaving his business in shambles, he died. On board the Queen Mary, just off Southampton.

His attorney phoned me to say there was no need for me to rush to New York: 'Your father had everything organised for his three months vacation ...' But papa's book-keeper begged me to sail there 'as soon as you can ...' Which I did on the Queen Mary's return voyage.

As if in a boxing ring, blows came at me from every side. Money was being paid out as normal, while — papa having placed an injunction on his distributors — none was coming in. Suppliers were screaming for payment. The Fire Prevention Officers ordered stacks of stock moved within twelve hours. Relatives and acquaintances from all over the world wrote, phoned, called for their papa-will-waved inheritance. Other map publishers threatened to kill me if I didn't join them in a deal against the City. Law cases were rife. Solutions beyond my ability, I left my apartment every morning with psalmist prayer (somewhat garbled) in my heart:

> *'In Thee O Lord I put my trust ...*
> *For Thou art my strong rock and my castle; be Thou*
> *also my guide and lead me...'*

Accustomed by now to making order out of chaos, and aided by unstinting co-operation from papa's staff, I restored the New York business to a going-concern. In the meanwhile, refusing a million dollar offer — conditional on my running it: 'I have my London colleagues to consider...'

From desperate problems with the English firm to as desperate in New York, I sailed back and forth across the Atlantic — once again becoming increasingly infirm.

'You can't go on like this!' vetoed Dr Wilberforce: 'You must give up the New York business. I've written to your father's executors to tell them so. As I'm tired of repeating, what good will you be to anyone if you flog yourself to death?'

Meanwhile, despite my lack of confidence in Mr Hetherington, I succumbed to renewed pressure from Harry Binder — 'You're away too often' — to promote him to Joint Director with Mr Stewart: 'The more troublesome a Johnnie is the better he'll respond to responsibility, m'dear, as I've told you before. What marvellous prefects the exuberant ones made at Harrow!'

Mr Stewart gladly agreed: 'He's got a lot on his plate ...' While Mr Connor sulked: 'Why not me?'

# CHAPTER 26

UNDER Mr Stewart's firm hand, Mr Hetherington now regularly submitted daily, weekly and monthly accounts to me; and through the
steadfast integrity and ability of Fred Bond in the drawing office, and Nigel
Syrett on sales and delivery, the A to Z Map Company steadily if slowly
progressed.

As did the shop. The long-finger-nailed glamour girl had long since departed
for more glamorous pastures; and a friend of mine had temporarily filled the
gap, until our chain-smoking houri also left — to marry one of our customers.
Replaced by a keen red-headed male manager, John Vince.

'I'm afraid you'll have to find another flat, Phyllis', warned my landlady
friend, Miss Avril: 'Druce's have applied for planning permission to demolish
our house ... and the others next to us. We're blocking their expansion, it
seems ... Only Ancient Lights could save us...'

Dora MacFadyean found me a flat-to-be in what had been Mrs Dudley
Ward's St John's Wood home — (notoriously visited by Edward Prince of
Wales before his imbroglio with Mrs Wally Simpson). Occupation in about six
months time, the rent unfurnished was £500 a year. For my furnished bed-sitter
I was paying £5 a week: 'I can't possibly ...' I said to Dora: 'It would mean
increasing my salary...'

'Why not?'

Echoed by Mrs Dent, my cleaner, in tune with her litany: 'Can't you allow
yourself better blankets, Mrs Pearsall, instead of these ragged army ones? ...
'Down pillows?' ... Linen pillowslips and upper sheets?' ... 'Egyptian cotton
for the lower?' — and when the faded curtains rent asunder: 'Can't you allow
yourself brocade?'

To celebrate my first night at 24 Cavendish Avenue, Dora and Andrew
brought a bottle of Bollinger and smoked salmon sandwiches: 'To happiness
here, and success in your business!' he toasted me: 'But above all don't ever
forget you're an artist!'

On a morning of November 1959 — convalescing from a major operation in
a Downderry hotel — I was called to the phone: 'A Mrs Stewart for you.'

'Jimmie's in hospital', she said: 'He collapsed last night after a severe
headache. I drove to the hospital with him in the ambulance ... a stroke the
doctor told me.'

Hardly had I put the receiver down when the phone rang again. It was Mr Connor: 'Terrible news. Mr Stewart paralysed. I'm coming straight down to see you.'

'Don't; we can meet in London tomorrow.'

'I'm not in London', he persisted: 'but on holiday in Bath. My wife and I'll be with you by six this evening'; and rang off.

By 9pm they had still not arrived. My friend, Mrs Pengelly, part-time waitress, offered to stay on to serve them dinner: 'They'll be famished after such a long drive...'

At 10 their car swung into our courtyard: 'When we reached Torpoint Ferry, we had to join a mile-long queue of cars and lorries,' he fumed.

'So sorry we're late', apologised his timid wife; but at dagger glance from hubbie, said no more.

'Please don't worry', I appeased: 'I've arranged for you to stay the night ... First you'll want a wash...'

In the dining room I introduced them to Mrs Pengelly: 'She's kindly waited to heat up your dinner ... instead of returning to her family.'

Without a word to her, they sat down at the places laid for them.

'Please do thank her', I mooted when she left for the kitchen.

Reluctantly — with an aside to me 'she's only a maid' — he did so. Nor did he thank her when she showed them to their room! — though 'Scrummy' ejaculated his wife.

'I know their sort!' smiled Mrs Pengelly when I apologised.

On my early pre-breakfast saunter along the sandy beach, he joined me: 'Poor Mr Stewart ... He was a bit of a stickler, I must admit ... Preferred to say no to any new idea ... I'll never let you down, Mrs Pearsall, I promise ...'

To my praise of Mr Bond for suggesting that county names and boundaries be shown in blue on a new quarter inch Road Atlas being prepared, his lips curled: 'Mr Bond? He's only a draughtsman...'

After breakfast, he drove me — his wife in the passenger seat — to Plymouth for my train to Paddington: 'It's on our way back to Bath.'

Before parting at the station, he paused expectant. For a Directorship, perhaps?

Instead, I naturally told him to add 'the two days wasted on me' to his week's holiday; and equally naturally to put in a petty cash chit at the office for petrol and expenses.'

Mr Connor was away on his second weeks' holiday, when Mr Bond phoned me: 'We've a serious problem ... Can I come round at once to see you?'

The shortage of experienced draughtsmen preying on Mr Stewart's mind, he had seriously blundered some months previously. By agreeing with Mr Hetherington and without consulting Mr Connor to take on applicant Mr Marsh, at the wage he demanded — though it was above that of our established draughtsmen: 'But please, Mr Marsh, whatever you do don't let any of the others know...'

Mr Marsh kept his word.

But no injustice can ever remain secret.

'I'll have a cup of tea ready for you', I said to Mr Bond.

Sipping it, he explained: 'Marsh's wage slip was found in a waste-paper basket; and its contents bruited to ready ears and eyes.'
To my suggestion that we raise everybody's wages above Mr Marsh's he wisely demurred: 'It'd look as though we give rises only when forced to, instead of as a just reward ... I'd wait three months or so...'

In the drawing office, when we arrived together, revolution. Over raised voices, Mr Bond appealed to his colleagues to listen to me.

'There can be no excuse for such an outrage' I said: 'I can only assure you it won't happen again. Mr Stewart's very ill. He'll no longer have any authority over the drawing office ... I'm ashamed...'

After some muttering, a young man recently out of his apprenticeship rasped: 'How can we be sure?'

'Mrs Pearsall has given her word', replied Mr Bond — with the serene authority of a good man, of a good craftsman.

Another day, he again called at Cavendish Avenue.

'Trouble?' I asked.

'Tall, upstanding, in blue blazer and darker blue slacks to match, his eyes blue and smiling, he shook his head: 'I gather you've turned down my idea of blue for the counties. So I've come to talk it over with you.'

'You do like blue!' I laughed: 'Of course draw the county names and boundaries in blue ... An excellent idea. As I told Mr Connor ... I can't have made myself clear ... So go ahead! ... Anything else?' And over tea, which he had helped me prepare, we happily spoke of many things — of cabbages and kings.

On Mr Connor's return, I sat them both opposite me at my desk; and said: 'You'll be delighted to hear, Mr Connor, that in your absence Mr Bond has looked after everything to perfection...'

Fury so distorted his face that to my own surprise as well as theirs, I added: 'So I'd like to make him Joint Head Draughtsman with you...'

He stormed from the room.

'Have I done wrong?' I asked.

'Thank you for your confidence in me', said Mr Bond.

A few moments later, Mr Connor, his whole body still contorted, burst back in: 'I'm handing you my resignation.'

Mr Bond, an arm about his shoulder, led him away.

Hours passed.

White-faced and shaken, Mr Bond reappeared: 'I'm afraid I haven't been able to calm him. Perhaps you could help change his mind. He's waiting outside.'

I too failed.

'If you're determined to leave us, and we all hope you won't' I finally said: 'please accept a full year's salary ... in addition I'll have Mr Hetherington make out a cheque for our contributions and your payments to your pension...'

'You can't mean it!' he exclaimed, tears flowing down his cheeks. Head in hands, he sobbed on: 'To be so generous! I've always tried to please you ... I've never understood what you wanted...'

Going round the desk to him, I raised his head, wiped his eyes, tried to comfort him: 'Pride's the very devil for all of us. Forgive me for hurting yours...'

Thus did Mr Bond find us on re-entering my office; and rejoiced: 'So all's well again, Les!'

But, awaiting him upstairs were his draughtsmen. With their leaving present of a Times World Atlas. 'Did that tip the balance?' Mr Bond and I asked ourselves. For after the presentation, Mr Connor became pensive; without a word left to catch his train ... and — except to collect his box of tools — never reappeared.

'You'd better have a word with the rest of the draughtsmen', advised Mr Bond: 'What he said against you before he broke down is nobody's business ... You've got another revolution on your hands...'

Not that I could sway the hostile assembly of men from blaming me. As Cliff Utting summed up: 'I've been here a year longer than Jack Archibald. Is something like this going to break our friendship?!

'Mr Bond is now Head Draughtsman. I'm sure you'll give him all the support he needs', I said.

Mr Connor having claimed some of our plate makers and litho printers as personal friends, I phoned to tell them he had resigned: 'You might not want to do business with us now...'

'On the contrary,' they each rejoined; one adding: 'Give me Fred Bond any day. In fact, can you send him round. We're having trouble with the fit...'

Said Fred: 'I've only tagged along once or twice; and went. To terryifying technical responsibility, as he recounted: 'I had to take off the England & Wales Road Map as there had been a change using screen blue for the sea and solid for Motorways. When the sea was correct the Motorways were too light, when the Motorways were correct the sea was too dark. New plates had to be made. Despite the cost...'

'The next job which was waiting to go on the machine was the Premier London in six colours which I thought would be all right. Next morning when called to pass the colours I had to take that job off as the blue boundaries were not in register with the black. Not only the disastrous cost of taking any job off the machine — make-ready wasted and the machine idle — but another set of plates required.'

The drawing office in safe hands at last, still left the Company at the mercy of Mr Hetherington. But of only one now instead of two small-time opportunists.

# CHAPTER 27

SINCE my plane crash and ensuing stroke I had been prone to any infection — contracting shingles, glandular fever, septicaemia, influenza, virus pneumonia, Aphthous ulcers — one after the other or concurrently; and subject in addition to blackout, faints and ceaseless headaches.

For Mr Hetherington, therefore, Mr Stewart's prolonged absence superimposed on my own, let him off the leash — 'I admit, Mrs Pearsall, I resented you bringing in the poor old dodderer over me!'

Back he plunged us into muddle and perpetual crises. Into nail-biting (his nails bitten to the quick) last minute salary tottings up every Friday; and as heretofore into lack of routine management accounts. His excuse: 'With all I've got to do! Running the business for you ...' I vainly countered: 'How can you run it without knowing where you are?'

To shame me for slave-driving, he arrived late one night at the hospital I was then in. Weighed down like a pack mule with bulging suitcase, sweating, red in the face, resentful: 'So you made me drag this load round!' he stormed; and snapped the cases open upside down. Out tumbled the Company books en masse onto my bed and floor. Loose papers too: 'Now are you satisfied!'

Sister ordered him out: 'What's the use of us working ourselves to the bone to cure our patients when you spread dust, dirt, disease, infection!'

Signing myself out next morning, I taxied to the office, dubbed Mr Bond and Mr John Vince directors.

'Only Junior Directors, of course', slicked Mr Hetherington; and, dashing off a Minute for me to sign 'for circulation to the staff', again outwitted me: 'And by the way' he added: 'Black's, the Camping people next door are offering to pay all our expenses and a premium of £6,000 if we'll move to Number 28. They want to enlarge their premises ... "Yes?" Mrs Pearsall or "No?"'

'If everybody else agrees, Yes.'

The move went smoothly; the draughtsmen carrying their equipment and originals across rooftops from our old building to the new — beautifully refurbished by Black's. On my first visit to the drawing office, there, leaning across the stairwell, weeping bitterly, was our young apprentice, Mike Manning.

'What's the matter?' I asked.

'The eye specialist's just told me I've got to stop drawing maps forever ...' he sobbed: 'or I'll go blind ... Maps are my life ... You can't understand...'

Henry Turner had long left for work more appropriate to his talents, and once again we had gone through a series of unreliable indexers.

Asked if he would mind indexing, Mike dried his eyes 'Anything to stay on. I'm so happy here! ... I think the world of Mr Bond.'

The specialist written to, approved: '... as long as Mr Manning won't be working on tracing paper...'

Sales increased annually — in 1960, from £72,000 to £89,000. Pre-tax Net Profit too — from £4,800 to £6,900.

'All my doing!' preened Mr Hetherington; and a month after Mr Stewart's stroke, handed me the salary cheque to sign.

'But it's blank...'

'And while you're about it, sign this batch too...'

'All blank cheques! ... Never!'

'Mr Stewart did ... to save me trouble.'

'He shouldn't have ... In future interleaf statements, payslips etc. with each cheque concerned...'

A fluttering of eyelashes and a change in tone: 'Don't you trust me?!...'

Evidence not to, proliferated. Absences, broken promises lies. Also riotous living. Rolling drunk with drunken companions at the Oval — witnessed by Sid Wells. Monday morning moans from our cleaner: of Board Room littered with broken glasses, empty beer cans and bottles, drink spilt over desks and carpets; half-eaten sandwiches, apples, bananas, cakes trodden in as well as left around: 'Disgustin! ... And today be'ind your desk M'm wot d'you thinks I find? A lace-up corset! Wot 'e and 'is toffee-nose skirt gets up to, Gawd knows!' Endorsed by neighbours: 'Orgies most Saturday nights after some match or other — cricket, rugger. Sing-Songs till all hours. Me and the Missus can't get a wink of sleep...'

At last he fell foul of bank manager Barry Bowman. On whose promotion from Bedford Row branch to Baker Street and 'the prestigious Marks & Spencer Head Office account' we had followed him with our much less so.

'Being in charge has gone to that man's head, Phyllis,' he said, having called me up to London from Backsettown: 'That's why I've asked you here, and have arranged for him to be shown into the waiting room. It's only a small pointer I know; but unlike you, his secretary — that supercilious Miss what's her name — won't put him through until she's got me on the phone...'

My own misgivings voiced, discussed, he rang a bell: 'Let's have that plausible mountebank in...'

The messenger returned without him: 'The gentleman's not yet arrived...'

'He always leaves things to the last moment ...' I apologised. When, panting, he rushed in, he gasped: 'The W. H. Smith & Sons' cheque I told you I was waiting for to pay into our account, Sir, didn't arrive till the second post! So here it is, Sir, as promised!...'

Shabbily debonair in unpressed suit, scuffed cuffs, rucked and matted brown suede shoes, he glanced uneasily from one to the other of us; and Barry nailed his lie: 'Ten days ago you told me you'd just put it in the post!'

'So that's the overdraft settled!' fawned Mr. H.

'Overdraft!' I exclaimed: 'We can't have an overdraft! 'Not with turnover up £200 a month over last year and retail prices based on costs plus profit margin!'

'But that's why!' he beamed: 'Reprints bounding forward because of increased sales ...' and having detailed every publication, added: 'Our Company's under-capitalised for the rapid expansion I've accomplished.'

Out in the street, he reproached me: 'Don't you realise I've got more important matters to attend to. We're bursting at the seams here. I've started negotiating for premises on a new Industrial Estate outside Sevenoaks. Only the foundations as yet ... Double the space for the same rent we're paying here. I spotted it a few Saturday's ago on my way for a game of golf. I'll run you down to have a look-see...'

The three adjoining units might have been made to measure: the outside one as Drawing Office, the centre as General and the third as warehouse.

'They can be adapted to our needs, the agent told us: 'You'll want the windows high so time isn't wasted looking out of them.'

'Let them look out', I said. He said: 'And of course the regulation number of toilets.'

'No. Double ... And date of completion?'

'September/October 1962.'

'Which gives us time to sublet all but shop and warehouse at Gray's Inn Road ...' and we referred him to our solicitor.

That was the trouble with Mr H. To deflect my Sherlock Holmes nose, always some entrepreneurial scoop. Such as Roy Dewar's excellent cover designs; the 24 Gray's Inn Road move to 28; the sale of a special linen bound edition of our new disappointingly slow selling Great Britain Road Atlas. To J. Wix (a Gallaghers subsidiary) as coupon Premium prize — though it proved a misery to slip them into the plastic folders needed to keep the white linen white.

Momentarily curbed by the Barry Bowman close-shave, he soon took the bit between his teeth for the longest gallop yet. My sustained pressure on him for routine accounts — by phone, letter and when possible in person — 'We're drifting rudderless!' he airly dismissed — 'What's eating you?' I'm settling every bill in 30 days as you laid down, and allowing 60 to our customers...'

Barry's suspicions and mine, Harry Binder pooh-poohed: 'Don't keep nagging at him Phyllis! Your Harry's got his eagle eye out for you non-stop! You're deuced lucky to have a chappy like that ... Treasurer of his Rugger club, dash it, and Cricket...'

But B.H., apprised at a pre-dinner chat, took action: 'Smells fishy to me ... I wouldn't give a tanner for Harry's assessment. That snobby son of mine hasn't got a thought in his head ... I'll send in our sleuth for the next audit.'

Which for the 1961 audit he did.

Exploding into the office, Mr Bernard Davis barked at Nigel: 'Hand me the Company books at once!'

'How can I get on with my Sales Entries?' he countered clutching his ledger to his chest.

'The Journal then, the Minutes ...' persisted Mr Davis.

'Mr Hetherington takes them home...'

'That's illegal!' stormed the sleuth; as Mr Hetherington strolled in. While Nigel yelled: 'For goodness sake Mr Hetherington take this man off my back!' Mr Davis stormed: 'If you're Hetherington, let me tell you it's illegal to take Company Books from the premises!'

'Who do you jolly well think you are to speak to me like that?' smoothly demanded Mr. H.; and when I introduced them, merely said: 'With all I have to do and interrupted every moment — there goes my phone! — I need the peace and quiet of home!'

'Fetch every Company book forthwith! Never again let them out of this office! We'll be starting the audit this afternoon!'

Months later, Mr Davis announced the result. Company profit down from £6,000 to £737: 'Mr H. must be expertly cooking the books. We followed the usual form: Backwards item by item until an error or errors are found. But not a single irregularity traced. Large sums must have been syphoned off for years. But how? My colleagues who've been auditing your accounts have left too much to him. Just one clue they've given me. Too late to track down. A deficit of £250 at the previous audit. On being told, Mr Hetherington, without further ado wrote out a personal cheque in settlement...'

On the 18th October, the office moved to Sevenoaks — organised by Nigel with military precision. Which even Mr Brown's concentration on work in hand could not disrupt. Unaware of the pandemonium of departure around him, he stayed working at his desk until Nigel on a last look round found him: — 'Come on Ernie!' and handing him bowler, scarf, umbrella, hustled him 'into the van with the others!' together with his desk, chair, Paying-In Book.

'I must get there before the others', Nigel's only thought; and, in his cherished green leather upholstered black Austin 10, held his foot down on the accelerator. Arriving in time to decant Mr Brown — 'Last in, first out!' — and tow him and his paraphernalia to his new allotted niche; where, taking up pen and Paying-In Book, Mr Brown neatly entered the next item. While Nigel and others — 'Grab yours and keep going!' — unloaded; and once under cover, carried everything to pre-arranged places. Amongst the few who left the firm was only one key draughtsman, Cliff Utting — whose wife, could not bear to leave her mother. (In his stead, Fred appointed Jack Archibald as Assistant Chief Draughtsman).

Not until a few days after the move did nostalgia for the roar of traffic milling multitudes and window shopping gazers hit Nigel: 'Gosh! It's deadly quiet here … I can actually hear that fly flying. Don't know how I'll adjust.'

Some members of the staff found accommodation nearer Sevenoaks; others, such as Fred, Mike Manning, John Frankel and Mustafa with his beautiful daughter, Rona, stayed where they were — 'for the present' — and commuted by train. As did Mr Brown: 'Never will I desert my dear Count and Countess … How could they do without me? Who'd clean their windows? Mow the lawn? Weed the gorgeous flowerbeds?'

Mr Hetherington, his home, like Fred's in South London was concerned about his secretary — 'Wouldn't it be dreadful if it's too far for her to travel and she left? …' Then he phoned me: 'Wonderful news! Guess what!'

'Overdraft slashed?' I hoped.

'Carla, I mean my secretary, is joining us after all … Her aunt in Beckenham's going to put her up.'

# CHAPTER 28

'MRS Pearsall, for six months I not be paid ...' said Mr Gerritt Groen as I was seeing him off at Liverpool Street station for his Harwich/Hook of Holland night ferry.

'But Mr Hetherington's assured me he's settling every account 30 days from invoice...'

'I don't trust that Mr Hetherington! ... Alway he promise. Alway he lie.' Gently my great big friend touched my arm: 'I'm sorry Missus ... I see I give you big agitation ... Of course you don't pay me a guilder until easy for you ... Sixteen years of good business together, you and I have confidence complete ... To be short of money when A to Z sell like hot cake is stoopid ... stoopid! When to-day in the Underground I see a man with our competitor street atlas I nearly punch him ... But look into that Hetherington! What's he getting from your suppliers? When he asked me for a sweetener, I pretend I not understand ... Scratch a liar and you find a thief ... If you need me I come over!...'

Bombshell which prescipitated me next day — the 2nd of November — to Sevenoaks. To book in at the crummy, pretentious Park Hill Residential Hotel. Like Backsettown away from town traffic pollution; and thus I hoped to guard my health for the long haul ahead.

Whence, phoning the office, I asked for Mr Hetherington.

'He didn't say when he'd be back ...' stalled his secretary, Carla.

'Tell him Mr Groen's been to see me...'

I could hear them muttering together; then as if with pleased surprise, she lied: 'He's just come in ... He'll have a quick word with you...'

'It's urgent, Mr Hetherington ...' I began.

'Oh God! What's the trouble now?'

'£50,000 owed to Mr Groen...'

'I sent his cheque yesterday...'

'Stop whatever you're doing, and make a list of our Creditors, overheads, commitments. All with dates of payments due. In date order. Bring it round to me by midday at the latest. Debtors too...'

'I've got appointments with Simpkin Marshall, Larby...'

'Cancel them!...'

At 2pm he arrived. I took the lists from him, sent him back to the office.

The papers revealed that by March 1963, we would be owing disastrously more than owed. Unless in the next four months the rot could be halted and reversed. Which, I assessed, it could be. By ruthless cuts (including my still modest salary to £15 a month) and extended credit from supplier friends. I thanked God for the past experience of pulling my business and my late father's New York one back from the brink.

The boardroom door next morning opened onto Mr Hetherington, his secretary and paper supplier, Ted Bould.

Their private chat interrupted by my unexpected arrival they volte-faced to bland welcome. 'If you'd only let me know you were coming, dear Mrs Pearsall, I'd have polished your desk ...' Carla reproached me; and to give her accomplices time to stuff away documents, burbled on: 'You'll want to read these carbon copies ... Four hundred and fifty letters I typed last week ... Are we busy!'

'Isn't she wonderful!' smiled Mr H., drawing my attention to the wall-to-wall deep piled royal blue carpet: 'What impeccable taste she has! She chose it...'

Mr Bould slapped a batch of invoices on my desk.

Picking them up, I phoned Mr Brown of Dickinson's to check on each. It was as Mr Groen anticipated. But instead of discussing the problem with me, Mr Bould barred my exit with arms outstretched: 'Unless you pay me ... And until you do so, Mrs God Almighty, I don't leave this room! *Comprenez?* Excuse my French!'

Aware of collusion between the two rogues to split the excess, I remarked: 'You didn't seem to be pressing Mr Hetherington for payment...'

'Oh Dave's all right...'

'Your account isn't due till December...'

'I don't care when it's due, damn it! I can smell bankruptcy a mile off...'

'Write out his cheque, Mr Hetherington, and I'll countersign.'

'No go!' smirked Mr Bould: 'It'll bounce! Like the last one did!'

Writing out my own cheque, I handed it to him: 'Not another order will you ever get from us...'

'You can't say that after a quarter of a century ...' began Mr H. Interrupted by his collaborator: 'Anyway if you do make it Mrs P. Dave'll have me back, don't you worry ... Ta-ta Dave, ta-ta Carla! And thanks a lot, Madam ... No sentiment in business, eh?'

The phone rang.

'Mr Leadbetter for you, Mrs Pearsall ... Our bank manager' said Carla: 'I'm putting you through.'

'(Some months ago, on Barry Bowman's retirement to run his family business, Mr Hetherington had transferred our account to the Holborn branch: 'So much closer to Gray's Inn Road. I don't have time to trek back and forth to the West End!')

'So I've got you at last, Mrs Pearsall', barked the manager: 'Be here tomorrow at 11am with your Company's overdraft repayment plan!'

Dreaded euphemism I knew for calling in overdrafts as prologue to enforced liquidation.

'The whole thing's cock-eyed!' laughed Mr H.: 'All right I have exceeded the £5,000 overdraft but only for a day or two.'

On his ringing off, I immediately phoned my creditors and future creditors for extended credit. Generously, Mr Brydone responded: 'for as long as you need it. I'll supply paper and printing for your many orders in hand ... and please go on sending us new work as normal ... I've always respected your integrity and your courage in adversity. How lucky your father is ... My son's not interested, and my nephew's not up to scratch ... If only I could persuade you to join my Board ...' (It was Gerrit Groen who had advised me not to: 'a printer needs a publisher ... a publisher doesn't need a printer. He must remain free to shop around...')

Sid Wells' response was to zoom to us in Sevenoaks; and leading me out of earshot into our warehouse, said: 'I've managed to save £10,000. It's yours if it'll help you out of the Dave/Ted shambles ... Saved over the years from A to Z earnings ... I feel part of A to Z.'

'Dear Sid, you need it yourself', I declined; but again heart-warmed.

Entering the bank's vast gloomy precinct with Mr Hetherington and David Churchill, we were led to a cubby-hole waiting room — redolent of failure, dashed hopes, suicides.

After the long wait inflicted on defaulters, the messenger re-appeared: 'Mr Leadbetter can spare you five minutes now...'

'I'd like to see him alone first', I said, leaving the others; and to the manager: 'I don't trust Mr Hetherington...'

'I'm glad you don't. Nor do I ... Nor this £6,000 loan to directors.'

'That's to me', I said: '£5,000 from our Insurance for injuries I sustained in an air crash; plus £1,000 from the airline — a pre-war Warsaw Convention limit on compensation...'

'All beside the point! ... Now sign this form giving us "first call on your Company's assets". And, effective from today, I'm withdrawing our facilities...'

'You'd be making a big mistake ...' I said: 'By May your loan will start to decrease; by September it'll be repaid in full; and we'll be showing an acceptable profit...'

'Women!' he snorted: 'Day dreamers!'

'Despite administrative mismanagement, our drawing office has remained conscientious. As you can see by the superb quality of this publication ...' and I handed him copy of our Greater London Atlas.

Without a glance, he shoved it into a desk drawer: 'Let's see your employees then ... I don't have all day...'

Neither were they offered a seat, nor a flat surface on which to display the books and the analyses David Churchill produced to confirm my forecast.

As he shooed us towards the door — 'I'm expecting the Chairman of the

Prudential, can't keep him waiting' — I blundered: 'My main suppliers are allowing us indefinite credit…'

'That's even more dangerous! Owing more than you've revealed!'

'We don't Sir', refuted David: 'Every creditor's entered. They trust us. That's why they're giving us time to pay!'

On leaving I again pleaded: 'Please trust me too, Mr Leadbetter, and give me the elbow-room we need…'

'I have to think about it … I'll let you know…'

For two weeks not a word from him. Then he phoned: 'My wife and I have been busy entertaining important clients…'

Determined not to show any weakness by asking for his 'Yea' or 'Nay', I sympathised: 'All that preparation and washing up…'

'My underlings and the caterers do that!' And he lapsed into social small-talk: 'What's the weather like in Sevenoaks? I do hope you're well …' At length, giving up hope that I would refer to the matter, he brusquely did: 'If you'll personally guarantee the overdraft, Mrs Pearsall, I'll extend the facility to the 5th of January 1963.'

'But I haven't £5,000…'

'It's your personal commitment I want.'

'And after the 5th of January?'

'That'll depend on your 1962 Balance Sheet. Which has to be brought to me that very day … In the meanwhile report here twice a week — 11am every Tuesday and Friday.'

In the drawing office next morning, I called Mr Bond aside: 'I'm afraid you'll have to hold up your new Manchester A to Z. We can't afford to print it…'

He blenched: 'That I can't tell the draughtsmen! Not after all they've put into it … Compilation, revision of the Premier area, drawing of the extensions, pagination … months of dedicated work … How soon before we can?'

'If we're lucky you'll be able to send the originals to Mr Groen mid-January…'

'I'll try to keep the hitch under my hat till then … They're too immersed in getting it out to ask about dates yet…'

Next, I joined Mr H. and his secretary in the Boardroom, where, riffling through Company Books I at last stumbled on a fiddle of his. In my personal ledger. Weekly withdrawals by him on my behalf of £10 or £20 cash. Which I had never asked for nor received. But, his word against mine could not be proved.

'Jolly rummy old top', agreed Harry Binder: 'But about that early audit your bank manager demands, I'll send my sleuth and a clerk straight along to start on it.'

I did not know where else to turn. With the exception as ever of Mr Brydone and Sid Wells, my suppliers and professional advisers all complained by letter to me personally of Mr Hetherington's failure to pay their accounts, and his promise after broken promise to do so. Complaints finally surging to 'We'll be issuing a summons.' Threats of which Mr Hetherington feigned amazement 'a pack of lies, the cheque must have got lost in the post...'

Said Harry: 'That's the same ballyhoo he gives Binder Hamylyn instead of settlement of our account.'

From him as well — though ashamed at preparing a Gestapo-like dossier — I asked for the facts in writing. These I showed to Mr Bond: 'I've warned Mr Hetherington. Now, according to the New Testament, he must be warned in front of a witness. So would you mind seeing him with me please?'

Reluctantly he agreed: 'I've always found him decent enough to work with...'

Faced with kind-hearted Fred, Mr Hetherington, — instead of his usual explaining away of old lies with new — Uriah Heaped: 'I've been so worried at home ... the twins needing blood transfusion; my newly-born son ill ... the move to Wrotham ... the worry and waste of time answering that Bernard Davis's queries ... Cross my heart and prepare to die, I'll keep the straight and narrow ... You've never had anything against me, have you Fred?'

Again he lapsed; by concealing a £500 bill we could not meet. Except by selling his car to bridge the gap: 'Our only asset, Fred,' I explained: 'Or have I become obsessed against him?'

'If we can get £500 for it we've got to.'

'How do you expect me to bring Carla to work?' inveighed Mr H. And next day, having himself bought back his car for £750 (the garage told me) drove her to the office as usual.

Unlike Mr Bond, my other director, John Vince, unaware of skulduggery, remained loyal to Mr Hetherington. Entrusted with counter-signing cheques, he brought one to my desk, derisively asked: 'What's this cheque then for £15 made out to you Mrs P.? I thought we were supposed to economise...'

At my answer — 'My reduced monthly salary' — Carla's and Mr H.'s sniggers ceased; the latter diverging to concern: 'On a cold windy rainy night like this, Mrs Pearsall, I can't allow you to walk back to your hotel ... As you can't afford a taxi, I'd drive you there myself ... But I'm up to my eyes with work ... till past midnight I shouldn't wonder ... John won't mind running you up there, will you John?'

Sullenly he did so; midway, burst out: 'What you hounding poor Dave for? Hasn't he enough to cope with at home!'

Recovery or failure on a razor's edge, I toyed with contingency plans.

Including a flight to Johannesburg to ask in person (I could not bring myself to do so by letter) for a loan from my friends Dora and Andrew McFadyean on a visit to their youngest daughter. And secondly — should illness re-incapacitate me — feelers about selling the business. But a lunch (arranged by son Colin McFadyean) with international publisher George Rainbird strengthened my determination to surmount the crisis and safeguard my honourable colleagues from tycoon indifference to employees — resulting in sell-outs, take-overs, mergers.

# CHAPTER 29

BOXING day 1962 dawned to a fairyland of snow. Harbinger of months of snow and ice. Twice a week Mr Roberts, my Rolls Royce Hire friend drove me to the Holborn bank — 'Pay me when things get better' — where the manager kept me waiting, then sent a message he was too busy to see me, and back to the office. Where other workers on our estate marvelled agog — 'Who's that in the Rolls? A film star?'

By the 4th of January, Bernard Davis completed a 'DRAFT, subject to Audit' Balance Sheet and Profit and Loss Account for the year ended 31st December 1962. It showed Assets of £58,332 and a Net Profit before Taxation of £4,879. (Though, as discovered later, Mr Hetherington had bumped up the Stock In Hand to £28,500, by the inclusion of unsaleable stock, unuseable paper and a fictitious invoice for more.)

Next morning at a quarter to 11, Harry, at my request — a little unsteady on his feet: 'a hair of the dog that bit me, ole gal' — joined me in Mr Leadbetter's defaulter waiting-room.

At 11.30, a messenger fetched us to the presence.

There in Charlie Chaplin style sat our Mussolini.

'Your overdraft Mrs Pearsall continues to creep up', he condemned: 'Well over the £5,000 I authorised ... My patience is at an end.'

But on my introducing Mr Harry Binder of Binder Hamlyn, he jumped from his chair, subserviently pumped Harry's hand: 'Good morning, Sir'; and asked us to sit down: 'What a pleasure it is to look after our dear Mrs Pearsall...'

With so august an auditor, the Draft accounts received only cursory perusal: 'Are you sure £5,000's enough, Mrs Pearsall?'

'Ample ... Please may I phone my office?' Put through to Mr Bond, I rejoiced: 'It's OK to go ahead with the Manchester A to Z!' and he: 'Thank God! Nobody's asked about it yet!'

Mid-February, tragedy struck John Vince. Commuting to the Gray's Inn Road shop as usual in our mini-van, he gave a lift to his father for a day out in London. On a chair in the back, for lack of a passenger seat. Skidding on the icebound road, the van overturned. John suffering only shock and bruises; but alas his father was killed. In sorrow and self-reproach, John later turned angrily on me: 'You've no right to give such responsibility to any of us!' and resigned: 'Mat Harford knows the job better than I.'

Mat's particular talent for solving customers' personal map problems was offset by his erratic time-keeping — 'I've got two alarm clocks going off one after

the other, but I can't seem to get up ... I just turn over and go to sleep again'
— and his overbuying from representatives of other map firms or allied trades:
'I just can't let them go away without an order.' I was there when he wrote one
out for over £100 for coloured pins and flags.

'But you've got boxes and boxes of them in stock!' I exclaimed, pointing at
three stacked shelves.

'They're out of date', said Mat. Echoed by the representative, who, on my
requesting a Credit Note as Managing Director, calculated the unsold stock and
handed it me for the full amount: 'to maintain goodwill...'

Meanwhile Bernard Davis and his clerk vainly continued to ferret for tangible
proof against Mr Hetherington. The rumour went round the office that they
were Time and Motion men — 'a jolly good idea' — said those subject
to fashion.

The Hetherington crux came unexpectedly low-key. The girl on the
switchboard asked to put me through to him replied embarrassed: 'He told me
to say he's incommunicado.'

'Where is he?'

'He told me not to tell anyone...'

'It's Mrs Pearsall speaking ... I remember now, he was going to Manchester
today...'

'Not Manchester. London ... He told me to say Manchester if you called ...
Oh dear I shouldn't have let the cat out of the bag...'

Next day, Friday the 22nd of March, Carla flounced out — 'I'm off! The way
you treat poor Mr Hetherington. After all he does for you! ... I would steal, lie,
and cheat to protect the man I love!'

Biting his nails as I joined him in the boardroom, he sat there wracked by
separation from his beloved: 'All your fault that Carla's gone...'

'What do you mean by telling the little girl on the switchboard to lie
yesterday? You know we never ask her to say ''we're in conference'' or ''away''
or any other untruth...'

'Everybody in business knows white lies are necessary...'

'Not here.'

'What do you want me to do?'

'I want you to resign.'

'I won't.'

'You were in London. Not in Manchester.'

Blotches suffused his golfer's ruddy complexion. Clue perhaps to guilt
unmasked, I bluffed: 'If you'll resign I won't take any action against you...'

Debonair again, he laughed: 'That a promise? All right then, I resign ... I've
enjoyed our long run together...'

Harry Binder whom I phoned for a formal resignation note for Mr
Hetherington to sign was about to leave his office: Spend the week-end with us,
Phyllis. Joan and I would like you to help us amuse Lord Remnant at a cocktail

party this evening ... He calls me "Harry" so I can call him "Jim" don't you think?'

On handing me the required note with carbon copy, he voiced my own fear: 'Let's hope that the So and So won't have changed his mind in the interim!'

But to my relief Mr Hetherington on the Monday signed.

Asked how and when he would like to leave he replied: 'If it's all right with you, why don't I just disappear quietly at the end of the week ... same as any normal Friday...'

'I won't give you away ...' I promised.

At 8 the following Monday morning Fred Bond phoned me: 'You're going to have to tell the whole sad story. Nigel's with me ... Dave Hetherington had them all down to drinks at the pub on Friday night. Where he told them he was leaving because of the clash of personalities between him and you ... They seem to have taken his side against you.'

'He knew better than to invite me!' said Nigel: 'Ken Palmer tells me twenty Greater London Atlases are missing...'

'Don't worry ... We don't have to accuse him of dishonesty ... It's all in the correspondence I'll bring round to show them...'

At 10 o'clock precisely, Fred, convalescent Mr Stewart and I sat behind my desk. Back to the inside wall. (Like the Spanish Guardia Civil in their historic last stand, I thought — forever commemorated by the flat-back to their shiny black hats.)

Carrying their own chairs, the disaffected staff filed in.

They neither greeted me nor I them.

At last, after much scuffling and moving ups and downs, they settled into place, facing us.

Handing them my batch of documents, I said: 'Please read these letters and pass them round ... As you'll see, they're from our solicitors, accountants, suppliers ... and explain why sadly Mr Hetherington has left us ...'

In silence, they read. In silence thereafter awaiting my summing up.

'One of the British qualities I love best is that we take the side of the loser ...' I said: 'But now, let's bury the past ... and on we go...'

Said Mr Bond, standing up: 'Isn't it better that Mrs Pearsall has had us here to tell us this, than that the business is broke and we've all lost our jobs.'

# CHAPTER 30

IN womanly desire to cleanse corruption out of the boardroom Mrs Stewart and I set-to with broom, mop, brush and pan, Hoover, duster.

While Bernard Davis rummaged at the shop; and phoned me: 'The scoundrel's been regularly going up to London to pay in the shop's takings. The cheques and Postal Orders, yes he did; but the cash he pocketed ... We can't prove anything though as he himself entered the amounts in the Paying-In-Book — "to save you trouble, Pete ..." But when you promised you'd take no action if he resigned, he thought you'd tumbled to it ... and so agreed to.'

Back in Sevenoaks, however, rummage in Mr H's locked desk drawer, brought forth acceptable proof: 'I've got him!' whooped the sleuth: 'Look at this cheque stub! There's been a scratching out here ... not quite obliterated...'

Confirmation came from the bank with a copy of the relevant cheque. Crowed Mr Davis: '£750 he purloined! See! So that's how the crook bamboozled us! and to boot, the Company's bought him a lawn-mower...'

'Well that's that!' I said.

'I've also found over £1,000 of cheques made out to you and not credited to your Glyn Mills personal account...'

'I'll still keep my promise not to prosecute him...'

'It's no longer a matter of promises ... We as auditors are bound by law to do so.'

Charged in Sevenoaks Magistrates Court, his barrister's plea for clemency — 'Trouble at home with his twins delicate, and new-born son ill; trouble at work with daily harrassment from his woman Chairman' — reduced the charge from embezzlement to Petty Larceny. He was given three years probation.

Before the Court case, Ted Bould called at the office: 'How's tricks, Mrs P.?' he greeted me, notebook in hand: 'Time for my next order!'

'No! Never do we buy another ounce of paper from you!'

'You can't mean it! You wouldn't want to force me to sell my pride and joy! My new MG ... The red one in your parking place...'

'I meant what I said at our last unpleasant meeting Mr Bould.'

'But that was in the heat of the moment ... I'll drop in on good old Dave! He'll look after me as I've always looked after him...'

'So you don't know what's happened! ... He's being prosecuted for embezzlement...'

Ted Bould's effrontery slumped to horror.

(Three months later, he phoned me in trembling voice: 'What's happened to Dave?

In happy contrast, Roy Dewar — whose simple but striking cover designs boosted sales — and whom we all liked, welcomed Mr Hetherington's departure: 'Never a friend of mine! ... Just our club's unreliable treasurer to say the least...'

Final repercussion came in September. From Mr Leadbetter. When, our overdraft paid off I transferred our account to the Midland's Sevenoaks branch.

'How could you!' he phoned me at my flat: 'After all I've done for you!'

'You never expected us to succeed, did you?'

'No I admit it ... With the rogues there are about I didn't see how a woman could...'

'All our debts are paid off, and our three months' profit is £16,000 ... Goodbye.'

Meanwhile, Fred and I asked Nigel to take charge of Sales and the General Office: 'We'll be supporting you ... Never must any single one of us have to bear anxiety alone.'

Taut, face chalk-white, Nigel accepted: '... If it'll help ... though I'd rather not.'

'Good!' said Fred: 'We'd all rather not. But we can't do better than our best'; and sadly mused: 'I gave my loyalty to the two of them, Les Connor and then to Dave Hetherington ... Now look what's happened...'

'Perhaps it's just as well', I tried to comfort him: 'At least we'll know never to cause such grief to those who trust us.'

Thus out of disaster — though it took a year to persuade Nigel to become a director — we formed the triumvirate which was to propel A to Z enthusiastically forward for the next quarter of a century and beyond — based on truth, care for the individual, quality of maps and service to the customer. And I thanked God:

*Behold, how good and joyful a thing it is brethren to dwell together in unity.*

# CHAPTER 31

'WE'VE been given a week's notice! The lot of us! Even poor old Mr Potter and Mr Trent who've been here fifty years! It'll be the death of them!' lamented Mr Rolfe. Curtain expert at Druce's soft furnishing shop on the corner of Baker Street, he had phoned me to come at once: 'to fetch your bathroom blind...'

This evil he explained in shocked spate of words 'leapt on us this morning like a wild beast ... They must have known ... they should have warned us ... so we could find other jobs; that's to say the lucky younger ones like me...'

The reason for such treatment, he went on to tell me, was the death of their owner Mr Druce some months ago — 'Only a few days before he'd popped in to see us ... to greet each of us by name, to admire our handiwork ...' Mr Rolfe's eyes filled with tears — 'a good governor. One of the best ... He'd never have sold us down the river. Steady profits like ours not big enough for them financiars, I suppose, so they close down our side of the business.'

Deathly pale and reduced to zombies were the victims.

Aghast, I took a taxi to my solicitors.

'How can I prevent any such catastrophe happening to my dear colleagues on my death?'

Asking for time to think it over, he smiled: 'Meanwhile you'd better stay alive...'

An appointment made, Mr Bond accompanied me.

'To safeguard your staff completely', begun Mr Ffrench: 'We'd have to form a Trust holding 100% of the Company shares for their benefit.'

'How?' I asked.

'Leave that to me ... As a matter of fact, I'm Chairman of a Trust that'd fit yours like a glove...'

'Oh no! It must be our own Trust...'

'That can be worked out later. Let's settle on the main issue. Do you want such a Trust or not?'

'Yes.'

'What does it entail?' asked Fred.

'Firstly that Mrs Pearsall and her brother would have to sell all their shares to the Trust...'

'Who'd pay?' I asked.

'The Company ... On its present showing there'd be no difficulty in raising a loan.'

'For how much? ... We've only just got over the Hetherington horror of debt.'

'That would depend on the valuation...'

'Valuation?'

'Of the shares.'

'But they're only worth £1 each...'

'When you started the Company, yes ... Not now. A reputable auditor will have to assess their present value. I know the very man.'

'What'll that cost?'

'Are we really going to have to quibble over every penny?'

'Yes. I like to know where I am. We run the business by housekeeping, don't we Mr Bond?'

'Can you give us some idea of the fee?' said Fred. To which Mr Ffrench replied: 'An established percentage of the total value...'

Then sitting back in his Chippendale armchair he warned me: 'You'd be committing yourself to a lifelong sacrifice. For a start, you, your brother and his issue will be forever totally excluded from receiving any Trust benefit. Secondly, you'll no longer own or control your Company, Mrs Pearsall...'

'But we need her to run the business!' exploded Mr Bond.

'The business, yes. But as an employee. And at that the only employee deprived of Trust benefits such as pension...'

'But that's not fair!' interrupted Mr Bond.

'Will you let me finish, Bond!'

'You can be pretty tough, Mr Ffrench!' I chipped in.

'Never with you my dear ... Now for your decision. Do you instruct me to let the whole matter drop? ... or to take the necessary steps to form your Trust? ... We could call it "The Phyllis Pearsall Trust"'.

'No. "Geographers' Trust" or "A to Z" ... If it weren't for my loyal colleagues there'd be no business'; and turning to Fred I asked: 'Are you ready for another plunge into what ship engineers call "grief" ... and for God knows how long?'

'For the sake of our future security, yes.'

'That does it! Go ahead, Mr Ffrench.'

A momentous decision; fraught with awesome responsibility and unforeseen consequences.

The shares valued at £82,500 (plus Stamp Duty and professional fees), the Company could not possibly affort to buy both Tony and me out.

'So I'll give mine', I told Mr Ffrench.

'I'm not sure I can allow that ...' he pondered: 'I've got to look after your interests, your security you know ... And there's no reason why the Company shouldn't go on borrowing for however many years it takes...'

'To you a Company is nothing more than a legal entity. To us it's blood, sweat and tears ... At last we've been able to climb out of crippling debt to comparative security ... a plateau where we can breathe pure mountain air and forge upward ... To put such an onerous financial burden on our business, is putting it onto us ... onto us flesh and blood people! ... Far easier for me to give from my pocket what I've never had ... My mother died destitute. What's it to me if I do?'

'Nobody's going to thank you for it ... Staff never do. Why worry about them? They won't worry about you!'

'"Give! And throw it away over your shoulder", say the Arabs.'

'Aren't you being a little emotional, my dear; and naive. In any case Inland Revenue wouldn't let you. They'd suspect some secret arrangement for future reimbursement ... You'd have to accept some token payment ... The real dilemma is that the Trust can't be constituted until financed; and a Trust account can't be opened until the Trust is constituted ... Anyway, have you ascertained whether your brother's willing to sell? ...'

'He's sure to ...' I predicted.

The raising of £55 or £60,000 the priority, I approached my friend Andrew McFadyean, now Chairman of Warburg's — (not only out of gratitude for having rescued the merchant banker and his family from Hitler Germany but because of proved ability.) Who made an appointment for me with one of the directors, Raymond Bonham Carter, at my flat for the following Friday 'after putting him *au fait* about you at lunch with Dora and me...'

Before such visits to London, my hair — wind-swept from painting out of doors and pre-breakfast walks in Knole Park — needed taming. About to pay the hairdresser, I found I had left my purse at home. 'Pay next time', said the proprietor; but the assistant, to whom I promised a double tip 'next time' wistfully renounced it: 'I'm leaving to-day. Going North ... to get married.'

The Midland Bank was just across the High Street. On an island formed by its convergence with London Road. A red brick edifice resembling a gargantuan corner cupboard; but at 3.40pm, closed against the public.

I pressed the bell. After a pause, I heard the turning of a massive key in the lock; bolts drawn back; the creak of the great door — held by its clinking chain — as it opened to a chink — and the angry voice of a man peering through: 'What'd'you want?'

'Half a crown...'

'The books are closed for the day!' he barked; slammed the door, re-locked and bolted it.

I rang again. Again he opened: 'You again!' But, foot in chink like any desperado, I asked if the manager were in.

'That depends who wants him and for why...'

My name brought him running: 'Your account's one of my most progressive!' he said; and red-carpeting me to his office: 'So good of you to call. What can I do for you?'

'I'd like half a crown please ...' Handing me the coin, he laughed: 'Only half a crown! Surely there's something more?...'

'Funnily enough there might be...'

Told about the Trust and the loan needed, he welcomed the chance of another good account and a safe investment: 'Your Company's got over £60 thou in credit! It'll be a cinch! ... I'd grant it here and now ... but at my Branch, any sum over £10,000 has to go to Head Office...'

'Don't do anything yet ... Warburg's have first option. I'm seeing one of their directors tomorrow...'

'Couldn't you tell him it's just an exploratory talk? ... After all you've banked with the Midland since the thirties ... and if we can lend 33 million to Imperial Tobacco we're not going to jib at your much lesser requirement...'

Mr Bonham Carter, briefed by Andrew, and shown our Balance Sheets, seemed favourably inclined: 'I like the idea of employees receiving full reward for their services. But' he added: *Sans indiscretion,* as the French say to preface one, how old are you?

'Nearly 59.'

'Rather too old for a long-term advance...'

'But the running of the business is totally delegated to my colleagues, and as you can see they're running it successfully ... I'm only called in for crises!'

'A company is only kept afloat by the person who meets crises! ... Which means, my dear, that Warburg's answer has to be NO.'

The Midland manager, handed my formal request for the loan, beamed with delight: 'Head Office will oblige, I'm sure ... You can safely go ahead with your public-spirited scheme.'

That preoccupation settled as I thought, another leapt to the fore — whether to join some existing trust or create our own. And I sought further advice.

'Your solicitor will be asking you for a Letter of Intent'. said Andrew: 'Write your intentions now; and make sure that they're embodied in the legal Articles they produce. Always weigh commonsense and truth against professional jargon ... But at the risk of repetition, never forget, Phyllis that you're an artist...'

Michael Robson (also a friend through my paintings) proposed I sell our Company to his international one: 'You'd be safer with us than with solicitors!'

'Take-over's just what I'm trying to avoid...'

'I'll pay you a quarter of a million now by cheque.'

'No Michael.'

'Good for you! I just wanted to make sure you mean what you say. Now for my advice which you needn't take. The nub is to choose the right Trustees ... and who can ever know until it comes to the crunch who are the right ones ... It's difficult for you to realise, Phyllis, how many would gain self importance by a trusteeship; possibly get overdrafts on it; try to borrow money from it — counting on your ignorance, exert accepted malpractice influence on the young and impressionable members of your staff even attempt to bribe them and eventually push you out in the cold. In addition to yourself, who are you considering as trustees?'

'My two co-directors. They've proved their loyalty, and their care for others; nor are they greedy. For money, status or restaurant show-off. But because we've just got over our second dishonest director I'd like one or two outside Trustees to ensure nothing like that ever happens again ... Would you, Michael?'

'I'm too often out of the country ... Anyway you know you can always count on me if any rotter tries to do you down...'

Helen Benham, whose house I was drawing on commission, warned: 'Whatever you do, don't give shares to the staff! It'll do them no good. My brother and I — on inheriting my father's electrical business — made the mistake of giving them the lot. To reward them, we thought; but in fact as we were architects, to be shut of the responsibility. So what happened. Within a few months their spokesman came to us: "We've got an offer for the shares. It's too good to be refused. Shall we sell?" ... "You're free to do whatever you want", I said: "But that'll be the end of your jobs." ...' "Oh no! They've promised to keep us all on!" ... "In writing?" I asked ... "They're gentlemen. Their word's good enough for us." ... So they sold, Phyllis. And within six months everyone of them was sacked...'

Bernard Miller, Chairman of The John Lewis Partnership, sent me a copy of John Spedan Lewis's book on its principles, formation and growing pains — with covering letter:

> ... When you're ready to form your Trust, please lunch with me and bring your solicitor — the legal side's very complicated — and I'll give you the benefit of my experience such as it is...

In his monk's cell of a sixth floor office, this small wiry man propagated his founder's beliefs. In humility, understanding of human nature and strong yet gentle directorship: 'Your Trust musn't be a welfare state within our Welfare State ... People need to be built into responsibility...'

'What do you think of lawyers?' I asked.

'A necessary evil. Good at lining their pockets. But know nothing of business.'

Mr Peter Foster, the solicitor's younger partner, was shown in. 'Mr Miller agrees with me that we've got to beware of solicitors in business ... and I suppose you're an academic too! ...' I greeted him in jest (unaware how hurtful to so sensitive a man.)

Legal and monetary aspects discussed over a canteen lunch included a query from Mr Foster: 'How many years before your founders' shares were fully paid up?'

'The bombing and re-building of our Oxford Street premises delayed it somewhat ... But over Mrs Pearsall's Trust, what's your thinking about Trustees?'

'She has intimated five. Three Inside ones: her two co-directors and herself. (She unpaid — excluded as donor of her shares from benefitting) and two Outside. For one of which Mr Ffrench offers his services as Chairman.'

Said Mr Miller: 'Any outside trustee would be anathema to me! Lacking day to day knowledge of the business and its staff, he'd be bound to meddle!...'

Nigel I knew felt as strongly; but — still obsessed with the Bird and Hetherington sagas — I agreed.

Mr Miller, seeing us to the lift, promised continuing support. (A promise kept throughout decades.)

As other outside trustee, I chose a wartime friend of mine. But on his being sent to Africa, by the Foreign Office (a bureaucratic waste of a Chinese scholar), I replaced him with one of our suppliers.


'High time to ascertain your brother's willingness to sell ...' said Mr Ffrench. Tony was in Minneapolis setting up a print department for their Art College on the lines of his own at the Slade, I told him.

'I'll see him in New York. Where I'm flying for another client — 'thus splitting the costs, Phyllis.' — There they rendez-vous-ed. There, ignoring Mr Ffrench's advice — 'It means giving up future rise in A to Z shares for money down?' — Tony joyfully accepted: 'A windfall!!! Daisy'll be ravie! ... *En tout cas,* I like the idea of the A to Z chaps running the business for themselves. And by the way what shall I do with all this money?'

'I'll invest it for you, Gross ...' offered the solicitor: 'a sound portfolio ... I know the very man.' A kind offer Tony gratefully accepted.

But the money to pay off Tony, plus other Trust expenses was still not forthcoming. Still no word from the Midland Bank's Head Office though they had been approached a year ago.

'Only a fortnight to our Trust's Consolidation date!' I urged the Branch manager: 'Whom do I phone or meet to get their Yes or No before Monday the 4th of April?'

'Of course it'll be Yes. Just leave it to me', he smiled: 'They must be overloaded with work!...'

Not until the Friday before D.Day — April Fool's day — did I hear from him. On the phone. In sombre voice: 'I'm afraid I've got bad news. Due to the government's new Credit Squeeze, Head Office have been forced to turn down your request ... We at the Midland stick by the rules. Then we can't go wrong ... I can't tell you how sorry I am ... What will you do?'

Fred Bond was at my elbow. For half a second — I had done all I could and failed — I was tempted to give up.

'What next?' asked Fred.

'I'll phone my friend Michael Robson.'

'Never! He wanted to buy us up!'

'Only to test me ... I trust him implicitly'; and, my hand still shaking, dialled his office number: 'A last minute hitch!' I told him: 'The Midland have just said "No"'.

'Where do you keep your personal account?'

'Holt's branch, Glyn Mills ... But I've never had more than £10 in it ...

through always ploughing back every penny into the business,

'Phone them in a quarter of an hour!'

I did so; asked for the manager; was put through, asked: 'Are you the manager?

'Yes.'

'I want to borrow £55,000...'

'I'd better put you through to the manager.'

A charming fellow, introducing himself as Mr Peachey Edwards, agreed to lend it.

'But you'll want to see our Balance Sheets', I demurred: 'I could rush up to London with them now...'

'No need, my dear. You can give us sight of them whenever it suits you.'

'I'll immediately move our business account to Glyn Mills.'

'There's no need to ... and by the way, we're not a merchant bank so the loan will have to be renewed every year ... But there'll be no difficulty about that...'

(Never — during the quarter of a century since — has Michael mentioned his part in it. But one of the funny stories he likes to relate is of tapping his umbrella against the outside window of Holt's Chairman's office, and teasing: 'Just to stop you getting pompous, Piggy!' — the obvious schoolboy nickname for surname Hogg.)

Rejoicing, I phoned the Midland manager: 'You'll be pleased to hear we've raised the money ... but sorry that you're losing our account to Glyn Mills.'

'Oh God! We've made a terrible mistake! How long can you give us?'

Still euphoric, Fred and I ran into the drawing office: 'Mrs Pearsall's got good news for you!' he said.

'It's our tea-break ...' objected Mike Manning to an echoed growl.

'We're turning the business into a partnership Trust! To prevent us being taken over, or outsiders put over your heads,' I rejoiced.

Said another: 'Better if we were taken over! More money would be put in ... an end to scrimping...'

'They take money out ... as Geographia's Dennis Stevenson has bemoaned to Mr Bond and me...'

Said Mustafa: 'So we'd be given shares?'

'No', I said; and Fred: 'We're only human and might be tempted to sell ... not just out of greed but because of family illness or such like.'

'Then it's not a Partnership!' scoffed Mike: 'I suppose we'll be able to elect the directors?'

'No', I said. Again Fred explained, 'That would mean popular showy directors instead of proven ones...'

'So all this song and dance isn't going to make the slightest difference to us!'

'Except that when I die it'll be up to you to carry the business forward ... to your advantage as a team. Instead of for outside shareholders interested only in Balance Sheets ...' I tried to explain: 'and to whom you as people wouldn't matter two hoots!...'

'Mrs Pearsall's giving up her security for us ...' chimed in Fred: '... not to speak of the fortune she's entitled to...'

Mr Roberts drove Mr Ffrench to our office. We lunched him well. 'An excellent claret', he declared after connoisseur ritual, as he did on accepting Fred's proffered Havana cigar and cutter: 'Now let's call in the *hoi polloi*, Bond, what?'

The table cleared and turned to face the room, and the Spanish episcopal chair of carved walnut upholstered in Cordova leather moved from its ornamental corner to the centre for him. Where, puffing regally at his Corona he sat in state.

A strange and impressive sight for his audience. So was his prolix speech on trusts in general as, through my own failure, to clarify my intentions he thought them to be; and at my sotto voce interruption benignly told me; ''it'll be your turn in a moment my dear to voice your feelings.'' Then, rising from his antique seat, he stretched out his arms towards them, perorated: 'From this day forth each of you owns the business! You! You! You! You behind there!' he said pointing at each in turn; and to the lad from the warehouse who flushed with self-importance: 'You!'

'Me too?' asked Mrs Griffin.

'Yes you Madam too! ... And now Mrs Pearsall would like to wish you well on this crucial day...'

''Devil's guts'' is the Sussex name for a particular rank and tenacious weed. As ineradicable were those true yet misunderstood words — and as quick flowering.

From next day on deputations about bad management streamed into Fred's office; particularly from the draughtsmen once a fortnight or so — despite his hope: 'We draughtsmen are concerned with drawing maps as well as we can, not with how the business is run...'

Finally, during a national paper shortage, he arranged for them to talk over their worries with me.

'Why don't we print in Yugo-Slavia?' asked one; having just spent a holiday in Split.

'Because the Yugo-Slavs are not reliable', I said: 'The Czecho-Slovaks are. The Director of a Prague photo-litho plant came to see us last week. Accompanied by a Politbureau watch-dog — as he whispered when the man left for the toilet: ''don't give me away, but we Czechs abhor our present masters ... Sh! I hear him coming!'''

'Here's his book on Prague', said Fred, sensing their disbelief.

'Look!' I said: 'Aren't these buildings beautiful ... the old bridge ... Just as I remember it.'

'You know it then', said Mustafa: 'And Yugoslavia?'

I nodded and continued: 'But he can't take on our printing as his machines are booked up for years on Hamlyn publications.'

Our answers to their other questions they also accepted.

Mustafa rose to his feet: 'As you've dealt with all the points we've been thinking about, we'd better get back to our drawing'; and they followed him out. Mike Manning too; though that evening he complained to Jack: 'Nobody's satisfied...'

So the two of them and I stayed on late.

'Who else?' I asked.

'I don't want to give anyone away...'

'Rubbish!' I said: 'This isn't the Politbureau. I suggest there isn't anybody else. So what's your personal gripe?'

'Very well then. After all the years I've worked here, I ought to be further on ... Not moneywise ...' he added quickly; (for he knew — as Fred had told me — that a today's "Situations Vacant" entry for "indexer with fluent French German Spanish" offered a lower salary than his.) 'What for instance?' asked Jack.

'I should be a Director by now.'

'And if you were a director what would you do?' asked I.

'For a start all that money you're holding for tax I'd give to us workers!...'

'You do a marvellous indexing job Mike ... But thank God you're not a director!'

In due course, with Fred and Nigel's warm approval, Mr Peter Foster took over our Trust's Chairmanship from his senior partner.

Nevertheless Bernard Miller had been right about Outside Trustees lacking day to day knowledge of the business. Only those within could eschew as passing fashion the clichés put to us as panaceas: — Diversify; Forecast; Advertise, with its spawn of Market Research and Opinion Polls; Time & Motion, that Office Equipment con. Their cliche thoughts they also expressed in catchwords of the time: Sophistication, Communication, Inducement, Relationships, Positive, Aggressive, Caring, Supportive. Though Housekeeping's reign brought momentary sweet harmony: 'How right you've been!' Permanent friction however stemmed from the generally accepted 'change of hats' policy for a person combining executive roles — in our case, that of Trustee, Director of the Trustee Company and Company Director.

'We always act simply to our conscience as in ordinary life', I objected; and once again asked solicitor Peter: 'Aren't we supposed to follow my letter of Intent?'

'Of course!'

'Most founders of Trusts are dead ... so their intentions can be misinterpreted ad lib', I laughed: 'But I'm alive. And won't let you! We'll stick to truth, kindness, high standards of quality, encouragement of talent and greater efficiency than rat-racers ... As Francois de Sales implies, if one is aspiring to a devout life in the world, one should excel in worldly matters without becoming attached to them...'

'I'm speaking of the law...', said Peter; and I: 'On that we rely on you to advise us. We're totally law-abiding: "Render unto Caesar the things which be Caesar's ..."' And, to myself, "and unto God the things which be God's" ... "God is spirit and God is truth" ... and "thou shalt love the Lord Thy God with all thy heart, and with all thy soul, and with all thy mind, and with all thy strength ... and thou shalt love thy neighbour as thyself. There is no other commandment greater than these." — Yet never abandoning commensense.'

As had been done in our Trust set-up. For due to a quirk in it — making it obligatory to pay tax on our Capital repayments — we could never redeem our Glyn Mills debt.

'It's breaking our back!' I told Peter. Whose outstanding legal brain at length found a way out: 'We'll form a new Company with Directors instead of Trustees; but the Trustees will still remain Trustees of The Map Trust ... Do you understand?'

'Of course not.'

'Well you'll have to. It'll involve the shares having to be revalued, and any Capital Gains paid by you and your brother.'

'But the declaration he and I signed stated that neither he nor I would be responsible for tax...'

'Income tax, not Capital Gains...'

'However much it is, I'll have to pay Tony's. I promised him there'd be no deductions from the capital paid him...'

'That's up to you...'

Yet another tax catch. In this new set-up, tax payment had to be brought forward a year, explained Peter.

'But how can they assess the profit?'

'They base it on the year before; and make any adjustment on the next.'

'Do we ever get the money back?'

'Only if you go into liquidation...'

'It's costing the Company a further £60,000!'.

'Non-recurrent ... You'll only feel it this year,' he assuaged.

And I speculated: 'What other unknowns are going to rear their ugly heads?'

Thus did we continue to drive blindfold through the arcane maze of cold-blooded legal gobbledygook; and through every Budget lassoo — lawyer and accountant enriching — thrown by Chancellors of the Exchequer.

An enigmatic load — added to our routine tandem of Net Profit and Cash Credit.

'Fret not thyself, or thou shalt be moved to do evil', I told myself.

But meanwhile, our turnover dropping, the business needed full attention. For paradoxically, whereas in the mid '30's, the trade wanted nothing new, now, 30 years on, our reps on showing their range were ad nauseum pestered for something new: 'Same old things?'

The drawing office were bogged down in the Master London scheme. Particularly, as Jack put it, 'by the headache of fudging the distorted edges of the L.C.C. area to butt onto the start of the extensions.' Thus Fred and I devised a One Way Street Map with Parking Places based on our 6″ Central London. Any drawing needed, he did; as well as plotting by dividers, from written regulations, the extent of Parking Meters. As to One Way Streets, I called at nearby Police stations where they marked them on a mounted wall map — but only those in their own district. At one, instead of marking, they pinned onto it little coloured flags — which, dusted off by their zealous cleaning lady, were stuck back by her, 'any old 'ow!' she admitted. Meantime Fred had obtained them all from Scotland Yard. From their department "for routing abnormal loads."

A bonus of working on the ground, was the discovery of map errors; such as a large hole in the ground instead of St Pancras Town Hall: 'The Town Hall's been gone ten years or more', complained the local librarian: 'Why are the Ordnance Survey and the rest of you map makers so appallingly out of date!?'

Brought out in May, this stop-gap map restored our sales: 'Something new at last!' said the buyers.

Said Nigel: 'I hope it'll see us through until the Master Atlas appears ...' But Jack could not promise it till January. We were now June.

'What's the hold-up? I asked him: 'You said the maps were already at Lowe & Brydone. Is it the Index?'

'Yes; Mike couldn't get started until we'd paged the maps.'

'We've got to have it on sale in September!' I said: ''To catch the Christmas market! So as to pay off the remaining £16,000 owed Glyn Mills.'

'Mike says he can't get it done any sooner.'

'Can't he get help?'

'You know Mike. He can't work with anyone. Nobody else'll be accurate enough for him!'

'Right! I'll do it!' said I: 'Of course he'll object even more to me ...' and to Mike: 'What page do you want me to start on?'

Soon in the swing (my pre-war indexing a boon), I worked from 6am to 8pm. To Mike's morose — 'What does it make me look like you here from dawn to nightfall while I start at 8 and knock off at 4.30!' — I responded sincerely: 'But look how much more accurate you are! The reputation you've helped build for us! ... Anyway there's only the alphabeticising left to do ... Let's do it together ... Shall I start at the "Ms"?'

On the 9th of September, the first lorry load of Master Atlases arrived at Vestry Road. 'Eureka!' cried the representatives as they carried them to their vans: 'Even at 57/6d it'll sell like hot cakes!' It did.

Thus in two years instead of ten, we paid back Glyn Mills. As David Churchill told the Sevenoaks Midland bank manager. Who replied — as ruefully reported to me — that Glyn Mills had had no right to ask for our account.

'That's libel!' I said; and phoned him: 'David and I'll be with you in ten minutes ... Oh! You've got a lunch appointment? Cancel it.'

White-faced behind his desk, the manager asked 'What's the trouble?'

Reminding him of the events leading to the transfer of our account — my need to borrow half a crown to tip the hairdresser, his offer to fund our Trust, his Head Office procrastination and ultimate refusal — and ended: 'It was I who decided to transfer our account to Glyn Mills. They never asked me. So never again please say they did...'

'How I envy you your memory', he said.

# PART IV
## 1963 to the Horizon

# ON WE GO

# CHAPTER 32

ALWAYS a relief to turn from law to the clarity and practical application of running Geographers' A to Z, it was joyous above all to continue as ever to discuss problems openly with my like-minded business associates — who by mutual respect and humour had blossomed into affectionate friends. Foremost of course — after what we had gone through together — my stalwart colleagues, Fred and Nigel. And, except for one or two "chip on the shoulder" grumblers and high-fliers, the rest of our growing conscientious and talented team. In particular, Company Secretary David Churchill; Stock Controller Ken Palmer; Chief Draughtsman Jack Archibald; and though with less over-all responsibility, Mustafa Zihni; John Frankel (wed to Mustafa's beautiful and skilled daughter, still working in the drawing office); and gentle Norman Dennison. Amongst the representatives: good loyal George Elston, Reg Peters, Bill Jaggs. And ultimate manager of the shop, David Taylor.

Gerritt Groen, about to retire, warned me of his successors: 'My son, sadly, is more interested in stationery than in the fine publications we pride ourselves on at the Drikkerij Thieme. So I wouldn't like your A to Z in his hands...'

They were giving me a farewell dinner in their Mathonsingel home; and Juup broke in: 'I know it's a terrible thing for a mother to say, but during the Nazi Occupation, we had to bring up our children with two moralities — to speak the truth to us but lie to the Germans. For at night, Gerritt printed for the Resistance...'

'Whenever I see a German, I still see the swastika on his arm ...' he brooded; and she: '... but remember how ashamed we were when the Americans bombed Nijmegen by mistake, and our own people tore the rings, jewels and clothing from the dead ... And then even the British soldiers were throwing away bacon fat when we were starving ... All right how could they understand. They were nice boys ... they didn't think.'

'So's my son a nice boy', warned Gerritt: 'But before he takes over you'll have to deal with my deputy.' Who at downward wobble in sterling, phoned our office in panic: 'Either you pay me immediately for all your work in hand and on order, or I take your London A to Z off the machine!'

'What did you do?' I asked Fred and Nigel phoning me at Backsettown.

'We can't risk running out of A to Zs., so we've agreed to send him the £25,000 ... though it'll leave us cash tight.'

Experience had taught me a better solution, I told them: 'Ring the bank, and buy Dutch guilders in advance...'

Following Gerritt's advice, we moved our A to Z printings to England. Our runs now too long for letterpress or sheet litho, we switched to web-offset. To Hazell, Watson & Viney at Aylesbury. Whose representative, Mr Ede, had persisted in calling on us since the David Hetherington days in Gray's Inn Road. No Mr Groen was he. We had to curb his habit of lunches, drinks and gifts to susceptible employees; and, because he peppered his conversation with — 'In confidence' — information about other publishers, had to be wary of what we told him.

Years on Sid Wells — 'I feel part of the A to Z family anyway' — wondered if he should merge with us to safeguard his wife and daughter: 'A lovely girl, my daughter. Terrible trouble with the husband she'd left.'

After a day's discussion over lunch in our boardroom, Peter Foster and our new kind local auditor, Philip Boobyer, decided against Sid merging with us; and advised him what steps to take. That his doctor had given him only a few months to live, he did not divulge. Nor soon after when he again asked to see me.

'Trouble Sid?' I asked, as he joined Fred and me.

'Yes. Serious.'

'If it's money, you can have any amount you need!'

'That's a dangerous thing to say!'

'You took a risk with me when we were desperate...'

'No. It's not money ... It's advice. I'm building new printing works on a site I've bought. It'll be a little while before I can shift my plant there. But I can't renew my lease short-term ... It's either 25 years or nothing...'

Said Fred: 'Have him repair the place before you sign for the lease, you can always sub-let...'

'You've got it, Fred! Thank you! The moment I crossed the A to Z threshold I felt better ... Bless you both for letting me clear my mind by talking my problems over with you! ... With true friends who won't pull the carpet from under my feet...'

'What a lovely friendship it's been!', I said as we hugged each other goodbye.

Mr Bernard Miller — now Sir Bernard — kept a paternal eye on our Trust, and rejoiced at the gradual development I reported of team spirit, the patient and generous passing on of the draughtsmens' skill to school leaver trainees, the aim of excellence in all departments; and the continued steady growth of a happy business: '... despite the bad augury of carping when I first announced the Trust', I added.

'Don't I know it!' he laughed: 'Staff are naturally apprehensive at any change. As to how it's going to affect them and their families ... On another tack, I'll never forget John Spedan's fear that his father would find out his plans for future staff participation. With me, for instance. Taken on by John, I had to wear morning suit and a silk hat: "So that if the old man sees you he'll think you're one of the floor-walkers…" Now it's I who — to carry out his wish — am training my successor, his nephew Peter Lewis. John Spedan's brother Oswald's son … God bless him.'

And now, on my beloved Mr Brydone's ninety seventh birthday, I visited him at Lowe & Brydone. Frail, but sitll working, because the fine young men he had trained to take his place had died before him or been forced by ill health to retire. Including Harry Williams, who today had driven up from Goring on Sea, to pay his respects to his old Governor. To our mutual delighted surprise.

'Isn't it wonderful, Sir!' he exclaimed: 'that we printed the very first A to Z! … And it's now a household name! … On our two colour quad demy at Perfecter price to keep the machine busy…'

With nostalgic smile, Mr Brydone took my hand in his: 'I knew the little lady would succeed … But more important than that, dear Mrs Pearsall, you've made better provision for your loyal staff than I have! By giving your shares to a Trust holding 100% for their benefit … Sadly, I've given mine to the wrong people! Out for what they can get! Money and status ridden everyone of them! Wasting my Company's hard-earned money on showy cars, on feasting customers in restaurants and pubs! I've never offered you more than a slopped cup of tea — "You're behind the times!" they tell me: "Nowadays everybody knows a big expense account's essential!"

Even their cliches "We weren't born yesterday" and "Too much like hard work" are a nefarious influence on the young … teaching them to scoff at generosity and duty … Not one of them understands! … Only when sorrow or disaster bring their pride down on their journey, will they learn! … But meanwhile, alas the business'll topple with them…'

(Prognosis fulfilled only too soon after his death.)

After a pause for breath, the firm's creator sighed: 'But I'm too tired to do anything about it … All we poor humans are in the hands of the Almighty…'

With a butterfly kiss on his paper-thin brow, I murmered my gratitude: 'I know I've thanked you for giving me credit whenever we were in financial trouble … for generous offers of money … for your trust in me … But have I ever thanked you for your example? The first business boss in my life I could respect and attempt to emulate. Combining mercy and truth, always kind and firm; patiently training the young men in skill and character — with never a raised voice … The keeping on of the aged and infirm whether capable or not … and so much more…'

I fell silent. Transcendentally behind his silver head of hair, rose a Fra Angelico golden halo.

At length he answered: 'Not unto us, not unto us, but unto Thee O Lord the praise! … It's rare indeed isn't it that we're shown how and when we're used …'

'How old were you when you first decided to tread this pilgrim path!'

'Twenty one ... I was reading my New Testament one morning — as, blessed with devout parents I do daily — when in a flash of heavenly light the words 'Be ye perfect as your Father in heaven is perfect' were illumined for me ... I've been trying and failing ever since.'

IN THE END IS THE BEGINNING.

Phyllis Pearsall painting Theatre Royal Haymarket Spring 1988, commissioned by the theatre management, photo N. Syrett.

# EPILOGUE
## 31st January, 1990

S TILL working at A to Z as Chairman and Joint Managing Director, and still painting, I have today — after many years, and in my 84th — finished writing this book.

Based almost entirely on memory (though from 1947 refreshed where relevant by colleagues), it spans only the years of greatest struggle: 1936 to 1966. For since then, whatever the hurdles encountered and surmounted, A to Z — manned by a superlative crew — has steadily sailed forward. Becoming ever more, through word of mouth recommendation, a household name.

In 1986, we celebrated our 50th Anniversary on a Thames pleasure boat with wives, husbands, children and babes in arms. And for me what happiness to see their joy and fun; to see the men and women I had known as boys and girls now parents — Fred Bond, Nigel Syrett even, grandfathers. A family business indeed, but the family not by inheritance but by worth. May God bless the ship and all who sail in her!

# APPENDIX A

## A-Z Publications with dates of first issue and up to 1966

*Pre-War 1936 to 1939*

Standard Map of the World
Standard Map of England and Wales
*A-Z Street Atlas of London
Standard Street Guide to London
*Premier Map of London
Ideal Guide to London
*35 Miles Round London
*London to the South East
*London to the South
London to the Sea
Famous Guide to London
Pictorial Souvenir of London

*War Maps 1939 to 1943*

The Western Front
Norway and Denmark
Holland and Belgium
Northern France
France from Rhine to Toulon
The Mediterranean
Finland
All-In-One War Map

*Still published though replanned
and redrawn

---

1946

**Pictorial Map of London
Handy London

1948

 Greater London Atlas
**55 London Views by Eliot Hodgkin

1949

**4 Sheet Map of London
England and Wales County
England and Wales Road

1950

Premier Leeds
Premier Birmingham
Premier Manchester

1951

Central London Map
**Premier Coventry
**Premier Glasgow
**Scotland County
**Scotland Road

1952

**Premier Wolverhampton
**Premier Walsall
Premier Bradford
**Premier West Midlands
**Bus — Underground Map

1953

A-Z Street Atlas of Birmingham
**Central London Atlas

202

**1956**

Main Road London
Postal London
**SE England ¼ "
**50 Mile Birmingham ¼ "

**1957**

**SW England ¼ "
**Wales ¼ "

**1959**

**Northern England ¼ "

**1960**

**NE England ¼ "
**S. Scotland ¼ "
**Scotland ¼ "
**NW Scotland ¼ "

**1961**

**GB Road Atlas ¼ "

**1963**

**City of London
**Essex
**Chertsey
A-Z Street Atlas of Manchester
Ashton-Under-Lyne
Altrincham and Sale
Bolton
Bury
Oldham
Swindon
Weymouth

**1964**

Birmingham Main Road
Exeter
Canterbury
Greater London Plan
Rochdale
Ramsgate, Margate and Broadstairs
Sevenoaks
Stockport
Stratford upon Avon
**Tunbridge Wells
Visitors' London Map

**1965**

Dover, Deal and Folkestone
Oxford
New Birmingham A-Z
Cornwall County
50 Mile Manchester
East Anglia
Plymouth
Reading
Taunton
Devon County

**1966**

Slough, Maidenhead

** Discontinued or replaced

# APPENDIX B

## Phyllis Pearsall's Letter of Intent to Trustees on foundation of Geographers' Map Trust (holding 100% of the shares for the employees)

I would like to write you this letter to put on record my personal approach to this Trust.

The reason I was willing to make any and every sacrifice to bring the Trust into being (and continue ready to do so to see it soundly established, God willing) is because of the human shock, distress and greed I have seen precipitated by the following present day accepted business practices:

1.  The selling up of a business where the staff were summarily dismissed. They were making curtains for me with care, personal attention and expertise. All working happily. One day I went in to find a black cloud over everybody. The life and purpose of many (some employees had served 30 and 40 years there) snapped by the shareholders' action. In U.S.A. I have seen people have strokes, die at similar treatment.

2.  Executives brought in from outside in a firm where the custom had always been to promote "its own timber", and as is the case so often, men or women with University qualifications put over the experienced personnel. Again, the life purpose of every individual right the way through, snapped. They were blocked for ever.

3.  Shares given or sold to employees. As the main shareholders usually kept share control of the business, this is often only a sop to keep employees happy. It adds to the already potential jealousy about wages and promotion — and leads to a less trustful working atmosphere.

    Where control was in fact given by share sharing, the temptation to sell was — despite previous owners' warning — "too good to be refused"; and the new owners' pre-purchase promise of continued employment was broken within six months. With hindsight, the employees regretted having accepted the lump sum — and lost their life's work and loyalties.

To make these three disasters impossible for the employees of Geographers' — as long as the firm quietly goes forward from its own inner map drawing growth, continues to be my aim. In the third case mentioned — even though our Trust would buy back shares, I feel that the extra greed and divisions caused by selling or distributing to our employees would more than offset any possible advantages of added incentive. It would kill the present happy and productive team spirit, carefully nurtured and maintained over many years.

Thus I make my aims clear. But we know that human foresight is limited, and the putting of a dead hand on anyone being abhorrent to me, the Trust Deed and Memorandum of Intent give my Trustees complete freedom. Nevertheless, the circular to the employees of July 1966 is a promise made to them which I regard as inviolate. Except in the event of wholly different circumstances I cannot foresee.

Background reminder of the spirit in which the business has been developed, and my interpretation of "to the benefit of the employees" in the formation of the Trust, is based on the conviction that "man does not live by bread alone", and is as follows:

1. Honesty and kindness in all dealings with everybody; staff, suppliers, representatives from would-be suppliers, professional advisers, Government officials, customers and each member of the public.
   For this it is necessary:

   a) That each individual be considered equally worthy of affection and respect (which includes trust — unless and until this should prove unfounded); that every form of prejudice, bigotry and discrimination be eschewed.

   b) That expediency be at all times eschewed. However vital it may appear to avoid trouble or attain success, it is less vital than to act honestly and kindly in each detail. The end never justifies false means; for the means we surely grasp, while the results are beyond human control.

2. Financial benefit to the employees to be related to their individual contributions to the Company's success. Remembering that effort, willingness and faithfulness in small matters as well as in big, be given due weight.

3. That meetings be conducted in a natural though correct manner to obviate two great dangers of formality:

   a) Self-importance

   b) The loss of ideas sparked off by some remark or fact (vide Lord Nuffield) because not on the agenda.

4. That integrity of character of each person in Geographers' be watched and fostered from the start with a view to future Manager, Director or Trusteeship. The ideal qualities at which to aim are (it seems to me after failing so often at most of them):

a) A good head and a good heart., i.e. unflinching truthfulness and unfailing kindness. Readiness to admit mitakes. Objectivity in assessing ideas; and unselfish thought and endeavour for the good of all. Readiness to reason and listen to reason. (Without running a line etc.)

b) Respect for the opinions and talents of others, without envy; recognition of own lack of experience, ability or expertise, together with a readiness to seek advice, weigh and adapt it. Flexibility of outlook, with ability to recognise and change priorities.

c) Self respect and independence of character. In particular, no hypocrisy, no aiming at popularity, no partiality. No trying to impress. No being impressed.

d) Protection and strengthening of the weak. This demands impartiality; no self-righteousness; but readiness to listen, kind firmness and definiteness; and the generous and patient imparting of one's own knowledge and experience. Even temper and no moodiness; praise for good work and gently constructive criticism.

e) Readiness to forgive offence, desire to conciliate the differences of others.

f) Fearless devotion to duty; fearless recognition of danger and steadfast confrontation; persistence in overcoming it.

g) Objective assessment of past experience with application to present and future.

h) The natural modesty of any person aware of human limitations and of his or her own particular ones; with happy giving of credit to others for ability and ideas, and with no feeling of superiority to any person or task.
The putting of the good of others before one's own.

This letter gives me the opportunity to thank you all, dear Trustees of the present, — and unknown Trustees of the future.

Unless you considered this Trust worthwhile in a human sense, and not just "big business", you should not be undertaking the responsibility for it. It should also be fun. The essence of it all, of course, is to love God and to love one's neighbour as oneself; to fail and still continue to try.

Bless you all.

Yours sincerely,